POETRY IN SPEECH

A volume in the series

MYTH AND POETICS

edited by GREGORY NAGY

A full list of titles in the series appears at the end of the book.

POETRY IN SPEECH

Orality and Homeric Discourse

Egbert J. Bakker

CORNELL UNIVERSITY PRESS

ITHACA AND LONDON

First published 1997 by Cornell University Press.

Printed in the United States of America

TCF This book is printed on Lyons Falls Turin Book, a paper that is totally chlorine-free and acid-free.

Library of Congress Cataloging-in-Publication Data

Bakker, Egbert J.
  Poetry in speech : orality and Homeric discourse / Egbert J. Bakker.
    p.   cm. — (Myth and poetics)
  Includes bibliographical references and indexes.
    ISBN 0-8014-3295-2 (cloth : alk. paper)
    1. Homer—Criticism and interpretation.   2. Epic poetry, Greek—
  History and criticism.   3. Discourse analysis, Literary.   4. Oral formulaic
  analysis.   5. Oral tradition—Greece.   6. Speech in literature.
  7. Poetics.   I. Title.
  PA4037.B33   1996
  883'.01—dc20   96-31979

Cloth printing   5   4   3   2   1

Contents

Foreword

GREGORY NAGY

Many of the books in the Myth and Poetics series center on the power of myth to make language special or specially formal: when language is stylized by myth, it becomes a culture's poetry or song. Egbert Bakker's *Poetry in Speech* approaches myth and poetics from another direction, asking how myth is shaped by poetics and, just as important, how poetics are conditioned by everyday language, language as it is actually spoken. Bakker calls everyday language *speech*, distinguishing it from the special languages of song or poetry (or even prose), and the word is aptly chosen, since the range of its meanings in contemporary English recapitulates the tendency of everyday language to become special in special contexts. In neutral contexts, as when we speak of the human capacity for *speech*, the word applies by default to any language situation; in special contexts, however, as when we speak of a *speech* delivered before an audience, the word refers to a special kind of discourse.

The criterion of everyday speech, it is essential to stress, is a cultural variable, depending on the concrete realization of whatever special speech or discourse is being set apart for a special context. In traditional societies, as the books in the Myth and Poetics series have argued in a variety of ways, the setting apart of such special discourse would normally happen when a ritual is enacted or when a myth is spoken or sung. The language of Homer is a prime example of such special discourse, as Richard P. Martin vividly demonstrated in the first book of this series, *The Language of Heroes: Speech and Performance in the "Iliad."* Homeric discourse is most sharply set apart from the reality of everyday language, no matter how we may reconstruct this reality for any particular time and place in ancient Greece, by its metrical and formulaic dimensions. Bakker traces these dimensions, which for Milman Parry and Albert Lord mark the orality of Homeric discourse, back to their sources in everyday language—a genealogy expressed in the book's full title, *Poetry in Speech: Orality and Homeric Discourse.*

Bakker has shifted the emphasis: poetry that is oral is in fact speech that is special, stylized by meter and formula. To put it negatively: it is not the absence of writing that makes oral poetry special. Nor is it the orality of oral poetry that makes it special, as if "oral" were a special category within a body of poetry that we generally experience in written form. From an anthropological point of view, poetry in and of itself is special speech. The real working opposition is the one between special speech—whether it be song or poetry or prose—and the everyday speech from which it derives. That derivation does not imply a binary distinction, of course, and the continuum that runs between everyday language and the varieties of special speech can be extended to include written texts. Speech that is written, because of the stylization involved, sometimes has a better claim to the "special" distinction than do any oral examples of special speech.

Understanding our inherited Homeric text as the reflex of a special language, Bakker transcends purely literary interpretation, refusing to be tied down by presuppositions of a text originally composed in writing and written in order to be read. In analyzing the principles of Homeric composition, he shows us how to rethink even the concept of the sentence and of the period, its classical analogue. Only in a text-bound approach, Bakker argues, can the sentence be considered the basic unit of speech. Following the methods of the linguist Wallace Chafe, he reassesses the building blocks of speech in terms of the speaker's cognitive system *as it actually operates in the process of speaking.* Chafe resists the artificial superimposition of literate grammar on the analysis of everyday language. Bakker frees his own analysis of Homeric discourse from such superimpositions and defamiliarizes our textbound mental routines in the reading of archaic Greek poetry.

Bakker's arguments about the shaping of the metrical and formulaic system of Homeric discourse by the everyday speech from which it is derived open many avenues for future research, particularly into the regulation of speech by this system at the posited moment(s) of performance in an oral tradition. The poetics of recomposition-in-performance, which are reflected in the patterns of wording and word placement within the fundamental rhythmical unit of the dactylic hexameter, can now be further examined from both synchronic and diachronic perspectives. Bakker's own explorations of these questions mark a monumental advance in our understanding of Homeric discourse as a linguistic system. A striking example is his success in explaining the syntactic functions of Homeric particles like *mén, mḗn, dé, dḗ, ḗtoi, ára/rhá, gár, autár/atár, kaí, allá, oûn.* In the wake of Bakker's analysis, the classicist cannot help but read the Greek of Homer differently: the reader's understanding of practically every verse is affected—and enhanced.

A vital question remains: why exactly is there a need for a special discourse in the self-expression of myth? The answers, which vary from culture to culture, have to do with the special contents of myth itself, which require special forms for their expression. In the case of Homeric discourse, as Bakker shows in minute detail, such answers can be found in the actual usage of the discourse itself. A case in point is the system of noun-epithet formulas. Through these formulas, as also through the deployment of evidential particles, Homeric discourse represents itself as the verbalization of a heroic world that is literally visualized by those very special agents of divine memory, the Muses. Whatever Homeric poetry *sees* through the Muses who witness the epic past becomes just as special as whatever it *says* through the Muses who narrate what they saw (and heard) to Homer. Homeric vision, as expressed by the metrical and formulaic system of Homeric discourse, claims to be something far greater than mere poetic imagination. The blind bard's inner vision becomes the ultimate epiphany of the heroic past.

FOR PETRA

Acknowledgments

The activities leading up to this book have taken some years, and it is a pleasure to express my gratitude for the help and support I received from people and institutions along the way. I have fond memories of a stay—one of the many pleasant things made possible by a Fellowship of the Royal Netherlands Academy of Arts and Sciences—at the University of California, Santa Barbara, where I was a guest at the National Humanities Center in 1990. I profited from seminars on discourse analysis in the Linguistics Department, particularly those given by Wallace Chafe and Sandra Thompson, who also kindly read the embryonic proposals on Homeric speech that I produced at the time.

At a later stage, I had the privilege of spending part of the academic year 1991–92 at the Netherlands Institute for Advanced Studies (NIAS), where I wrote the earliest version of what is now Part 1. At NIAS the project benefited from my participation in an interdisciplinary theme group, "Orality and Literacy." To some of the participants in particular I owe a debt: to Franz Bäuml (University of California, Los Angeles) for opening up the discussion of orality and literacy in the Middle Ages for me, and to David Rubin (Duke University) for his comments on my work from the standpoint of cognitive psychology.

In 1992–93 I was among the Fellows at the Center for Hellenic Studies, Washington, D.C., a stay that was made possible by a grant from the Netherlands Organization for Research. During this most pleasant and fruitful year I not only had the opportunity to work on earlier versions of what are now Chapters 3 and 6 through 8, but also to present my ideas to a number of patient audiences: the Directors and the Fellows at the Center for Hellenic Studies, as well as audiences at Columbia, Brown, Yale, Harvard, and Duke Universities. I thank Suzanne Saïd, Alan Boegehold, Victor Bers, Gregory Nagy, and Keith Stanley for their invitations to present my ideas in their departments.

Even though I was supposed to teach, not write, in the Department of Classics of the University of Virginia in 1993–94, I made much progress during that year, not least because of the graduate seminar I gave there in the winter of 1994, from which the writing of Chapters 4 and 5 gained momentum. I thank my colleagues at UVA for the opportunities they gave me to discuss my work with them. The work saw its completion, finally, at the Université de Montréal, where it benefited not only from a generous teaching schedule but also from a research grant from the university. In this final stage, presentations at the University of Ottawa and the UCLA Center for Medieval and Renaissance Studies helped to shape my thought. I thank Denis Brearly and Franz Bäuml for their invitations.

Welcome advice and encouragement came from many friends and colleagues along the way. I thank Ahuvia Kahane and Ian Rutherford for reading parts of the manuscript in its final stage. Mark Edwards has always been willing to read the results of my projects, finished or unfinished. I thank him for his interest throughout, his faith in this project, and his personal support. I would like also to express my special thanks to Gregory Nagy, for the inspiration that his own work has given me, for the attentive way in which he followed my work from the beginning, and for his advice, both practical and theoretical, during various stages of the project. In the final stage, Terence McKiernan was a most helpful editor, whose criticisms and suggestions enhanced the final form of the text and the articulation of the argument.

Finally there was someone who was not always near but always present, and who in the end, with a logic untainted by too much Homeric special speech, saved the manuscript from some of its more glaring idiosyncrasies. This book is for her.

EGBERT J. BAKKER

Montreal, Canada

POETRY IN SPEECH

Introduction

Poetry in Speech examines the poetic discourse of the *Iliad* and *Odyssey* in terms of spoken discourse or speech. Such a project needs to be justified at the outset. The most influential type of criticism of Homeric poetry in the twentieth century, the oral-formulaic approach of Milman Parry and Albert Lord, holds that text, the medium opposite to speech, is absent in the composition of the epic tale. And more recent research, focusing on performance, is reaching consensus on the idea that even if an archaic Greek poem has been written down, its text is at best a marginal factor in the reception and transmission of the poem. What, then, is new in the study of Homeric poetry as speech?

While most research dealing with oral poetry views orality as belonging to times and places other than our own, the orality that is the subject of this book is a less remote phenomenon. The performance of Homeric poetry in its institutional setting may be something of the past, of a culture different from our own with regard to the role and importance of writing; but the discourse that was presented in these performances had one very obvious property in common with something in which we all participate: it was a matter of speech and voice, and of the consciousness of the performer and his audience. This is orality too, but not in a historical sense. The difference here is not one of time or culture but of medium; speech as a medium "other" than writing. In treating Homeric poetry as oral in this "medial" sense, we leave, at least initially, the poetic or literary perspective and view Homeric poetry against the background of the spoken medium, considering it as speech or discourse. I have tried, where appropriate, to

I

think of terms and concepts that apply to speech in its own right, rather than to speech as viewed from the standpoint of writing. Part 1 offers some thoughts on the opposition between the oral and the literate in this connection. Having argued in Chapter 1 against a conception of orality from the point of view of writing, I then proceed in Chapter 2 with a possible scenario for Homeric writing seen from the standpoint of speech.

The criticism of Homeric discourse as speech is the subject of Part 2. In Chapters 3, 4, and 5, I discuss those features of Homeric style (such as parataxis, adding style, and ring composition) that I believe are better accounted for as naturally occurring strategies of speakers who present their discourse to listeners than as elements of poetic style that have to be characterized as early or primitive with respect to the poetic styles of later periods. My discussion of this Homeric speech syntax—which includes an account of certain Greek particles that differs from the usual descriptions based on classical, written Greek—is at the same time an attempt at establishing links between the level of syntax and higher levels in the flow and composition of the epic tale.

Yet such a discourse analysis of Homeric poetry does not ignore or diminish the importance of the difference between Homeric language and everyday speech. On the contrary, the speech perspective is meant to accommodate the common features of epic style, such as meter and formulas, providing a basis on which they can be studied: in the method that I have followed, the *Iliad* and *Odyssey* are not so much poetry that is oral as speech that is special, a matter of the special occasion of the performance. Thus in Part 3 (Chapters 6 and 8) I argue that poetic meter and formulas, rather than removing Homeric poetry from the realm of the ordinary and the everyday, derive from what is most natural in spoken discourse: the "chunks" that make up the adding style. I argue that meter and formulas entail the stylization of ordinary speech, rather than some inherently poetic principle.

Special attention is paid to the noun–epithet formula, the type of expression that plays a key role in the metrics as well as in the thematics of the Greek epic diction. I argue in Chapter 7 for a function of the noun–epithet formula in Homeric discourse over and above its evident metrical importance, as noted by Parry. Starting from the premise that speech is necessarily a matter of behavior, I analyze the noun–epithet formula as the characteristic articulation of a speech ritual specific to the epic performance: the privileged moment where past and present, heroic action and poetic action, find joint expression in the epithet as the principal bearer of the hero's epic *kléos* 'renown.'

Much of the effort that went into this book had to do with the apparent paradox posed by the study of Homeric poetry as speech: the *Iliad* and *Odyssey* are texts, and as such they firmly belong to the medium in which most of our scholarly discourse is conducted. Working within the speech perspective implied by my methodology and forcing myself to read Homer as the transcoding of one medium into another, a flow of speech through time that has become a transcript, I began to realize just how much of the vocabulary and the notional apparatus used for our study of language and style is overtly or covertly literate, pertaining to our writing culture, and thus perhaps more indicative of the perspective of the philologist than of speech studied in the form of a text. The result is an attempt to combine the concepts of Greek philology, stylistics, and linguistics with insights drawn from discourse analysis and the study of oral poetry, and most of all to remove the boundaries between these disciplines.

PART ONE

PERSPECTIVES

CHAPTER I

The Construction of Orality

L'oralité est une abstraction; seule la voix est concrète, seule son écoute nous fait toucher aux choses.
—Paul Zumthor, *La lettre et la voix*

In our culture, speaking and writing are distinct activities, with one often happening in the absence of the other, or even to the exclusion of the other. So we telephone instead of writing a letter, and increasingly we e-mail instead of speaking on the phone. It would seem that the two activities—speaking and writing—constitute a symmetrical contrast, in which either term can be used to define the other; but in practice this is not so. Often we use the one term, "writing," as vantage point for our conception of the other, in ways that betray a distinct cultural bias. Our use of the term "oral" and related expressions is a case in point. We may speak of "oral" simply when a discourse is spoken; but more often we endow the term with a cultural value. So we routinely speak of "oral poetry," not to characterize a given poem as "spoken" but to oppose it to the dominant form of poetry in our culture. And we speak of "orality" not to describe what happens when someone talks, but to label a period or a culture as different with respect to our own writing culture. Oral poetry and orality, in short, are abstractions derived from the property of *not writing or being written*, and as such they are literate constructs: they define speech as the construction of a writing culture that uses its own absence to define its opposite.

It may be useful, at the outset of this study, to put this cultural bias in perspective by distinguishing between two dimensions in which something can be oral. We may use "oral" in a *medial* sense, meaning simply that something is spoken and as such is a matter of sound and the voice of the speaker. In this sense, a neutral, medial opposition between spoken and written discourse obtains, the one being "phonic," the other "graphic."

7

This neutral, medial opposition gets compounded by the fact that each medium comes with its own set of associations, and even its own mentality: speaking and writing are different activities that call for different strategies in the presentation and comprehension of a discourse. Thus "oral" may also be a matter of *conception* and may enter into an opposition—not so much with "written" as with "literate"—that is far less neutral than the medial one: whereas no one would question the simple existence of medial orality (speech), our acceptance of conceptional orality as a phenomenon in its own right is much less obvious. For it is here that we have to become aware of the inbuilt biases of our writing culture in order to arrive at real understanding.[1]

In the conceptional sense, "oral" can designate the mental habits of persons who do not participate, or who do not participate fully, in literate culture as we know it, a phenomenon we associate with societies other than or earlier than our own. When applied to texts, "oral" in this sense implies that a given piece of writing does not display the features that are normal and expected in a writing culture: it came into existence without the premeditation that is usually involved in the production of written texts. Such a discourse has been written down and is "graphic" as to its *medium*, but it may be called "oral" as to its *conception*. In the conceptional sense, then, "oral" may denote the absence of characteristics of written language, whether a discourse is spoken or written. Thus even though the two senses of "oral" have a certain affinity to each other, it is important not to confuse them. A discourse that is *conceptionally* oral (such as a conversational narrative) is often *medially* oral as well, but it is also possible for such a discourse to be written. And a medially oral (phonic) discourse is often conceptionally oral, but instead it may be fully literate as to its conception (as in the case of an academic paper read out loud).

Finally, a third sense may be distinguished. The term "oral" has been used to refer not to a set of mental habits or to a mode of communication, but to a property of literary language and hence of literary texts. Parry is one of the first to speak systematically of orality as a property of literature, in opposition to the property of being written, a distinction that serves as the basis for a classification of literature in general: "Literature falls into two

---

[1] The notion of "medial orality" as opposed to "conceptional orality" derives from Koch and Oesterreicher 1985 (see also Oesterreicher 1993, 1997). For more discussion of the various ramifications of the opposition between spoken and written, see also Brown and Yule 1983: 4–19; Tannen, ed. 1982 (esp. Chafe 1982); Olson et al., eds. 1985 (esp. Chafe 1985); Chafe 1994: 41–50; Givón 1979: 207–33.

great parts not so much because there are two kinds of culture, but because there are two kinds of *form: the one part of literature is oral, the other is written."* [2] In this sense, "oral" denotes not so much an absence as a presence: that of the *formula* as the prime feature of the oral or traditional style. We shall turn later in this chapter to the notion of the formula. Here we simply note that the concept of oral poetry as a class of literature is insensitive to the distinction between medium and conception just made: it applies to both. The oral poem is considered a spoken discourse, but at the same time a text with properties that make it very different from texts in our culture. We shall have occasion later to consider the problems that this may cause. [3]

The relation between orality and its opposite seems to be unproblematic and straightforward in the conceptional and medial senses. "Oral" and "literate" in the conceptional sense can be considered prototypes, or opposite end points on a continuum: as properties that come in degrees, they need not exclude each other. Someone's mental habits may be oral to a greater or lesser extent, and that person's degree of literacy will be inversely proportional. Likewise, societies as a whole may be oral or literate in various degrees, and since the transition from a preliterate to a literate society in which writing is institutionalized is never an abrupt one, the notions of orality and literacy, though distinct, do not exclude each other, either diachronically or synchronically. [4] The same point applies to orality as a textual feature: texts may be oral to a greater or lesser degree, depending on the nature of the conception underlying them. [5] The notion of an oral medium, however, seems to exclude its opposite on first sight, in the sense that whoever speaks does not write, and vice versa. The exclusion is superficial, of course, since speech and writing as media are coexisting strategies, both of them being available to most members of a literate community and chosen according to the communicative needs and purposes at hand.

But what about "oral" in the sense used by Parry in the quotation above? As a subclassification of poetry, Parry evidently means "oral" to exclude "written," thereby turning a mere opposition into what seems a contradic-

---

[2] Parry 1971: 377.

[3] See also Bakker 1997b.

[4] The sociological or conceptional sense of "orality" often implies a historical perspective, focusing on the arrival of literacy and its implications (e.g., Goody and Watt 1968; Ong 1982; Stock 1983); on the residue of orality left after this arrival (e.g., Havelock 1963, 1986); or on the coexistence of the two (e.g., Thomas 1989). Thomas (1992: 19) warns against approaches in which each and every aspect of progress and innovation is attributed to literacy.

[5] Oesterreicher 1997.

tion in terms: for how can poetry like Homer's be "oral" and therefore "not written," if we experience it as a written text? By "oral" Parry means, as is well known, "orally composed" as against "composed with the aid of writing," yet that does not really alter the picture, and by conceiving of "oral" in terms of form and style (i.e., *formula*) Parry and many researchers after him believed that "oral" could be made to apply to written texts, provided they have certain oral (-formulaic) properties.

Traditional Style and Homeric *Kunstsprache*

The dichotomy between oral style and literate style is not the original form in which Parry cast his conception of Homeric discourse. First came the notion of traditional style as opposed to the individual expression of later poetry, an idea that remained closely attached to orality throughout Parry's writings. Owing to its formulaic nature, Homeric diction is traditional, by which Parry means that it cannot possibly have been the individual creation of any one single poet. "The nature of Homeric poetry," he writes, "can be grasped only when one has seen that it is composed in a diction which is oral, and so formulaic, and so traditional."[6] And again: "*Oral poetry is formulaic and traditional*. The poet who habitually makes his poems without the aid of writing can do so only by putting together old verses and old parts of verses in an old way."[7]

For Parry, the traditional nature of Greek epic diction is reflected in the distinctly systematic character of the Homeric formula.[8] Going well beyond the usual treatment of Homeric diction in terms of gratuitous cosmetics or poetic style *tout court*, Parry introduces two key concepts that are central to his conception of the traditional nature of Homeric style: extension and economy.[9] Economy is the one-to-one correlation of a given formula and a metrical form, or in Parry's own words, the absence of "phrases which, having the same metrical value and expressing the same idea, could replace one another."[10] Extension, on the other hand, is the

---

[6] Parry 1971: 328.

[7] Parry 1971: 377.

[8] See Parry 1971: 276: "It is the system of formulas, as we shall see, which is the only true means by which we can come to see just how the Singer made his verses."

[9] Parry originally spoke in terms of "extension" and "simplicity" (e.g., Parry 1971: 6–7, 16–17); later he came to speak of "length" and "thrift" (e.g., Parry 1971: 276).

[10] Parry 1971: 276.

degree to which such a unique pairing of a meaning and a form applies to a whole class of formulaic expressions (a formula type), for example, metrically interchangeable expressions for a range of gods and heroes. Thus, according to Parry, a system of formulas is economical in that all expressions with the same meaning are different from one another in their metrical form (e.g., *polútlas díos Odusseús* 'much-suffering godlike Odysseus' vs. *polúmētis Odusseús* 'many-minded Odysseus', both expressions having as their meaning "Odysseus"). And the system is extended, conversely, in that all formulas with the same metrical form are different as to their meaning (e.g., *polúmētis Odusseús* vs. *pódas ōkùs Akhilleús* 'swift-footed Achilles').

The arrangement of formulas in systems is treated by Parry as an indication that the whole of Homer's diction is organized in this way. An analysis in terms of economy and extension, in Parry's view, can show the way to a better understanding of why and how Homeric diction in general has the specific form it does. For example, the systems of formulaic expressions for gods and heroes in the nominative case are for Parry not an isolated observation; they merely offer a clearer and more striking case of systematic economy and extension than do other areas of Homeric diction,[11] a case yielding proof that Homeric diction as such, not just some parts of it, is schematized, systematic, and hence traditional.[12]

This proof has been controversial,[13] with much discussion, both inside and outside oral-formulaic theory, devoted to defining the formula. The debate, which took as leitmotiv Parry's own definition of the concept ("a group of words which is regularly employed under the same metrical conditions to express a given essential idea"[14]), tended to start from the "inten-

---

[11] "In the case of this system, as in that of other formulas, such as those of the types πολύμητις Ὀδυσσεύς and δῖος Ὀδυσσεύς, the length and the thrift of the system are striking enough to be sure proof that only the very smallest part of it could be the work of one poet. But for the greater number of systems which are found in the diction of the Homeric poems we cannot make such sure conclusions, since their length is rarely so great and their thrift never so striking. This does not mean that the proof by means of the length and thrift of the system is possible only in the case of the noun-epithet formulas. It is clear without need of further search that the greater part of the system quoted above must be traditional." Parry 1971: 277–78.

[12] See Parry's analysis (1971: 301–14) of the first twenty-five lines of the *Iliad* and *Odyssey*.

[13] For the argument against Parry's systematic treatment of noun-epithet formulas, see Vivante 1982: 158–59, 164–67. The most recent and extended argument against economy is Shive 1987. For a general discussion of the reception of Parry in current Homeric studies, see Martin 1989: 1–5. The term "formalist," although sometimes used with hostile intent (e.g., Fenik 1986: 171, cited by Martin 1989) can, if used in a more neutral sense—as in "formal linguistics"—quite adequately characterize Parry's conception; see below, as well as Bakker 1995.

[14] Parry 1971: 272. Cf. Parry 1971: 13; Lord 1960: 30. Discussion of Parry's definition in Bakker 1988: 152–59.

sion" of the concept (What is a formula?) and move to its extension (How much of the Homeric text is formula?). It was hoped that clarity as to the essence of the basic unit of oral composition would clarify the concept of oral composition as such.[15] But this strategy made the definition of "formula"—in itself already more a *definiendum* than a *definiens*—dependent on each scholar's position regarding the wider issue of oral-formulaic composition and created circularity problems that oral-formulaic theory has never satisfactorily solved.[16] The question of systematicity and of the essence of the formula will be addressed in Chapter 8 below, where I will attempt to view Parry's insights from the perspective developed in this book.

The participants in the debate on formulas are divided about how traditional and formulaic Homeric diction really is: from entirely or almost entirely traditional and formulaic, as Parry and Lord claimed, all the way to mostly or entirely nontraditional, except for the core of formulaic systematicity that Parry had established irrefutably for noun-epithet phrases.[17] But whatever one's position on this continuum, there was one thing that bound most participants in the discussion together. Most scholars took the traditional and formulaic as the phenomenon to be accounted for, the figure against the ground. Such a position assumes that whereas the definition of the formulaic (and so the traditional) may be problematic and the subject of inquiry, the definition of the nontraditional and nonformulaic is not.

We notice here the same perspective as the one with which this chapter began: Homeric poetry, whether under the aspect of oral or of traditional, is seen in terms of an opposition in which the one member (oral or traditional) is defined with respect to the other (literate) which functions as

---

[15] For discussion of the development in Parry's thinking about the formula, see Hoekstra 1965: 8–18; Bakker 1988: 152–64; 1990a. Well-known critical statements of Parry's notion of formula include Hainsworth 1964; Minton 1965; Austin 1975: 11–80; Mueller 1984: 14–21. Just how large a portion of the debate on the formula in the 1970s was devoted to problems of definition can be gleaned from most of the papers in Stolz and Shannon, eds. 1976.

[16] As is well known, the number of clear-cut noun-epithet formulas (conforming to a system and as such the core of Parry's theory as well as of any theory of Homeric formulas) is almost negligible compared to the bulk of the *Iliad* as a whole, and to make Homeric diction acceptably formulaic, Parry had to work with a vague concept of similarity (1971: 313), which later scholars would develop into the notion of the structural formula (e.g., Russo 1963, 1966). But statements to the effect "x is like y" are not very useful, in that anything uttered in hexametric rhythm is *as such* like anything else uttered in that rhythm. The statistics in O'Neill 1942 are revealing in this respect. Discussion and criticism of structural formulas in Minton 1965; Bakker 1988: 159–64. See also my remarks below on analogy.

[17] See, for example, Bassett 1938: 15–19; Hoekstra 1965: 15–20; Austin 1975: 11–81.

framework and norm. Language, we almost unconsciously assume, is written and individual by default, and it takes some special conditions for it to become the "other" with respect to these notions. This same perspective, again, is apparent in the third and last dichotomy we will discuss, that between artificial and natural.

Before Homeric style became traditional or oral, it was artificial. Philological criticism found in Homer an artificial diction that could never have been spoken in ordinary discourse at any time or place, a *Kunstsprache*, as it came to be called in the dominant publications on the subject.[18] The notion of *Kunstsprache* originated in nineteenth-century historical and descriptive linguistics, the backbone of linguistic thought in philology, and was based on a thorough investigation of the morphological, phonological, dialectal, and lexicographic features that distinguish Homer from other authors. These features include the geographic and temporal mismatch of Homeric forms and the use of inherently "artificial" forms, words that do not exist elsewhere. As a simple example we may cite the accusative phrase *euréa pónton* 'wide sea', created on the analogy of the dative formula *euréï póntōi*, to replace the "natural" but metrically undesirable *eurùn pónton*;[19] or the accusative form *hēniokhêa* 'charioteer', created on the basis of the "artificial" form **hēniokheús* (instead of the "natural" *hēníokhos* and its accusative *hēníokhon*).[20] These artificialities were seen as dependent on the exigencies of the dactylic hexameter, an observation epitomized in Kurt Witte's words: "The epic language is the creation of the epic verse."[21]

Parry is a direct heir to this approach: his oral-formulaic analysis amounts to a continuation of the research of Witte, Karl Meister, and their predecessors. The essential dimension that Parry adds is the perception that the dependence of language on verse is not merely an issue of aesthetics, the result of the hexameter functioning as a poetic generative principle, but a matter of functional motivation. Parry shows that the bewildering variety of epithets and morphologically heterogeneous dialectal "forms" is not an arbitrary feature of "epic style" but conforms to a system designed to facilitate oral composition in performance. It is within the context of this system that the "artificial" element in Homeric style, or generally the

---

[18] Witte 1913; Meister 1921. These works can be seen as the culmination of extensive nineteenth-century research on the decisive influence of the verse on Homer's language. See also Ruijgh 1971: 106–12. Up-to-date bibliography in Janko 1992: 8–19.

[19] Witte 1912: 113 (=Latacz, ed. 1979: 112).

[20] Chantraine 1948: 95.

[21] Witte 1913: 2214: "ein Gebilde des epischen Verses."

characterization of Homeric language as *Kunstsprache*, comes to be rein-
terpreted as that which exists in service of the traditional, and ultimately, the
oral: "A whole new word no poet could make, since no one would understand him if he did, but he may make a form like another. That is to say, he
may make the *artificial* by analogy with the *real*. The reason for such a
creation is of course the same which leads the singers to keep the old and
foreign forms, namely the need of a formula of a certain length which can be
gotten only by this means."[22]

It appears, then, that in order to account for the Homeric formula
various interrelated concepts have been used and are still in use: artificiality,
traditionality, and orality, differentiating Homeric poetry respectively from
the naturalness, the individuality, and the writtenness of ordinary poetic
language. The phenomenon thus created, however, may be more a product
of the perspective used than an objective reality. For when we change our
perspective, shifting our focus from poetic language to language, and particularly language as it actually functions in speech, the three opposites of
natural, individual, and written are not such distinctive features anymore.

From Poetry to Speech

We may wonder how "natural" ordinary language is when we realize
that analogy, the creation of one form on the basis of another, is not at all
confined to the creation of formulas in the oral style. Analogy is a regular
feature of language change in general, part of a general drive of languages to
make grammatical paradigms more "regular" when phonetic changes or
unproductive morphology have made certain forms obsolete and "irregular."[23] A simple example in Greek is the "artificial" but regular form *oída-
men* 'we know', created on the analogy of the "natural" and regular form
oída 'I know' to replace the "natural" but irregular form *ísmen*.[24] Natural
and artificial, then, do not seem to be viable concepts in the study of
language change, where creating the artificial by analogy with the real is a
very natural phenomenon. Nor does the artificial as such seem useful as a
concept to characterize Homeric language. True, the motivation for ana-

---

[22] Parry 1971: 339, emphasis added; cf. Parry 1971: 68–69.

[23] This process is sometimes called leveling; see Hock 1986: 168–71.

[24] The oldest attested uses of the new form seem to occur in Herodotus (4.46, 7.214) but it is
not until the New Testament that the form has become normal; the older form, however,
continues to be used.

logical formation in Homeric diction is metrical, and therefore artistic; but that does not mean that the resulting form is inherently any more artificial than analogous formations in ordinary language.[25]

Analogical change in language, whether ordinary or poetic, is traditional in that no individual speaker or singer can impose a given newly made expression on the language community and make it enter the system. The very concept of system, in fact, which Parry sees as the key element in the traditionality of Homeric style, is not left unaffected by the shift in perspective from poetry to language. The system consists of the systematic differences between formulas as forms. A very similar account, however, can be found in structuralist linguistics, the approach to language introduced by Ferdinand de Saussure.[26] Just as Parry himself does in the case of formulaic language, the structuralist linguist sees language in general as a system or code, a coherent set of differences and similarities between linguistic forms that serve the purpose of the efficient transmission of their content or meaning. An just as in the case of Parry's formulas, the form of linguistic expression is seen as determined by an autonomous structure or system that is distinct from the content of the message transmitted (Parry calls the latter the "essential idea" of a given formula).[27]

But the problem of how to define Homeric traditional diction is not confined to the way in which the Homeric formulas relate to one another; it affects the concept of formula itself. The study of language has long been concerned with creativity and originality, with how speakers are the individual composers of expressions within the system of rules that makes up their language. In recent years, however, very different voices have been heard, drawing attention to the traditionality of speakers, their use of phrases of which they are not the original makers or authors. Indeed, repetition is a

[25] After Parry, the issue of the relation between Homeric formulaic language and ordinary language has occasionally been raised; see, for example, Lord 1960: 36; Wyatt (1988: 29), who in criticizing Schein's treatment (1984: 2–13) of Homeric language as artificial and never spoken by anyone as an ordinary language, submits that "Homer's language was as natural for him as is English to us." For the acquisition of poetic language as a second language, see Rubin 1988; 1994: 136–44.

[26] Structuralist linguistics conceives of language, partly in opposition to nineteenth-century diachronic and historical linguistics, as a synchronic system, consisting of functional differences between its constitutive elements. For elementary expositions of Saussure's work (1972) see Jackson 1991: 20–56; Holdcroft 1991.

[27] Parry 1971: 13, 272. More on the affinity of Parry's account of the Homeric formula with structuralism and other formalist linguistic paradigms in Bakker 1995: 118–22 (see also Lynn-George 1988: 55–68). Notice in this connection that Antoine Meillet, Parry's teacher, was a pupil of Saussure.

pervasive phenomenon when language is conceptionally oral. In the third part of this book we shall consider some implications of this observation. For now, we may simply reconsider the concept of traditional or oral formula, the exclusive feature of oral epic as proposed by Parry.[28]

If formulas as traditional "prefabs" also occur in ordinary language, we might do better than opposing Homeric poetry to ordinary poetic language, viewing it instead in connection with ordinary spoken language. True, the formular nature and function of expressions in Homeric poetry is determined, in ways to be explored further in Chapters 6 and 8, by metrical factors that do not, as such, play a role in ordinary speech. But the difference between metrical and nonmetrical is not as clear-cut as it seems, and even a predominantly metrical function for a Homeric expression does not preclude its also having a function akin to that of formulaic expressions in ordinary speech.

All this is not to say, of course, that there are no important differences between Homeric discourse and everyday speech. The point is rather that the phraseology of Homeric poetry may not be most fruitfully characterized by calling it chiefly and inherently artificial or traditional. And when we add orality to the mix, we risk running into outright paradox. In explaining artificial by means of traditional, and traditional by means of oral, Parry gave the notion of *Kunstsprache* an entirely different conceptual load, causing a revolution in Homeric scholarship. This revolution, however, was in a sense a conservative one. Earlier analysts of the Homeric *Kunstsprache* focus on poetic style; Parry keeps that perspective and analyzes oral poetic style as a special case. In explaining the artificial, poetic element in Homer's diction, Parry comes to equate the oral with what distinguishes Homer's speech, treated as poetic style, from ordinary speech. In the oral-formulaic analysis, stylistic features like formulas, repetitions, and rhythmical patterns are studied by explicitly confronting them as a special case, isolated as a research object sui generis, a traditional oral style and a separate formulaic language.[29] But this research project ignores, and has continued to do so till the present day, that the oral is all around us, not as a special poetic style but as everyday speech.

It is with respect to this pervasive but therefore neglected and ill-

---

[28] "It is the *nature* of an expression which makes of it a formula." Parry 1971: 304. On formula as a natural category of language vs. formula as a function of language, see Bakker 1988: 153–57.

[29] See, for example, Parry 1971: 328: "Clearly a special language for the hexameter could come into being only when poetry was of a very different sort from that which we ourselves write, and which we know to have been written throughout the history of European literature."

understood phenomenon that I attempt to define Homeric poetry in the chapters that follow. My starting point and main assumption in this book is that orality is not so much a phase in the development of culture, or literature, to be overcome in due course, as it is the primary manifestation of language. Orality is language in the spoken, phonic medium along with the conceptional process that it implies: a conception that has to be studied on its own terms, rather than with respect to writing. The study of speech as a phenomenon that can be observed all around us is an empirical discipline. In the chapters that follow, we will draw on some of this research, highlighting those approaches and methodologies that provide the best opportunities for the study of Homer.

We are concerned, then, not with oral as the special case of poetry, but with poetry as the special case of oral, in other words, with poetry in speech. We will view Homeric discourse not as oral poetry but as special speech.[30] A general catchword for the poetry in Homeric speech is the term "stylization," which implies, just as imitation or parody, two discourses: the discourse that is the object of stylization and the stylizing discourse itself. The stylizing discourse is meant to be distinctive, but in order to be recognizable as a stylizing discourse, it has to display some essential features of its model.[31] In the same way, Homeric discourse can be said to stylize ordinary discourse by departing from it and yet retaining, or even highlighting, its most characteristic features. An important part of the program of this book will be to identify those most characteristic features, and to present them as the basis for an account of Homeric poetics.

Our main task, then, will be to ask what it means for language to be spoken, so that we can define what it means for speech to be special. The first question will concern us in Part 2; in Part 3 we will then be in a position to deal with the second one. But let us first finish our preliminary discussion of perspectives: if it is of interest to ask, for the benefit of the interpretation of a text, what it means for language to be spoken, then we may also want to ask what it means for speech to be written.

---

[30] Cf. Nagy's concept (1990a: 5–6, 29–34) of marked speech, or "song," as an anthropological notion.

[31] See Bakhtin 1981: 362; 1984: 185–204, on "double-voiced discourse," which "is directed both toward the referential object of speech, as in ordinary discourse, and toward *another's discourse*, toward *someone else's speech*" (1984: 185).

CHAPTER 2

The Writing of Homer

Let us say that a text is any discourse fixed by writing. According to this definition, fixation by writing is constitutive of the text itself. But what is fixed by writing? We have said: any discourse. Is this to say that discourse had to be pronounced initially in a physical or mental form? that all writing was initially, at least in a potential way, speaking? In short, what is the relation of the text to speech?
—Paul Ricoeur, "What Is a Text? Explanation and Understanding"

The orality-literacy dichotomy is not so much an objective distinction as a reflection of a particular perspective. It creates orality as what happens in the absence of writing. But it may also create orality as what happens in the presence of writing, diminishing its strange alterity in favor of a conception that is compatible with what we call literature. A case in point is Ruth Finnegan's monograph *Oral Poetry*. This book argues against a "deep gulf" between oral and literate poetry, and tries to correct some of the "dubious" and "romantic" generalizations about oral poetry in our modern literate culture.[1] This knowledgeable contribution to the subject of oral poetry considered as a cross-cultural social phenomenon has had quite a surprising effect on its classical readership. Finnegan's insistence that there are no hard boundaries between the oral and the literate has blurred the distinct senses of oral discussed in the previous chapter and has led to a new conception of orality as a phenomenon not essentially different from literacy. Instead of helping readers gain greater insight into the various aspects of oral poetry, Finnegan's book has actually contributed to the new spread of a literate and antioralist stance in Homeric studies. The feeling that no special categories of criticism and analysis, like those of oral-formulaic

---

[1] See, for example, Finnegan 1977: 2, 16–24, 30–41.

theory, are needed for the study and appreciation of Homer has been reinforced, paradoxically, on the authority of an acknowledged specialist in oral poetry.[2]

Finnegan's attempts at bridging the chasm between oral and literate poetry may indeed yield some insights into the nature of both that have been obscured by the oral-formulaic analysis of epic poetry and by the study of modern written narrative. In Homeric studies, however, they cause confusion by evading what I take to be the real issue. Homerists have drawn support from Finnegan's work for their position in what, since Parry, has been a major controversy: the question whether the Homeric poems were composed orally or not.[3] Yet this question is less central and productive than has been assumed, in that either answer to it misses the point by excluding the other. The mere acknowledgment of the existence of the text of the Homeric poems and of its importance in antiquity, for example, might in the dichotomized orality-literacy debate be taken as a statement to the effect that the Homeric poems have not been composed orally; or at least that they were composed by a poet who had liberated himself from the constraints of oral composition or was in the process of doing so.[4]

More interesting than either opposing oral and literate or blurring the distinction between them, however, seems to be the question—even if it does not lead to a clear answer—what it might have meant for the *Iliad* and *Odyssey* to have been written in their historical context. And if reading is the intended reception of a written text, we have to ask what it means for the texts of the Homeric poems to have been read in that historical context. Instead of manipulating oral and literate, then, as immutable primary elements that either coexist with or exclude each other, we should try to endow these terms with cultural value. Such an attempt requires of us a readiness to question the assumption that our conception of writing is a norm for writing in all times and places. In other words, we will have to make the effort to defamiliarize our culturally and professionally determined habits and preconceptions, to make them more meaningful, or rather, less self-evident. The resulting sense of relativism is what we surely need when it comes to the study of Homeric writing.

---

[2] See in particular Griffin 1980: xiv; Lloyd-Jones 1992. For a similar critique of Finnegan, see Nagy 1992b: 318–19.

[3] For the lingering importance of this question, see most recently Erbse 1994.

[4] See now Nagy 1996, a forceful antidote against this view.

Speech and Text

What are the possibilities when we try to bring speech and writing into closer contact with each other than they are in the binary contrast between written and oral composition? The most exciting possibility imaginable would be that the text of the Homeric poems is directly related to the real event, as the faithful recording of an epic oral performance, with traces of this actual event still present in our text. This would reconcile the *Iliad* and the *Odyssey* as performances with the existence of a written text and leave orality in its strong sense of textlessness intact. But this possibility is highly improbable. While it is true that text and performance have much to do with each other (in fact I will argue later on in this chapter that they are interdependent), the notion that the text is a faithful recording does not seem a viable one. It would lead to blatant anachronism and turn the Homeric text into the published version of the field notes of some ancient anthropologist, an interested scribe who was present at the performance of the master, but who had no part in the dynamics of the speech event, and in whose writing dynamics the performing poet had no part.[5]

One could also separate in time the composition of the *Iliad* and the *Odyssey* from their writing (and thereby save the notion of oral composition): the Homeric poems could have been written down long after their composition. This is the position that G. S. Kirk defends.[6] Kirk argues for a Homer who made no use of writing, a truly oral poet whose highly atypical, colossal poems were transmitted orally until they were committed to writing. Kirk's views rest on the common assumption that a creative phase in the development of the oral tradition (that of the *aoidoí* 'singers', of whom Homer was allegedly the last and the greatest), in which new poems were composed, was followed by the reproductive phase of the *rhapsōidoí* 'rhapsodes', who merely recited the creations of their great predecessors.[7] But this is a very literate, not to say literary, presentation of the matter; Kirk assumes that repetition is the reproduction of a first, normative, and superior original, and hence the creation of something derivative.[8] In his conception

---

[5] Lord himself admits (1960: 125, 149) that written texts of actual performances are extremely rare.

[6] Most recently Kirk 1985: 10–14.

[7] See, for example, Kirk 1976: 126–27: "In Greece there are reasons for believing that the *Iliad* and *Odyssey* came very near the end of the creative oral tradition. The introduction of writing, and the supremacy of the monumental poems themselves, no doubt hastened the decline of creative oral poetry."

[8] More on repetition as a literate concept in Chapter 7 below.

of Homer's creative orality (as opposed to the rhapsode's repetitive orality) Kirk thinks in solidly textual categories. What he neglects is the notion of performance, in which the concepts of repetition and reproduction are not as appropriate as those of reinstantiation, recreation, reiterability.[9] The insight that repetition across performances is crucial, not reprehensible, not only for the epic performance but also for speech in general, makes Homer somewhat less original than we like him to be, but the reciting rhapsodes become a great deal more creative; in fact the distinction between the two might well collapse.[10]

Which brings us to the position of Gregory Nagy and his elaborate argument in defense of the anonymous rhapsode. In Nagy's view, the single genius poet, whether composing orally or not, recedes in favor of a concept of Panhellenism, a "cumulative process, entailing countless instances of composition/performance in a tradition that is becoming streamlined into an increasingly rigid form as a result of ever-increasing proliferation."[11] This increasing rigidity, according to Nagy, eventually led to the textual fixation of the Homeric tradition, but the final stage of fixation was not reached until the performance tradition of Greek epic had completely vanished.[12] In Nagy's account, writing is seen as inherent in the fixation of the tradition, not as an external phenomenon superimposed on the tradition from outside. In what follows we will elaborate on a similar conception of writing, focusing more than Nagy does on the precise interrelationships between speaking, writing, and text.

We are dealing, then, with the role played by a poet who was capable of recomposing the *Iliad* in the actual production of the written text. The best-known scenario here is Lord's conception of "oral dictated text," in which a poet and a scribe engage in a deliberate communication, with the production of the text as intended outcome.[13] Owing to the changed communicative situation in which it was produced, the oral dictated text,

---

[9] See, for example, Foley 1991: 56–57; Hymes 1981: 82–83; Lord 1960: 99–102; Zumthor 1990: 49. The transmission of songs is not so much a matter of verbatim recall per se as of constraints on the memory of the performers; see Rubin 1995.

[10] See also Bakker 1993a. For another critique of Kirk's position, from a different perspective, see Parry 1966.

[11] Nagy 1979: 8; see also Nagy 1990a: 52–56.

[12] See now Nagy 1996, esp. 109–11, on the "five ages of Homer," and the transition from genuine oral poetry via "transcript" to "scripture," a process involving various centuries of transmission, that is, fixation in (re-)performance. See also the Conclusion below.

[13] Lord 1953; 1960: 126–28, 148–57; 1991: 38–48; see also Jensen 1980: 81–95; West 1990; Janko 1990; 1992: 37–38.

the reasoning goes, can be longer, covering more detail, than any single normal performance. Taken by itself and viewed from the right perspective, dictation remains a plausible conception for the fixation of the *Iliad* and the *Odyssey* in writing and for the initial stages of their text. To the extent, however, that the idea of dictation arose from a conception of orality that is opposed to literacy in the binary contrast that we are discussing here, the proposal must be viewed as born out of necessity.

As we have seen, in the original conception of Parry and Lord, oral and literate are always mutually exclusive concepts: a poet is either oral or literate, and an oral poet has an entirely different technique from the literate poet. Lord puts the dichotomy as follows: "The written technique . . . is not compatible with the oral technique, and the two could not possibly combine, to form another, a third, a 'transitional' technique. It is conceivable that a man might be an oral poet in his younger years and a written poet later in life, but it is not possible that he be *both* an oral and a written poet at any given time in his career. The two by their very nature are mutually exclusive."[14] Statements such as this one reflect the direction of the discussion of oral composition and the climate in which it has been conducted; oral composition has often been conceived of as a fragile flower that is immediately killed off when it comes into contact with its mortal enemy, literacy.[15] Lord's conception of the oral dictated text, in the context in which it was proposed, amounts to an effort to account for the existence of a text while leaving the much cherished idea of a monolithic oral tradition intact. Oral dictation in Lord's sense is the tangential contact between the oral tradition and writing, in the form of a special, abnormal performance of an unspoiled oral poet.

Historical and sociological research outside oral-formulaic theory, however, suggests that the picture is not so simple. Even if we adhere to orality vs. literacy as a meaningful opposition (a policy which I try to question in this chapter), it is clear that the advent of literacy in a society by no means kills off the phenomena that we conceive of in terms of orality: as we saw in the previous chapter, conceptional orality is a matter of degree. Eric Havelock, for example, proposes an oral residue in archaic and classical Greek societies, which are well beyond the phase of primary orality, the age of complete textlessness in all respects and on all levels. An even better picture

---

[14] Lord 1960: 129.

[15] See, for example, Kirk 1985: 15–16: "For the oral tradition, which would have been killed off by any immediate and serious extension of literacy. . . . Writing had spread too far by the early years of the seventh century B.C. for the creative oral genius to flourish much longer."

of the interaction of orality and literacy is provided by the Middle Ages, another period of early writing, which has yielded much more evidence than archaic Greece on what people actually did with written texts. The medieval record has made it clear on a large scale that people can live graciously with written texts while retaining degrees of orality in the reception or transmission of those texts that would surprise the doctrinaire oralist.[16]

A first step toward bringing more nuance into the one-dimensional dichotomy between orality and literacy might be to fraction it into dichotomies of composition, reception, and transmission. This would allow texts to be both oral and written, according to the parameter chosen. For example, texts may be written and still be oral in their reception (i.e., in performance/recitation), an oral text may be written down so as to be distributed and read, and so forth. On this basis we could argue that pure orality, in which neither the poets, nor their audiences, nor the tradition has any contact with writing, is a phenomenon much more limited in its occurrence than the earlier oralists would allow. In practice there is always some aspect of the oral tradition that is no longer oral. And the very existence of texts pertaining to an oral tradition, as in the case of Homer, seems to prove that the tradition does not belong to the pure type.[17]

The fractioning of the orality-literacy contrast into composition, transmission, and reception may seem to have an advantage over the one-dimensional dichotomy, but in reality it amounts to nothing more than a multiplication of the contrast. In themselves the three components still yield absolute, binary distinctions between the written and the oral: a text is conceived of as orally transmitted or not, orally composed or not, with our literate notion of nonoral writing still intact as a cultural universal. The fractioning of the orality-literacy contrast, we may note, is Finnegan's way of bridging the "great divide" between orality and literacy.[18] Yet the result of this solution is the reconciliation of literacy with orality as a concept defined in literate terms, and a conception of orality as entirely encapsulated within a literate universe: with orality being confined to certain aspects of an oral poem, it is possible to continue studying it as if it were a written poem, without questioning or rethinking any of our common

[16] On medieval literacy and illiteracy see Bäuml 1980, 1984, 1993; Clanchy 1993; Schaefer 1991, 1992; Zumthor 1987.

[17] See Bäuml 1984 on medieval "oral" texts and the problems those texts pose for the theory of oral composition, given the social context in which they have to be situated.

[18] See, for example, Finnegan 1977: 17–18.

literate assumptions. In order to avoid this anachronism, we need to view writing and written composition from the perspective of speech, instead of looking at oral composition from the point of view of writing. This shift will mean reexamining our notions of writing and oral composition. These two concepts have been maintained as mutually exclusive alternatives by an anachronistic approach to writing and an idiosyncratic treatment of orality. Both the anachronism and the idiosyncrasy are due to the perspective discussed in Chapter 1: a tendency to see oral poetry as a special case whose characteristic properties must be studied in terms of production. This emphasis on composition has led scholars to neglect the importance of reception in the creation of the Homeric poems.

Lord's writings, and indeed most writings in the oral-formulaic tradition, leave no doubt as to what is meant by "oral composition": for oral theorists, oral composition is the use of the formulaic system provided by the tradition. The use of this system, or better, the dependence on it, is for Lord the quintessential feature of oral composition, and since written composition is not dependent on the formulaic system, there is a hard distinction, formulated by Lord as follows: "The oral singer thinks in terms of . . . formulas and formula patterns. He *must* do so in order to compose. But when writing enters, the 'must' is eliminated."[19]

This treatment of the formula as the necessary condition for oral composition has led analysts to make a sharp distinction between such composition and writing.[20] But it has also led to a distinction between the oral style and ordinary speech; in fact, these two oppositions are related, and if one is invalid the other is too. At the end of the previous chapter I hinted that, rather than separating Homeric discourse from ordinary language, the formula helps create that discourse by stylizing everyday speech. This relation between Homeric discourse and ordinary language (indeed between special speech and speech) necessarily implies a certain amount of listening knowledge on the part of the poet's audience within the tradition. Beside composition, then, reception is an important factor in the function of formulas, and to the extent that this is the case, the formula ceases to be irreconcilable with writing. For the intended effect of formulas as speech

[19] Lord 1960: 130. Yet formulas do persist after the introduction of writing, and in a later publication, Lord (1975: 18) denies these phenomena the status of formulas because they evidently had not facilitated oral composition. Convincing criticism in Smith 1977: 141–44.

[20] Consequently, the alleged weakening of the concept of formula has been thought to bring Homer closer to writing. See Shive 1987.

units stylizing the units of ordinary speech was not in any way changed by their being written down, especially since the text produced was meant not to be read but to be heard.[21]

The allegedly destructive effect of writing on the capabilities of the poet is an artifact not only of the formulaic view of oral composition, but also of an anachronistic view of written composition. Lord may seem to see writing as the absence of the dependence on formulas, but in reality his conception is much broader: it is based on what writing means in our culture. Lord's use of the terms "writing" and "written composition," in fact, is underspecified and ignores a distinction that derives directly from the differentiation in the semantics of "oral" presented in the previous chapter: there is an important difference between "writing something down" and "composing something with the aid of writing." In the former case, writing is a medium transfer, the transcoding of a phonic discourse into a graphic discourse. One could do this without having anything to do with writing as composition, the production of a text that is written as to its conception.[22] In other words, one could write in a technical and physical sense, without one's thought processes being governed, or even touched, by writing as a compositional process. Lord, in his discussion of the opposition between oral and written composition, restricts "writing" to our notion of compositional activity or process, ignoring the fact that this notion is the highly developed end point of a long, evolutionary process of interiorization, and applying it to the very earliest stages of that process, where a quite different sense of "writing" is much more appropriate.

It is essential to realize that for us writing is a way of organizing thought and texts, and that its underlying technology has become entirely transparent and taken for granted. Earlier stages in the development of the technology were very different. The technology and psychology of medieval writing has been investigated by M. T. Clanchy, with results that should be of great interest to classicists.[23] In the writing culture of the eleventh century, composition in writing and writing technology were

---

[21] This liberation of the formula from production in the oral-formulaic sense stems mostly from the work of medievalists; see, for example, Schaefer 1988; 1992: 59–87.

[22] Oesterreicher (1993: 269–70) brings out this distinction by means of the terminological opposition between *Verschriftung* (writing in the medial sense, the transcoding of a discourse into text) and *Verschriftlichung* (writing in the conceptional sense, the textualization of a discourse). See also the Conclusion below.

[23] Clanchy 1993. I cite from this second edition.

entirely different fields, with their own specialists. As Clanchy notes, "Just as reading was linked in the medieval mind with hearing rather than seeing, writing (in its modern sense of composition) was associated with dictating rather than with manipulating a pen. Reading and writing were not inseparably coupled with each other as they are today."[24] In other words, writing in the sense of composition was a *form of speaking*, a matter of *voice*, separated from writing in the technological sense, which was the *transcription* of the sound produced by the voice.[25] A person, as Clànchy notes, might be able to "write" and still be illiterate by our standards: the writing that we couple with reading (in the visual sense) was an art in itself that was practised by highly trained scribes.[26] But even on the relatively rare occasions when the writer took pen in hand, the concept of dictation and voice did not lose its relevance, because writing then amounted to dictating to oneself, writing down what one heard one's own voice saying.[27] The central insight to be gained, then, from Clanchy's detailed investigation of early writing is that our distinction between speaking and writing is anachronistic and artificial when applied without further consideration to earlier stages of the literacy evolution. In particular, it appears that the distance between speech and text need not be so large as it is in our culture, either from the point of view of production, or from the point of view of reception, as we shall see in the next section.

Returning to the dictation of the Homer text, we now face the paradoxical situation that whereas Lord's conception of writing has to be rejected, his scenario for the writing of the *Iliad*, at least in the earlier stages of the transmission of the text, is highly plausible, if not compelling, provided that the dictation of the Homeric poems is viewed in the right perspective. What I am suggesting is that the dictating bard "wrote" by his own standards and "spoke" by ours. The *Iliad* is real speech: in recomposing it, the poet actually produced every sound of which the poem consists and his thought processes, and hence the presentation and structure of his discourse, were not in any way governed by writing in our conceptional sense. And yet he produced a written text that is the basis—at first probably in

---

[24] Clanchy 1993: 270–71.

[25] On transcription and inscription, see below.

[26] Clanchy 1993: 125–26; 131–32. But even literates would make use of scribes; see Zumthor 1987: 111; Clanchy 1993: 126.

[27] This is the suggestion made by Magoun in a discussion (1953: 460) of the Anglo-Saxon poet Cynewulf. The ultimate consequence of this idea, writing as performance and the scribe as performer, has been recently pursued by Doane (1994).

competition with other, similar variants of the same discourse[28]—of the tradition that has eventually yielded our Homeric text.

So I agree with Lord that a poet (who might well have been illiterate by our standards) dictated the *Iliad* to an amanuensis. But to distinguish this dictation event from writing, as Lord does, is to draw lines that do not seem relevant for the earliest stages of literacy, when speaking and writing form a continuum that runs counter to our own cultural routines. The relation between the earliest Homeric texts and their speakers must have been one for which no close parallel exists in our culture. The speaker was neither a disinterested party in the dictation event (and hence external to the text produced there), nor the very "maker" (the literal sense of *poiētēs* 'poet') and hence the author or owner of the text; in the textual fixation of his activity, he was rather a link in the transmission of Homeric discourse, and hence an agent in its survival. A possible scenario for this survival I consider in the final part of this chapter.

The Interdependence of Text and Performance

Texts are usually not created as self-contained objects; they have to be read.[29] Being read, in fact, is no less than the completion and fulfilment of any text.[30] The manner of this completion quite crucially depends on the nature of the text, its function and its manner of composition. A discussion of the writing of the Homeric text, then, is incomplete without a treatment of how it might have been read. In fact, a discussion of reading has the potential to deepen our understanding of writing, insofar as nothing is likely to be produced without some idea of the use that will be made of the product. We are concerned, then, with how the Homeric text might have been used in its original historical context.

[28] Medieval philology again provides suggestive, if indirect, evidence for what must have preceded the Alexandrian recension and redaction of Homeric poetry. See, for example, Zumthor 1987: 160–62, on *mouvance*, the dynamism of a poetic tradition, with textual variants resulting from its expansion in time and space (on which see now also Nagy 1996: 7–38). See also Cerquiglini 1989; Fleischman 1990b: 24–25; and O'Brien O'Keeffe's 1987 study of the coexisting textual traditions of Caedmon's *Hymn* in Old English, Latin, and vernacular. The manuscripts in the last-mentioned tradition provide less spatial organization (resulting in *scriptio continua* and rudimentary punctuation) and more textual variants than the manuscripts in Latin, and thus constitute a case of "the accommodation of literate to oral" (20) rather than the reverse.

[29] The remainder of this chapter is based on Bakker 1993a: 15–18.

[30] Cf. Ricoeur 1991: 151–52; Svenbro 1993: 45–46.

Even without the preceding discussion, it would hardly be controversial to label as anachronistic the notion that the first text(s) of the Homeric poems were read by silent readers, or that the ancient reception of the poems was somehow a "written reception."[31] Less evident, but still unmistakable, is the anachronism in the suggestion that the first text of the Homeric poems was kept by its commissioner as a valuable possession, in principle not to be read at all.[32] Such a conception separates the text from the oral tradition, just as it separates the oral poet from the production of the text; it reinforces the awkward coexistence of orality and literacy described earlier and leaves us with the idea of the Homeric text as an anomaly in an oral milieu, waiting to be discovered by someone who would treat it in the way in which *we* would treat it, by reading it or copying it.

In the context of archaic Greece, the idea of a text as a thing, or rather the idea of a thing as text, is more suitable for inscriptions, texts inscribed on stone or pottery. As Jesper Svenbro has argued, the term "inscription," denoting the activity of inscribing, may be used to refer not so much to the text as such in its physical medium (e.g., stone), as to the speech situation created by the earliest archaic Greek inscriptions: it is the inscribed tomb that "speaks" in the first person (e.g., "I am the tomb of so-and-so"), thereby functioning as substitute for the speech of the author. Contrasting with this speech situation are inscriptions in the third person ("This is the tomb . . ."), presenting not so much a speech act that takes the place of speech as a transcription of an earlier speech.[33] The transcript inscriptions, according to Svenbro, do not seem to appear before the middle of the sixth century. Whether the text on stone is an "inscript" or a transcript, however, its effect is always one of *addressing a reader*, in the presence of the text and in the absence of its author.[34]

---

[31] Harris 1989: 49; see also Taplin 1992: 37: "Not even the most zealous of the vigorous new school of scripsists would claim, I think, that Homer wrote his poem for a reading public. The important thing is that it was created to be delivered orally and to be heard." Contrast Lord 1960: 131: "Writing as a new medium will mean that the former singer will have a new audience, one that can read." See also Kirk (1985: 12), who indirectly makes the same assumption: "It [the *Iliad*] was still designed for a listening audience, since the spread of literacy cannot possibly have been such, by say 700 B.C., as to allow for a proliferation of copies and readers."

[32] See, for example, West 1990: 48.

[33] Svenbro 1993: 28–43; see also Nagy 1992a: 35.

[34] The presence of the text is discussed by Svenbro as the presence of the reader, who has to lend his voice to the speech act of the text during sonorous reading, being dispossessed of his own "I" (1993: 44–63), a conception of reading that runs counter to "animistic" interpretations of early writing (1993: 41). The magical or minatory use of early writing, however, cannot be completely discarded. See for example Harris 1989: 29 and Thomas 1992: 59, both citing the

The idea of texts as an address to a reader and as a substitute for speech is applied by the philosopher Paul Ricoeur not to the earliest stage of alphabetic writing, but to our writing. Like Svenbro, Ricoeur opposes the notion of inscribed discourse to the notion of transcription: "What is fixed by writing is . . . a discourse which could be said, of course, but which is written precisely because it is not said. Fixation by writing takes the very place of speech, occurring at the site where speech could have emerged. This suggests that a text is really a text only when it is not restricted to *transcribing* an anterior speech, when instead it *inscribes* directly in written letters what the discourse means."[35] Inscription is here opposed not to a subsequent stage (as in Svenbro's opposition) but to an earlier stage of the development of writing; it may be characterized as the fixation of the meaning of the speech event, whereas the transcript is the fixation of the speech event itself.

Transcripts, then, find themselves wedged between two types of inscription, one ancient and one modern. The transcribed text differs from either type in a number of ways. It does not come in the place of speech, but rather crucially depends on speech. It does not speak itself, as a physical inscribed object does. Nor does it speak in the metaphorical, fictional way of the modern written text. Rather, it is the recording of speech, as the transformation of speech into a different medium.[36] Finally, it does not directly address a reader in the way the inscriptions do: instead of directly transmitting a message to its recipient, it defers this activity to the speaker that gave rise to its existence, or to the speaker who acts as his substitute.[37] And in doing so it has recourse to a reality outside: not a context that is constituted by the text as a physical object, nor a reality contained in the text,[38] but rather a reality that must precede the text in time.

Now what does it mean to read a transcript, a text that according to

---

well-known text (seventh century B.C.E.) inscribed on an aryballos from Cumae: Ταταίες ἐμὶ λέκυθος· hὸς δ' ἄν με κλέφσει θυφλὸς ἔσται, "I am the jug of Tataie; whoever steals me will be blind," cf. Jeffery 1961: 238. Magical writing occurred in the Middle Ages as well; see Clanchy 1993: 314–17, 333–34.

[35] Ricoeur 1991: 44, emphasis added.

[36] Cf. Oesterreicher 1993: 269–70, on *Verschriftung*, the medial transformation of speech into text.

[37] For functions of early texts other than transmission, see Forster 1989; Goody 1987: 54.

[38] On the closure and autonomy of the written text as opposed to the contextual openness of speech, see Olson 1977: 264; Bäuml 1980: 251–52; Schaefer 1991: 119–20; 1992: 52–54. Ricoeur (1991: 47) speaks of "interception" to characterize the modified "referential contract" a written text entertains with the world.

Ricoeur is not really a text? The question cannot be seen in isolation from another question: what does it mean to write a transcript? Both questions lead us back to the most important transcript the archaic Greek period produced, the Homeric text. Being neither the physical embodiment of the speech act it represents, nor its autonomous container, the transcribed text needs voice to become physical, to accomplish the speech act that led up to its existence. In other words, in the case of the Homeric text the medium is different indeed from the message, to invert McLuhan's well-known dictum. An analogy between the ancient transcript and the transcripts of our time, the fruits of advanced technology, might help here: like the musical compact disk or computer diskette, the Homeric text in its original transcript stage preserves an original message in a format that is quite alien to the message as such. To read such a text is not to receive the information transmitted but to restore the medium of the original message, to convert it to a format with which the user is familiar, or rather, which is understandable to the user at all. And the writing of the text is not the act of transmitting the information it contains, but saving it in a medium that is more suitable for that purpose.[39]

Writing and reading as "medium shifts": this is the original use of the Homeric text that is proposed here. If this text, a transformation of speech into a different medium, owed its existence to speech and voice, then its reading was nothing other than the reversal of this process: the transformation of text back into the medium of speech, the reenactment of the speech represented by the text. It appears, then, that not only the distinction between speaking and writing, but also the one between writing and reading, begins to break down: if speaking is a matter of cognition, of the activation of ideas in a speaker's consciousness, as I shall argue in detail in the next chapter, then reading is a matter of the re-cognition and re-activation of those same ideas, both in the reader's and in the listeners' consciousness.[40] The reader of the *Iliad*, then, as well as of the other transcribed texts of early Greek literature, was no less a speaker than the writer

[39] In referring to CD-players and computer drives as *lecteurs* and to "saving" as *enrégistrer*, French usage for the management of computer files brings out the transcript status of "texts" in the new technologies more clearly than English.

[40] I owe the play on "cognition" and "recognition" to the meaning of one of the Greek verbs for "reading" (ἀναγιγνώσκειν 'to know again', 'recognize'), as well as to Svenbro's discussion (1993: 165–66) of it. See also Nagy 1990a: 171. Svenbro repeatedly emphasizes the practice of writing in *scriptio continua* which made the reader's voice necessary for the sounds of the text to be "recognized."

of the text was, which amounts to saying that writing and reading were related to each other as performance and re-performance.

That the *Iliad* is a text to be heard, not read, may have anyone's consent, but the present discussion aims to show that such a claim does not go far enough. Whoever wrote the *Iliad*, or gave orders for it to happen, did not merely write down a poem that was meant to be heard rather than read, still engaging in what we would call literary communication. Nor did the writing of the *Iliad*, whether as a unique event or as a series of events, a process, put an end to the public performance tradition of the Homeric epics. On the contrary, the writing of the *Iliad* was a masterful attempt—and a successful one, we may say—to secure this tradition by regulating the ongoing flow of performances and supplying it with a firm basis, a model for the rhapsode's act. This model was a written text that was authoritative precisely because it derived from, and was meant to give rise to, authoritative speech (speech that, in its turn, derived its authority from being stylized and special).

The writing of the *Iliad* did not constitute the first literary text, with a strong footing in the oral tradition; nor did it constitute the often mentioned culmination (i.e., the death) of the oral tradition, as the Homeric poems were transformed into the higher medium of writing. The writing of the *Iliad* was not an oral tradition becoming a literate one, unless one sees this process as indissolubly connected with the oral conception of a written text: the original text was meant to represent the *Iliad* in its essential quality of speech and performance, and to be as such a normative model for reenactment. As the fixation of an ideal performance, the original text of the *Iliad* was an attempt to establish a canon, a means to exert power over future performances in the Homeric tradition.[41] Or in other terms, the text of the *Iliad* is a transcript of the previous performance, and hence a script for the next one. In other words, the reading of the *Iliad* is the reenactment of its writing, with the actual text as nothing more (but also nothing less) than the preservation of the actual wording.[42]

[41] On power in the relation between a writer and a future reader who is forced to lend his voice to the vocalization of words that are not his own, see Svenbro 1993: chap. 3. On canons, value, and power, see Most (1990), who stresses the close link between literacy and canonization. Outside classical philology see Smith 1983; 1988: 30–53. Among the possible motives for establishing the Homeric tradition as canonical are Panhellenism (Nagy 1979: 1–11; 1990a: chap. 2); propaganda for aristocracy (Morris 1986; Latacz 1989: 85–90; Janko 1992: 38); and competition with new performance genres (Burkert 1987).

[42] See Herington's comment (1985: 45) on the absence of all mention of writing and texts,

Returning now to the orality-literacy contrast, we may assume that the contact between the Greek oral epic tradition and writing did not result in a mixture of what *we* conceive of as oral and literate features, with the almost inevitable outcome that those features that are oral are accommodated to the literate framework. Rather, the mixture goes deeper, resulting in a text the study of which is crucially bound up with the analysis of speech, considered as a phenomenon in itself, rather than as a concept defined from a literate point of view as the absence of writing. Accordingly, the body of this study will be a reading of the *Iliad* as a transcript, in an attempt to arrive at the speech that must once have been its primary referent.

To the extent that the orality-literacy contrast turns Homer into either an oral poet whose poems have somehow become texts, or a literate poet who in having liberated himself from the limitations of orality is one of us, it has to be rejected. Homer is not an oral poet, one of *them*, whose poems have been overheard, as it were, to be transcribed into the text which we possess. And because his writings need voice to become alive and do what they are meant to do, he is not one of *us*. It is the crucial importance of the human voice in the production, transmission, and reception of poetry whose essence lies in performance that led the medievalist Paul Zumthor to coin the term "vocality."[43] His coinage is gaining in popularity among medievalists as a way to characterize phenomena that are misrepresented by the orality-literacy dichotomy in its classical form.[44] More important than terms, however, are the perspectives they reflect. And the importance of perspectives lies in our being aware of them.

---

not only in the Homeric poems, but also in archaic poetry in general: "The texts were no part of the performed poem as such, but merely a mechanical means of preserving its wording between performances. You could hardly expect the archaic poem to allude to its own written text any more than you could expect a violinist in the concert hall to interrupt the music with an allusion to his printed score."

[43] See Zumthor 1987: 21: "C'est pourquoi je préfère, au mot d'*oralité*, celui de *vocalité*. La vocalité, c'est l'historicité d'une voix: son usage." See also Zumthor 1987: 19: "Lorsque le poète ou son interprète chante ou récite (que le texte soit improvisé ou mémorisé), sa voix seule confère à celui-ci son autorité. Le prestige de la tradition, certes, contribue à le valoriser; mais ce qui l'intègre à cette tradition, c'est l'action de la voix."

[44] Schaefer 1992: 5–20.

PART TWO

SPEECH

CHAPTER 3

Consciousness and Cognition

Consciousness is the crucial interface between the conscious organism and its environment, the place where information from the environment is dealt with as a basis for thought and action as well as the place where internally generated experience becomes effective—the locus of remembering, imagining, and feeling.
—Wallace Chafe, *Discourse, Consciousness, and Time*

In the preceding chapters I have argued that a binary distinction between orality and literacy does not quite capture the way in which speech and written texts may coexist and interact in cultures other than our own. Whereas written texts are medially different from speech in any culture, the conception underlying their production and use may in some cultures be so close to the conception of spoken language that a simple distinction between "oral" and "literate" becomes inappropriate. To study such texts, we need to ask what it means for language to be spoken. The search for an answer to this question where the Homeric text is concerned requires concepts and methods that are not to be found in classical philology, a discipline that has historically been concerned with the study of language as text. Below and in the chapters that follow I shall draw on such recent work in discourse analysis, the empirical study of speech, as seems relevant and useful for our purpose. Discourse analysis will provide a basis for discussing those features of our Homeric text that go unnoticed and unaccounted for in the textual perspective.

But this proposed change in perspective will not only lead us to look outside the philological discipline, but also require us to rethink some of what lies within. This takes us into the realm of the style of Homer and other archaic Greek poetry and will prompt us to reexamine such central concepts as parataxis, adding style, and ring composition. We shall deal in some detail with the phenomena denoted by these terms, paying attention to the question whether they do indeed reveal pertinent properties of the object de-

35

scribed—Homeric discourse—or are more indicative of the literate perspective of the stylistician. Our discussion of Homeric discourse in terms of the style of spoken language, then, will be concerned throughout not only with *medium*—spoken vs. written language—but also with the *conception* underlying each medium—oral vs. literate—and in particular with avoiding literate concepts in the study of the medium of speech.[1]

Periodic and Unperiodic Style

If the classical ideal of sentence structure, the rhetorical period, is taken as a norm, then Homer, who was held in antiquity to be the standard for many rhetorical virtues, falls short of it. Many ancient analysts of discourse, followed by the students of Homer in modern times, have observed that the style of Greek epic is different from the later, classical style characterized by a balanced and complex syntactic design that we call periodic structure. In fact, Homeric style is decidedly unperiodic, as Parry noted in a discussion of Homeric verse structure and sentence structure inspired by the analysis of these phenomena by the Greek critic Dionysius of Halicarnassus (first century B.C.E.): "The period . . . [is a sentence] in which there is a planned balance of the thought. The unperiodic sentence is one which lacks this balance and in which, to cite [Dionysius], 'the clauses are not made like one another in form or sound, and are not enslaved to a strict sequence, but are noble, brilliant, and free.' That is, the ideas are added on to one another, in what Aristotle calls the *running* style."[2] Parry is referring to Aristotle's well-known concept of *léxis eiroménē* 'strung-on way of speaking', that is opposed, as an archaic way of expression, to the *léxis katestramménē* 'turned-down way of speaking', the periodic style that comes to a natural end:[3]

---

[1] On medium and conception, see Chapter 1 above.

[2] Parry 1971: 252. Immediately before the quoted passage, Parry discusses Dionysius on enjambement in *Od.* 14.1–7 (*De comp. verb.* xxvi, in which the phrase occurs to which Parry's term "unperiodic" goes back: ὁ ἑξῆς νοῦς ἀπερίοδος ἐν κώλοις τε καὶ κόμμασι λεγόμενος 'the sequence of ideas is unperiodic, uttered in clauses and phrases'). In Parry's description of periodic and unperiodic sentences, the passage quoted from Dionysius is, oddly, from *De comp. verb.* xxii, a discussion not of Homeric unperiodic style but of the so-called grand, emotional style as a possible register in public oratory. See also Parry 1971: 262. Parry uses the term "unperiodic" to designate an important type of enjambement in Homeric verse, in which the end of the verse falls between two constitutive parts of an unperiodic sentence (see further Chapter 6 below).

[3] The translations "strung-on" and "turned-down" are borrowed from Kennedy 1991: 239. Aristotle's use of the term λέξις lies somewhere between "style" in the philological sense and

λέγω δὲ εἰρομένην ἢ οὐδὲν ἔχει τέλος καθ᾽ αὑτήν, ἂν μὴ τὸ πρᾶγμα τὸ
λεγόμενον τελειωθῇ. ἔστι δὲ ἀηδὴς διὰ τὸ ἄπειρον· τὸ γὰρ τέλος πάντες
βούλονται καθορᾶν· διόπερ ἐπὶ τοῖς καμπτῆρσιν ἐκπνέουσι καὶ ἐκλύονται·
προορῶντες γὰρ τὸ πέρας οὐ κάμνουσι πρότερον. ἡ μὲν οὖν εἰρομένη [τῆς
λέξεώς] ἐστιν ἥδε, κατεστραμμένη δὲ ἡ ἐν περιόδοις· λέγω δὲ περίοδον λέξιν
ἔχουσαν ἀρχὴν καὶ τελευτὴν αὐτὴν καθ᾽ αὑτὴν καὶ μέγεθος εὐσύνοπτον. ἡδεῖα
δ᾽ ἡ τοιαύτη καὶ εὐμαθής, ἡδεῖα μὲν διὰ τὸ ἐναντίως ἔχειν τῷ ἀπεράντῳ, καὶ
ὅτι ἀεί τι οἴεται ἔχειν ὁ ἀκροατὴς τῷ ἀεὶ πεπεράνθαι τι αὐτῷ· τὸ δὲ μηδὲν
προνοεῖν εἶναι μηδὲ ἀνύειν ἀηδές. (*Rh.* 1409ª29–1409ᵇ4)

I call "strung-on style" a type of discourse that has no inherent end point
other than the completion of the discourse topic in question. This style is
unpleasant by its unbounded nature, for all want to see an end point. This is
why it is [only] at the end of the course that [athletes] are out of breath and
exhausted: having the end point in view they do not tire beforehand. Such is
the strung-on style; the "turned-down style," on the other hand, is the
periodic style. I call "period" an utterance with an inherent beginning and
end as well as a length that can be beheld at a single glance. Such a type of
discourse is not only pleasant, but also easy to learn. It is pleasant by the fact
that it is the opposite of what is unbounded, and because the listener at every
moment has the idea of having hold of something, by the fact that every
moment is bounded in itself. For having no anticipation of what is to come
or not completing anything is unpleasant.

Aristotle seems to take as periods not the long balanced sentences that
the modern handbooks cite from the oratory of Isocrates or Cicero, but
rather the constitutive elements that make up such elaborate linguistic
structures.[4] Immediately after the passage quoted above, Aristotle claims
that a period is easier to understand because meter makes it easier to
remember than unperiodic discourse, an observation to which we will
return in Chapter 6. A second difference between Aristotle's account and
the conception of periodic style that we find in the modern handbooks of
Greek grammar is that the former is hearer-oriented, whereas in the mod-

---

"presentation strategy" as the phrase might be used by modern sociolinguists or discourse analysts. On the one hand, the term is used by Aristotle to designate properties of language as text; on
the other, λέξις never quite loses the meaning that is inherent in its morphological status as an
action noun.

[4] See Kennedy 1991: 239. See also Chapter 6 below.

ern accounts the emphasis is on the hierarchical relations in a sentence as marked by the syntax of subordination. In fact, Aristotle seems to deal with a different medium: his concern is with spoken, not written discourse.

Central in Aristotle's account of periodic style is hearers' anticipation (*pronoeîn* 'to have a sense as to what will come next'). Any present moment in the comprehension of a discourse, according to Aristotle, should be connected in expected ways to the next present moment, and it should be clearly defined with respect to a given end point. The teleology of periodic discourse, moreover, implies a "beginning" that is just as clearly marked as the "end," yielding a conception of periodic style as "bounded": it gives the listener a sense of "having hold of something," a mental disposition that is not only conducive to the comprehension of a discourse, but also adds to the listener's pleasure.[5]

In Aristotle's account, the strung-on style of speaking is all that the periodic style is not: it is unpleasant because of its unboundedness. Without beginning, middle, and end, it does not provide the listener with a sense of being somewhere, of knowing where the discourse will lead and from which point it started. In other words, the *léxis eiroméně* is not viewed as a phenomenon in its own right; it is negatively defined with respect to the positive qualities of the periodic style. Aristotle may differ from us in his emphasis on the listener and in his attention to the spoken medium, but he is a clear precursor of modern stylistic practice in using a given conception of language as a norm to which some discourses conform and others do not.

It was not until Parry that Aristotle's stylistic perspective came to be seen in the terms that are familiar to us today. Parry turned Aristotle's well-known stylistic distinction between periodic and unperiodic style into a basis on which Homeric adding style, as he called it, could be considered an oral style and opposed to the literate style of later authors. Within Parry's perspective and the conception of orality discussed in the first two chapters of this book, the adding style is what distinguishes Homer's oral poetry from other literature. It is a necessary consequence of the fact that Homeric poetry is produced under circumstances that are quite different from those applying to written composition: "Oral versemaking by its speed must be chiefly carried on in an adding style. The Singer has not time for the nice balances and contrasts of unhurried thought: he must order his words in

---

[5] It is not clear whether this quality applies to the relation between periods or to the internal structure of periods. See further Chapter 6.

such a way that they leave him much freedom to end the sentence or draw it out as the story and the needs of the verse demand."[6]

Just as in the case of the formula, the other major characteristic of the oral style, Parry puts strong emphasis on production as the criterion for distinguishing between oral and nonoral discourse and as the explanation of the distinctive features of the adding style. The hurried thought underlying oral verse-making renders the oral adding style a necessity, insofar as anything more complex is in practice unattainable under the specific circumstances in which oral verse is produced. In this way, Parry's perspective is still (however implicitly) the primacy of writing and written language as a norm to which oral language does not yet conform, even though his work did much to establish oral poetry as a legitimate form of literature with its own poetics.

The strung-on style with its unbounded nature has indeed been upgraded from vice or necessary evil to stylistic virtue by some scholars working in the wake of Parry's discoveries, the idea being that there is a need for an oral poetics opposed to and coexisting with the traditional literate view of language and texts.[7] Such work, however, does little more than reinforce the binary and unproductive opposition between orality and literacy that I argued against in the first two chapters. It still views the unperiodic strung-on style from the point of view of periodic style; what is forbidden or reprehensible in the latter is simply permitted or even desirable in the former. We need an account of unperiodic style in its own right, without the bias of periodic style or its post-Aristotelian form, the literate conception of language. Such an investigation does not deal with orality or oral style but with something that lies outside the realm of style: ordinary speech. In this chapter and the next two I offer such an analysis, arguing that Homeric unperiodic discourse, if studied from the appropriate angle, involves just as much boundedness and controlled anticipation as Aristotle attributes to periodic style. The difference lies in the means used to that end, means that belong to the spoken, not the written medium.

Apposition and Parataxis

Parry's conception of Homeric discourse in terms of adding style has been refined by later authors, leading to a proliferation of terms for what re-

[6] Parry 1971: 262.
[7] See, for example, Notopoulos 1949; but cf. Austin 1966: 295–96.

mains essentially the same observation. Kirk, for example, speaks of "cumulation," the crucial property of a style in which "each new piece of information, as the story proceeds, can be envisaged as being heaped upon its predecessor."[8] From a different angle, using syntactic rather than stylistic terminology, Antoine Meillet, Pierre Chantraine, and others have singled out the "appositional construction" as the crucial property of Homeric syntax.[9] By a syntactic principle inherited from Indo-European, according to Meillet, phrases or even single words in Homer tend to have considerable syntactic autonomy, being loosely attached to each other by appositional relationships and having the semantic autonomy of independent sentences. As an example of appositional syntax in the adding style consider the following piece of Iliadic battle narrative:[10]

Πρῶτος δ' Ἀντίλοχος Τρώων ἕλεν ἄνδρα κορυστὴν
ἐσθλὸν ἐνὶ προμάχοισι, Θαλυσιάδην Ἐχέπωλον·
τόν ῥ' ἔβαλε πρῶτος κόρυθος φάλον ἱπποδασείης,
ἐν δὲ μετώπῳ πῆξε, πέρησε δ' ἄρ' ὀστέον εἴσω
αἰχμὴ χαλκείη· τὸν δὲ σκότος ὄσσε κάλυψεν,
ἤριπε δ', ὡς ὅτε πύργος, ἐνὶ κρατερῇ ὑσμίνῃ.

(*Il.* 4.457–62)

Antilokhos was the first to kill a chief man of the Trojans,
valiant among the champions, Thalusias' son, Ekhepolos.
Throwing first, he struck him, on the horn of the horse-haired helmet,
and the bronze spearpoint fixed in his forehead and drove inward
through the bone; and a mist of darkness clouded both eyes
and he fell as a tower falls in the strong encounter.

To the first mention of Antilokhos's victim (*ándra korustền* 'chief man', 457) are added two pieces of information, which according to Meillet's analysis have to be seen as loosely added appositional phrases (*esthlòn enì pro-*

---

[8] Kirk 1976: 152; Kirk's notion of cumulation is criticized for imprecision in its relation to enjambement in Higbie 1990: 13.

[9] Meillet 1937: 358–59; Meillet and Vendryes 1968: 598–99; Chantraine 1948–53: 2:12. See also Ammann 1922: 9; Schwyzer 1947: 8; and esp. Thornton and Thornton 1962, an account of apposition in terms of temporal experience. See also Chapter 5.

[10] Translation is from Lattimore 1951, except for the insertion of "him, on" in 459 and different transliterations of the proper names.

mákhoisi 'valiant among the champions' and *Thalusiádēn Ekhépōlon* 'Thalusias' son Ekhepolos', 458) that acquire a large amount of syntactic autonomy (they are equivalent to separate clauses: "he was . . . ; his name was. . . ."). Furthermore, the recapitulative phrase *tón rh' ébale prôtos* 'Throwing first, he struck him', 459 is followed by a phrase (*kóruthos phálon hippodaseíēs* 'on the horn of the horse-haired helmet', 459) that can be seen as an added piece of information, specifying the verb *ébale*: 'he struck him, [namely] on the horn of the horse-haired helmet'. The passage as a whole, finally, is characterized throughout by a paratactic structure, in that the clauses are added to one another, without there being the kind of complex syntactic interrelationships that come with hypotactic structure and periodic composition.[11]

Now adding style, appositional syntax, and parataxis are themselves apt characterizations of the passage cited, though I will be replacing them in the next two chapters with other terminology, but the way in which these terms are used may still to a certain extent be indicative of the perspective of the user. We have already seen that Parry's use of the term "adding style" is entailed by his view that Homeric oral poetry is an art form composed under specific circumstances. Meillet's and Chantraine's appositional construction, on the other hand, is a concept from historical syntax: Homeric style is viewed, from a diachronic point of view, as archaic, conforming to inherited Indo-European patterns to a greater extent than do later texts from the Greek corpus. The closely related notion of parataxis frequently and typically conveys qualities such as primitive or crude. Paratactic discourse, it has been thought, fails to express certain logical relations and has to put ideas of unequal importance and syntactic status simply beside each other, in the absence of any grammatical means to effect syntactic subordination. Criticism of such a "prelogical" way of expression was frequent in the preoral era before Parry and continues to be heard occasionally. Thus Eduard Norden calls *léxis eiroménē* the prime characteristic of the language

[11] The literature on parataxis in early Greek literature is vast and covers not only parataxis as the stylistic appearance of single passages (e.g., Perry 1937: 410–12; Chantraine 1948–53: 2:351; Fränkel 1968: 40–96), but also parataxis as the primary compositional principle behind whole works (e.g., Van Groningen 1937, 1958; Notopoulos 1949). Notopoulos (1949: 5–6) proposes parataxis as the core element of a non-Aristotelian poetics: "The *Iliad* and *Odyssey* have a unity; but unlike that of the drama it is inorganic and, moreover, the digressions far from being, like Homer's similes, for purposes of relief, are actually the substance of the narrative, strung paratactically like beads on a string." A more recent account of parataxis as compositional principle is Thalmann's (1984: 1–6), who argues that parataxis by no means excludes planned design. For a more detailed discussion, see Chapter 4 on parataxis as movement.

of "children and primitives,"[12] and Kirk writes of "the unsophisticated tendency to state logically subordinate ideas as separate, grammatically co-ordinate propositions," a very common characterization of "archaic style" in classical philology.[13]

The three terms all reflect an assumption that style is a set of properties assigned to what the researcher perceives and conceives of as a text, a text that is different in a number of ways from other (i.e., later) texts. Homer may be said to use an adding, appositional, paratactic, even an oral style, but these qualifications ultimately derive from a comparison with other texts that lack certain properties; even the notion of style may itself imply a textual perspective, in that texts other than the *Iliad* serve as a basis for the characterization of Homeric style as archaic or oral. This comparison is understandable, given the necessarily textual orientation of classical philology, but is it necessary? Must the analysis of the appositional, paratactic passage just cited be a matter of comparing supposedly primitive archaic texts with sophisticated classical texts? And is style, considered as a textual property, at all an appropriate concept for defining the passage's nature and design?

Those questions might best be answered by considering a very different example. The following text is a transcript drawn from a linguistic investigation of spoken narrative under the supervision of Wallace Chafe and known as the Pear Film project, in which subjects were shown a short film and were asked afterward to verbalize what they had seen and experienced. The fragment has many of the features that we noticed in the passage from

---

[12] Cf. Norden 1909: 37 n: "Daß die λέξις εἰρομένη überhaupt das wesentliche Kennzeichen primitiver Rede ist, weiß jeder aus der Sprache der Kinder und Naturvölker." Similar prejudices exist against repetition in discourse, as noted by Finnegan 1977: 131–32.

[13] Kirk 1962: 169. See the introduction in Kühner and Gerth 1898–1904: 1–2, where the task of grammar is defined as the description of how the Greek language has developed from the primeval form of the simple clause to the elaborate perfection of the Attic periodic sentence. See also Kühner and Gerth 1898–1904: 2:224–26, where parataxis is described as a primitive stage of linguistic expression, the precursor of more sophisticated stages in the development of text and the human mind. See also Denniston 1952: xl: "As expression develops, subordination largely replaces co-ordination, the λέξις κατεστραμμένη the λέξις εἰρομένη." Notice that Kirk's phrase "logically subordinate ideas" testifies to the widespread tendency in classical philology to treat style as the *form* of a text in a binary opposition to content or what the text represents, the underlying idea being that the text "contains" logical, subordinating relationships but that the style used by its author is still too primitive to express them. This way of thinking applies also to suprasyntactic levels, as appears from Immerwahr's characterization (1966: 307) of the structure of Herodotus's *Histories*.

the *Iliad*, but its style does not seem to fit the historical and textual paradigms just discussed:[14]

> And he rides off, [1.55] with the basket, [.3] in front of his handlebars, [.8] balanced, . . and he hits some bumps, and a few pears spill out. [.85] He goes down the road, [.75] and he passes a girl on a bicycle, [.35] and in passing her, his hat comes off, [.55] and he turns his head, and he looks back, [.5] then his bicycle hits a rock in the road, and he falls over, [.2] spills his pears, . . hurts his leg.

This text displays the appositional syntax and adding style attributed to Homer: one piece of information is heaped on another in small, relatively autonomous units (e.g., "with the basket | in front of his handlebars | balanced" or "and he falls over | spills his pears | hurts his leg"); furthermore, the passage is paratactic throughout, with almost each new clause that contains a verb being linked to what precedes by the conjunction "and." This parataxis may seem to be a textual feature, because we also find it in the Homeric text, but the Pear Film passage is, of course, a transcript of a spoken narrative. Its parataxis may be better understood if we study it not as a feature of the transcript as such, but of the speech serving as its model. Such a perspective quickly reveals that speech, our own everyday language, is pervasively paratactic too—the feature appears to be an inherent property of spoken discourse, naturally resulting from its production, and essential in some ways to its comprehension. If this is the case, parataxis can hardly be an archaism or a mark of primitive language. To question such a conclusion, we would have to say that we all "speak in an oral style." But the very strangeness of that phrase brings us back again to the central issue: the concept of an oral style involves applying literate standards to what was once a spoken reality. What if we were to reverse that approach, applying what we know of speech to our received Homeric text? My brief discussion of the Pear Film passage would seem to allow such an experiment. It is suggestive, first of all, that a collection of spoken narratives should contain speech that in certain respects resembles so closely the language of Homer. Notice also that we have not listened to the original Pear Film narrative or

[14] Chafe, ed. 1980: 319. Numbers in brackets indicate pauses measured in seconds. Two dots indicate brief pauses up to one-half-second long. Punctuation marks show intonation contours: a period indicates falling pitch, and a comma indicates rising pitch.

to a tape of it. We have examined a transcript, using comparisons with other examples of spoken narrative as a way of understanding the style of the transcript. I would suggest, then, that we use a similar approach to the transcriptions that have come down to us as the Homeric poems.

Consciousness and Cognition

Perhaps the most striking difference between speech and written text—modern written text—is that the former is a *dynamic process* evolving in time, whereas the latter seems to be better characterized as a finished and hence static *product*. To call a text static may seem strange at a time when reader-response criticism and reception aesthetics have left their mark on literary studies. Texts are more and more conceived of as dynamic and protean, rather than static, shaped in the ever changing dynamics of their reception. Yet the shift to considering reception and comprehension as subjective and dynamic processes tends to stress the relative autonomy of written texts, and this emphasis makes it even more likely that in its production or composition the written text will not be perceived as a process. More precisely, the actual production of written texts does not show in the text, the art of written composition being directed to hiding the processes related to production and to the presentation of a finished product.[15]

Speech is a process evolving in time, and not just because it takes time to utter words and sentences. The processlike quality of speech, less trivially, has to do with what happens in the minds of the speaker and his audience. As an act of socialization, speech may be public, an observable event occurring in the world, and words may, in the formulation of Mikhail Bakhtin, be "performed outside the author";[16] but this observable, public event is nonetheless closely associated with what is inherently private and non-observable: the consciousness of both the speaker and his or her listeners.

In introducing consciousness, not only as the source of speech, but also as a constraint on speech that determines important aspects of spoken

[15] Of course, this distinction between product and process is not a clear-cut one, just as the orality of a discourse is not a matter of "yes" or "no." As pointed out at the beginning of Chapter 1, discourses may, according to their conception, be oral to a greater or lesser degree. The processual features that result from orality may even be imitated; see Oesterreicher 1997.

[16] Bakhtin 1986: 122. The public nature of words and utterances is the basis of Bakhtin's ideas on the "joint creation of meaning" by the speaker or author, the listener, and "those whose voices are heard in the word before the author comes upon it" (121).

discourse as it is publicly performed, I am following the ideas on the relation between language and consciousness of Wallace Chafe, whose earlier Pear Film project I mentioned above.[17] Spoken discourse, Chafe argues, represents the consciousness of the speaker in a more direct way than written discourse does the consciousness of writers, and hence the observable, physical properties of the speech process are best explained as reflecting some characteristic properties of the flow of consciousness of the speaker. This flow, as Chafe notes, is a matter of activation, the flow of successive ideas through the mind: "Although every human mind is devoted to modeling a larger reality within which it (or the organism it inhabits) occupies a central place, only one small piece of that model can be *active* at one time. At any given moment the mind can focus on no more than a small segment of everything it 'knows.' I will be using the word *consciousness* here to refer to this limited activation process. Consciousness is an active focusing on a small part of the conscious being's self-centered model of the surrounding world."[18] Hence consciousness can be understood in terms of vision, a particularly important aspect of Homeric poetics.[19] Consciousness is like vision, according to Chafe,[20] in that both can focus on no more than a very limited amount of information at any one moment. The eye's area of foveal vision, where visual acuity is greatest, is small compared to the total field of vision and is continuously shifting. In the same way, a focus of consciousness, as Chafe calls it, containing the information that is activated in a person's mind at a given moment, is small in comparison with the huge amount of inactive information, of which one could be but is not conscious at any given moment.[21] This focus of consciousness is also much smaller than the amount of information that is of immediate relevance for it, and that other information is analogous to the background in a field of vision: in order to be meaningful, any conscious experience, be it visual or introspective, needs a certain amount of information of which one is half-conscious (or which constitutes the periphery of the field of vision).[22] And like vision, consciousness is continu-

---

[17] Cf. also Bakker 1990b; 1993b: 5–8; 1993c: 278–80. Chafe's ideas are now most fully presented in Chafe 1994.

[18] Chafe 1994: 28.

[19] See further Chapters 4 and 5 below, as well as Bakker 1993b: 15; 1997a.

[20] Chafe 1994: 31, 53; see also Chafe 1980: 12–13.

[21] On activation and inactivity considered in terms of presence and absence, and in the context of the Greek epic tradition, in terms of *kleos* and forgetfulness, see Bakker 1993a.

[22] Such a background (both in visual and in cognitive terms) is what Chafe (1987: 28–31;

ously moving, not in an uninterrupted, smooth flow, but owing to the seemingly discrete nature of a focus of consciousness, in small jerks from one focus of consciousness to the next.[23]

Consciousness, moreover, is closely related to time and memory. Not only is the movement from one focus of consciousness to the other a process evolving through time; the notion of focus is itself a matter of time, in that its short duration can be related to the essence of time: the experience of a now, a present moment. Human experience of a now has to cover a time span that is short enough to be adjusted to the rapid changes in the environment, but long enough to make possible a reaction to what might happen during this now. Cognitive and neurophysiological research suggests that this time span is a two- to three-second period.[24]

The activation and conscious experience of a small amount of information during this period, furthermore, appears to be the proper domain for what in psychology has been called short-term memory, the evanescence of which matches the restless movement of conscious experience itself. Short-term memory can either be visual, retaining for a few seconds what was on the eye's retina a few moments before, or nonvisual, keeping strings of digits or other elements of information that, once focused on consciously, can be held in memory for a short period after the activation. And finally there is the short-term remembering of sound, by which acoustic signals (e.g., words spoken) can be retained for a limited duration after the moment of hearing.[25] So our consciousness, with its successive shifts in focus, seems to be limited both in capacity and in the duration of each active state, limitations that also apply to foveal vision and short-term memory, as is suggested by intuition and confirmed by experimental research.

Now when we consider focal consciousness and short-term memory in terms of linguistic expression, we have to think of short strings of words, conveying the information that is in focal consciousness and not exceeding the capacity of short-term memory. Furthermore, we must assume that

---

1994: 71–80) calls semi-active information. Further details, in connection with the particularities of Homeric discourse, in Chapter 5 below.

[23] Chafe 1994: 29–30. See also Flanagan 1992: 159.

[24] In Turner 1992: 86–88, the three-second period is called a "fundamental parcel of experience."

[25] On short-term memory, see Miller (1956), who states that short-term memory typically can hold seven items (plus or minus two). The short-term memory of sound is sometimes called echoic memory (e.g., Chafe 1994: 55). Rubin (1995: 69) speaks of "working memory."

when a consciousness is engaged in turning its successive foci into speech, these foci are apparent in the flow of speech produced by a verbalizing consciousness in order to be processed by a listening consciousness. And this appears to be in fact the case.

If we see speaking as a turning of what is private into public speech, or in Bakhtinian terms, as the creation of an object or the objectification of consciousness,[26] then listening to and making sense of speech is necessarily the reverse of this process: it involves turning what is public into private sense, or alternatively, the subjectification of speech. But it is also possible to listen to speech as an object of study in its own right. In adopting this empirical stance, Chafe is one of the relatively few linguists who have noted that spoken discourse comes in a series of "spurts of vocalization" beginning every two or three seconds and often (though not always) preceded by a pause which may last from a slight break up to several seconds. These units are above all characterized by a coherent intonation contour, that is, they are uttered as integral wholes and end with a pitch contour that signals a sense of closure.[27]

On the basis of the last property, Chafe calls these units "intonation units," emphasizing their physical, empirically observable quality as units of speech.[28] It is intonation units that are mainly responsible for what might be called the fragmented style of spoken discourse, as opposed to the more fluent and integrated quality of written discourse. But this public, readily observable reality is intimately connected with the private consciousness

[26] See also the psycholinguist Goldman Eisler (1958) on what she calls subjective and objective speech.

[27] See Chafe 1980: 13–16; 1987: 22–25; 1988: 1; 1990: 88–89; 1994: 56–62. See also the general discussion in Brown and Yule 1983: 153–69, with special reference to the work of Halliday (1967); as well as Turner 1992: 88; Devine and Stephens, who list (1994: 412–14) other prosodic features as well.

[28] Other researchers making the same observation have proposed different terms, such as "tone unit," "information block," or "idea unit." As often in linguistics, there is a proliferation of terminology that does not seem to be entirely justified by the researchers' differing interests and points of view. Chafe uses "idea unit" in earlier publications (1980, 1982, 1985), a term that seems to apply more to units of consciousness than to units of speech. Devine and Stephens (1994: 411) speak of "major phrases" as intonational, prosodic units that are "important not only as phonological cues to syntactic, and consequently semantic, structure, but also as cues to processing units. Our brains seem to process the utterances we hear in clausal chunks." Hymes (1981: 309–41) speaks of "lines" in this connection, a term stressing the importance of "intonation units" in poetry, which is also one of the main themes in Turner 1992: 61–108. Intonation units and meter are the subject of Chapter 6 below.

that drives the speech: the intonation unit is the linguistic equivalent of the focus of consciousness, the amount of information that is active at any one time in a speaker's consciousness. The intonation unit is the largest linguistic unit that is still available in its entirety to consciousness, the typical sequence of speech sounds that is within the grasp of the speaker's, and listener's, echoic memory: any stretch of discourse that is longer will have to be processed as more than one of these basic chunks.[29]

It is in terms of the segmentation of spoken discourse into intonation units that we have to view the characteristics of the Pear Film passage presented above. We present it here again, this time with each intonation unit displayed as a separate "line:"

a. And he rides off,
b. [1.55] with the basket,
c. [.3] in front of his handlebars,
d. [.8] balanced,
e. . . and he hits some bumps,
f. and a few pears spill out.
g. [.85] He goes down the road,
h. [.75] and he passes a girl on a bicycle,
i. [.35] and in passing her, his hat comes off,
j. [.55] and he turns his head, and he looks back,
k. [.5] then his bicycle hits a rock in the road,
l. and he falls over,
m. [.2] spills his pears,
n. . . hurts his leg.

Most of the intonation units in this stretch of spoken discourse are short clauses, consisting of a verb with a subject and/or object (such as units a or m), and most of these clauses are introduced by the particle "and." Intonation units may also be something other than a clause and are in principle not predetermined by any kind of linguistic structure. In terms of syntax,

[29] Chafe 1994: 55. Cf. Rubin 1995: 68–69, 104–5. See also Turner 1992: 88: "A human speaker will pause for a few milliseconds every three seconds or so, and in that period will decide on the precise syntax and lexicon of the next three seconds. A listener will absorb about three seconds of heard speech without pause or reflection, then stop listening briefly in order to integrate and make sense of what he has heard." Turner's connection between the brain and poetic meter will prove important in Chapter 6.

intonation units can be anything from complete clauses to all kinds of nonclausal elements: prepositional phrases as in units b and c, phrases involving participles as in unit d, or even separate noun phrases when they are the verbalization of the idea on which the speaker focuses.

The little jumps from one focusing to another, furthermore, are mainly responsible for what Aristotle would have called the unperiodic or strung-on style of the passage: there is no inherent end point in the discourse of this speaker. The transcript is punctuated to suggest intonation: the comma transcribes a rising intonation, which conveys the idea that more is to come, whereas the period represents the falling pitch that signals closure in spoken English, the sense that something has been completed.[30] In the composition and comprehension of written discourse, we conceive of such moments of closure in terms of the end of a sentence, and we tailor our syntax in such a way as to make that moment a meaningful and a pleasing one for the reader.

Such planned organization is quite absent from the above fragment, whose speaker merely passes from one scene to another in recalling the story. Syntactically, the beginning of the second "sentence" (unit g) is marked only by the absence of the particle "and" in the middle of a whole string of clauses introduced by that particle. The concept of sentence, then, the primary stylistic unit of written discourse and the principal domain for the operation of written syntax, is much less relevant in spoken discourse. Speakers may regularly produce sentences by intonational means (sentences that may or may not correspond to what is for us a finished, syntactically correct sentence), but the syntax of their speech is the syntax of the intonation unit as it reflects the flow of ideas through their consciousness.[31]

The same kind of nonsentential segmentation becomes apparent when we re-present the *Iliad* passage that was cited above, changing the hexametric lines of our modern printed text into the lines of cognitive production:[32]

---

[30] Chafe 1988: 6–10; 1994: 143.

[31] On "sentences" see more in Chafe 1980: 20–32, where the frequent discrepancies between intonational and syntactic closure are noted; 1987: 45–47; 1994: 139–44. See also Devine and Stephens 1994: 418–19.

[32] In this and every similarly presented example in this book, I have retained the punctuation of the *OCT* for the Greek text in the left column and have used Chafe's intonational punctuation of transcripts (see above) for the English translation in the right column. I have sought to strike a balance between a literal rendering enabling the Greekless reader to follow the discussion of each passage, and English idiom as required for an independently readable translation.

a. Πρῶτος δ᾽ Ἀντίλοχος	And first Antilokhos,
b. Τρώων ἕλεν ἄνδρα κορυστὴν	of the Trojans he took a helmeted man,
c. ἐσθλὸν ἐνὶ προμάχοισι,	valiant among the foremost fighters,
d. Θαλυσιάδην Ἐχέπωλον·	Thalusias's son Ekhepolos.
e. τόν ῥ᾽ ἔβαλε πρῶτος	He first struck him,
f. κόρυθος φάλον ἱπποδασείης,	on the crest of his horse-haired helmet,
g. ἐν δὲ μετώπῳ πῆξε,	and he planted [it] in his forehead,
h. πέρησε δ᾽ ἄρ᾽ ὀστέον εἴσω	and it pierced right through the bone,
i. αἰχμὴ χαλκείη·	the bronze spearpoint,
j. τὸν δὲ σκότος ὄσσε κάλυψεν,	and darkness covered his eyes,
k. ἤριπε δ᾽ ὡς ὅτε πύργος,	and he fell as when a tower [does],
l. ἐνὶ κρατερῇ ὑσμίνῃ.	in the tough battle.

(*Il.* 4.457–62)

My argument, here and in later chapters, rests on the assumption that the lines into which I divide Homeric extracts must have been a prosodic, intonational reality. Our text obviously does not record that reality as such, but it provides some cues. First of all there is meter. The metrical dimension of Homeric speech will not concern us until Chapter 6, but we can already note that boundaries between the units in this fragment coincide either with the end of the hexameter line or with the middle caesura (penthemimeral or trochaic). The coincidence of intonation with metrical units is a universal characteristic of performed poetry in oral traditions, and in the study of Homer it seems justified to use the latter as evidence for the former.[33]

Furthermore, the content of phrases can be used as criterion for division—in fact, this is the very reason of being for intonation units in Chafe's analysis: each unit represents a single focus of consciousness. In an analysis of the Homeric text, this semantic criterion is to a certain extent arbitrary, but in practice the often observed coincidence of metrical units and semantic units in Homer can guide us, each metrical *colon* being the verbalization of a single idea in a satisfyingly large number of cases.[34] Thus each of the

[33] See Bakker 1993b: 8; 1997b; Devine and Stephens 1994: 410, 424–28; Rubin 1995: 86, 206. Notice that the significantly greater tolerance as regards hiatus and *brevis in longo* at the middle caesura, which since Parry's (1971: 197–221) seminal discussion has been discussed in terms of the modification and juxtaposition of formulas (e.g., Hoekstra 1965), is primarily an intonational phenomenon, because formulas are stylized intonation units. See further Chapter 6.

[34] See Parry 1971: 256–62; Lord 1960: 145; Edwards 1966: 121–25; Turner 1992: 73–79. In Bakker 1990b: 17–18, I show that certain ideas may be so strongly associated with a given metrical contour as to influence the surface realization of an adjacent unit.

phrases that in the above analysis of the passage were called appositional (here units c, d, and f) can now be seen as the verbalization of a focus of consciousness. Besides meter and semantic content, syntax is an important cue for the division of Homeric discourse into speech units. As noted above, intonation units are in themselves not determined by a syntactic structure, but the reverse does frequently occur. Like many languages, ancient Greek has enclitic particles that occupy, as postpositives, the second position within a "domain" that is intonational rather than syntactic.[35] Consequently, we may consider these particles as textual evidence of an intonational boundary. In our fragment the particle *rh'* (unit e), a phonetically attenuated form of *ára*, is an example. Even more significant is the conjunctive postpositive particle *dé* (units a, g, h, j, k). This particle can be described as a *boundary marker*, setting off discourse segments against each other.[36] In written prose, those segments tend to be larger, with textual structure and cohesion being the rationale for the boundary. In Homer, on the other hand, the segments marked by *dé* appear to be much shorter, the size of Chafe's intonation units, so that *dé* becomes an important feature of the Homeric text considered as speech. *Dé* plays a role similar to "and" in English speech, and is the prime feature of Homeric parataxis, as we shall see in more detail in Chapter 4.[37]

It appears, then, that metrical and syntactic cues may be of help in determining the way in which Homeric discourse is segmented according to the cognitive principle noted by Chafe and others. Many readers of Homer will find this segmentation intuitively satisfying. Yet not all of Homeric discourse is as clear-cut as the extract presented above, with meter, syntax, intonation, and cognition all in perfect agreement. There are passages that are more complex and sophisticated, with deliberate, rhetorical *mismatch* between the various levels. I discuss some of those in Chapter 6 below. In other cases, a division into foci of consciousness is simply not as clear as in the fragment just cited, or less well supported by meter or syntax. The reader will encounter such examples in the chapters below, and may or may not agree with the division I propose in each case. Instead of invalidating the general principle, however, such less-than-prototypical cases are

[35] See Ruijgh 1990; Devine and Stephens 1994: 422–23; H. Dik 1995: 31–38. More on the details of this phenomenon, known as Wackernagel's Law, in Chapter 5 below.

[36] See Bakker 1993c.

[37] Other postpositive particles whose occurrence signals an intonational boundary are *mén*, *dé*, *gár*, and *oún*, to be discussed in Chapters 4 and 5 below.

inevitable, as in any investigation of an observable phenomenon. Even Chafe's acoustic data are not always clear-cut.[38]

To return to our Homeric passage, each unit specifies the image or idea evoked by the preceding unit in a way that is no different from what we see in Chafe's transcribed stretch of ordinary speech. And just as in that fragment, the notion of syntactic closure as a criterion for "sentencehood" is a precarious one. Indeed, the editorial business of punctuation, in this passage and throughout the Homeric corpus, is no more than arbitrary. Especially when it comes to using the full stop, the modern editor is making decisions not unlike the ones the conversational narrator makes in uttering units with a falling intonation. What matters much more is the kind of relation between units in Homer that a discourse analyst editing a transcript would mark with a comma.

In the next two chapters we shall be concerned with more details of the progression of Homeric discourse through time and with the nature of the relations between Homeric speech units, the syntax of epic discourse. Here we simply observe that Homeric speech is amenable to the analysis of speech that is demonstrated in Chafe's work. The segmentation of Homeric discourse, as evidenced by the length of the linguistic units of which it consists, can be seen as the manifestation in speech of the flow of the speaker's consciousness, each unit being the verbalization of a focus of consciousness. The length and duration of the units fits the acoustic short-term memory of the performer, or in other words, the ability to process linguistic expressions as wholes, which is determined by an "auditory buffer" of two to three seconds.[39]

No less important than the similarities, however, are the differences between the ordinary and the epic passage. Chafe's text is the transcript of a recording, made in order to study the evanescent sounds of his speaker's narrative. The Homeric text is a transcript, too, but one that was obviously

---

[38] See Chafe 1994: 58: "The physical manifestations of psychologically relevant units are always going to be messy and inconsistent. If one breaks eggs into a frying pan, it may or may not be easy to tell where one egg leaves off and another begins. It may be similarly easy or difficult to read off the boundaries of intonation units directly from displays of acoustic data."

[39] Notice that my position with regard to the relation between speech and thinking—speech is closely related with mental processes—is the reverse of the usual conception of mental processes in Homer—thinking is closely related with interactive speaking—noted by Russo and Simon 1968 and by the classic writers on Homeric psychology (Snell 1975: 27; Dodds 1951: 16; Onians 1951: 13–22). The two possibilities complement each other, of course; together they point to the fact that in a speaking culture, speech will be conceived of in terms that are very different from our own.

made for purposes very different from linguistic analysis. The speech which it records is not a onetime event; it will be repeated by future speakers, and heard by future listeners. In fact, these speakers are listeners themselves, insofar as each of them receives the discourse from a consciousness other than his own. The segmentation displayed by the Homeric passage, then, is not merely a matter of production and cognition, but also of re-production and re-cognition.

The reuse of the Homeric passage and of the narrative to which it belongs, as well as the special nature of this speech, has important consequences for the status of its constitutive units: to bring out the resemblance between them and the intonation units of ordinary spoken discourse may be an important step, but it does not exhaust the complexities of the phenomenon. Homeric discourse is obviously not an ordinary discourse, and its constitutive units are better known as formulas than as intonation units. In fact, formulas are stylized intonation units, and the cognitive approach to Homeric narrative is incomplete without some idea of how it might serve as a step toward a psychology of the Homeric formula. The Homeric formula and its metrical dimension will occupy us in Chapters 6 through 8. But first, in the next two chapters, we continue the discussion of Homeric speech units as a sequence that progresses through time. A picture will emerge in which Homeric discourse is much more bounded and goal-oriented than Aristotle's concept of unperiodic style or Parry's account of adding style might lead us to believe.

CHAPTER 4

The Syntax of Movement

Die bloße, aus dem Innersten herausgeholte *Wahrheit* ist der Zweck des epischen Dichters: er schildert uns bloß das ruhige Dasein und Wirken der Dinge nach ihren Naturen, sein Zweck liegt schon in jedem Punkt seiner Bewegung.
—Schiller to Goethe, 21 April 1797

Like any speech act, the epic performance is constituted and constrained by time in various ways. In the previous chapter we saw that the very act of verbalization, as it turns the flow of ideas in a speaker's consciousness into a flow of speech, is intimately connected with temporal progression. But time is also a factor external to the speech process as such: a speaker or performer may get tired from speaking for too long a time. Or there may simply not be enough time available: whereas writing may be confronted with a shortage of space, speaker and listeners may not have enough time to bring a speech to its natural conclusion, or cover all the topics related to a given subject or theme. It is because of the potential shortage of it that time becomes an important factor in the meaning of a discourse: listening to a discourse, giving it your time, is not an automatic thing, and a speaker will have to secure this cooperation on the part of his public by marking the units of his speech as steps through time, taken by him and the listener in joint anticipation of what is to come.

As a concession to time, speech is always a selection. Telling a story "as it really was" would require unlimited time, a situation that is humanly impossible. This is reflected in what might be called the Homeric *recusatio*, "a refusal to give a full presentation of complex things."[1] The characteristic formula is "as for X, I could not tell, nor could I name it," which is used by Homeric speakers when they see themselves confronted with the mismatch

---

[1] Ford 1992: 73.

between human limitations and the vastness of a given subject about to be presented. The most famous of these moments occurs when the Homeric narrator is about to name the Greek leaders and their contingents:[2]

πληθὺν δ᾽ οὐκ ἂν ἐγὼ μυθήσομαι οὐδ᾽ ὀνομήνω,
οὐδ᾽ εἴ μοι δέκα μὲν γλῶσσαι, δέκα δὲ στόματ᾽ εἶεν,
φωνὴ δ᾽ ἄρρηκτος, χάλκεον δέ μοι ἦτορ ἐνείη,

The multitude I could not tell or name,
not if I had ten tongues, ten mouths,
not if there was unbreakable voice and a heart of bronze within me.

(*Il.* 2.488–90)

It is at the moments when the speaker is most acutely aware of the shortness of time and breath that the positive side of time becomes most apparent. Whatever is dealt with at length, as in the full, catalogic coverage of epic material, takes time, which is a precious commodity, and the subject gains in prominence for that reason.[3]

The time-consuming nature of speech appears particularly clearly in Homer when we realize that epic speech is presented as a verbalization of things *seen*. In their original performance milieu, epic tales are typically presented by performers who adopt the stance of an eyewitness or even a sportscaster—not so much a narrative stance that we would call fictional, as a psychological state shared by the performer and his audience (whether or not that state is thought to involve mediation and verification on the part of the divine, as in the case of the Muses in the Homeric tradition).[4] Seeing or

[2] Cf. *Od.* 4.240–41 (Helen on the exploits of Odysseus) and *Od.* 11.328–30 (Odysseus on the women he saw in the underworld). In Hes. *Theog.* 369–70 the problem of time, and of human shortcomings, is essentially that of the Panhellenic poet who is expected to produce a catalogue of all the rivers and their gods but is unable to do so, whereas a local poet in an epichoric tradition would have no problem. Cf. also *Od.* 14.192–98.

[3] On another level of narrative organization, one may think of digressions in Homer, as discussed by Austin 1966. For a recent discussion of the expansion techniques inherent in Homeric discourse, see Russo 1994. An awareness of the importance of time in the dispensation of material in Homeric discourse may also serve as a necessary modification of Auerbach's discussion (1953: 3–23) of Homeric style as essentially concerned with detailed description. See also Chapters 5 and 8 below on the principle of expansion in Homeric discourse.

[4] For vision and visualization as prominent features of Homeric poetics and psychology, see Bakker 1993b: 15–25; 1997a. The visual quality of epic discourse in general is discussed by Fleischman 1990a: 265–66, who focuses on medieval Romance epic (*Chanson de Roland*, *El Cid*). More on eyewitness poetics in Homeric epic in Kannicht 1988: 11–12.

visualizing a scene from the epic tale—the difference between the two is less great for an epic singer than it is for us—requires much less time than putting that perception into words, especially when the scene that is selected for verbalization is one of complex and rapid action. The more fine-grained the detail in which the imagined scene is observed, the more time it takes—potentially more time than is available—to transform it into speech; the sharp focus that we usually attribute to pictorial representation (designated in post-Homeric Greek by words like *akríbeia* 'sharpness' or 'precision', *akribés* 'exact', and the like) yields to another quality: the fullness and truth of speech.[5]

As David Rubin has recently demonstrated, mental imagery is an important factor in the recall of stories and thus in the stability of an epic tradition.[6] Even without a cognitive interest, any reader of Homer can testify to the graphic, concrete images in which Homeric narrative proceeds. Images as aggregates of visual information are easier to remember than verbal, sequential information. Still, in telling the epic tale, such sequential organization, that is, the flow of speech, is necessarily what the epic poet has to produce. Verbalizing the image, in fact, is like looking at a picture: the consciousness of the speaker resembles that of the observer, who can focus only on one detail at a time, the area of foveal vision. So for the study of that verbalization we need concepts and terminology not so much pertaining to the image itself as to the way in which it is *perceived*. In other words, the sharpness of the image or picture is there, but it is projected onto the dimension of time and represented as a succession of verbalized foci of consciousness.[7] Owing to the discretizing nature of the speech process (and to the limitations of the consciousness which drives it),

[5] Often characterized in Homer with terms built on the verbal root τρεκ- (cf. Latin *torqueo*): ἀ-τρεκές 'unswerving' or 'exact', ἀ-τρεκέως 'exactly', and the abstract noun ἀ-τρεκείη 'accuracy' (e.g., Hdt. 4.152). Significantly, this term is frequently used in combination with καταλέγειν 'give a full, catalogic account', mostly in the formulaic line ἀλλ' ἄγε μοι τόδε εἰπὲ καὶ ἀτρεκέως κατάλεξον 'but come on, tell me this, and give a full, exact account', a verse that, as often with metalinguistic terminology, is more frequent in the *Odyssey*. On catalogic accounts, see below. For the difference between visual perception and the account of it in speech, see also Ford 1992: 75–76, with formulations very similar to the terms used here.

[6] Rubin 1995: 39–64. Imagery is for Rubin one of three major constraints on memory in the recall of discourses in oral traditions, the other two being theme and sound.

[7] See the discussion of consciousness and speech in Chapter 3 above. The perception of pictorial representation has long been a topic of interest in psychology; cf. Buswell's discussion (1935) of remembering in terms of perception, used by Chafe in his analysis (1980: 15) of speech and consciousness.

the action or object seen is broken down into its component visual details, which are presented in linear, temporal order.[8] The most obvious example of this linearization of speech in the Homeric context is ecphrasis, the description of pictures or works of art.[9] The example is paradoxical, for although the describing speech cannot but linearize the descriptive items, thus reflecting the order of the perceptions made by a mediating consciousness, the pretension of this kind of discourse is that it provides unmediated access to the object seen, as a natural icon, a real picture, would do.

One of the goals of the present chapter is to argue that ecphrasis as a descriptive discourse mode, distinct from narration, is an un-Homeric phenomenon. More precisely, the contention is that Homeric narrative is on the whole ecphrastic, and that in Homeric discourse narration and description cannot be separated: all narration is description. A case in point is battle narrative. The linearization problem here is no less prominent than in the overt description of a visual object: in battle narrative the speech process clearly imposes its own properties on the representation of the scenes depicted; it creates a temporal relation between events, or details of events that is peculiar to the flow of speech. The paradigmatic example of this linearization is the *androktasía* 'man-to-man slaying', in which the poet zooms in on a detail that is selected for verbalization from a mental image of mass fighting over an extended area, and thus effects a transformation of the spatial dimension of the battlefield into the temporal dimension of speech. Not only are the component visual details of the killing put into a linear order that does not belong so much to the event itself as to its representation in speech; the killing event as a whole is also necessarily sequenced in speech between other, similar events that occur simultaneously on the battlefield.[10]

The narrator of the *Iliad* is fully aware of this. At the beginning of his account of the great battle around the walls of the Achaean camp, he puts the matter, just as he did at the beginning of the catalogue of ships, in terms of an opposition between divine power and human limitations:[11]

---

[8] See also Fleischman 1990a: 273.

[9] See on this subject Fowler 1991; Becker 1992; Krieger 1992, with more citations, ancient and modern. The term "linearization" is borrowed from Levelt 1989: 138–40.

[10] Important points have been made by Latacz (1977: 75–81) in a discussion that successfully collapses the traditional distinction between single combat (the concern of the ἄριστοι 'best fighters') and mass fighting (the work of the λαοί 'soldiers').

[11] For discussion of this passage see Latacz 1977: 98, with the references cited there; Ford 1992: 78, who mentions the similar passage *Il.* 17.257–61.

Ἄλλοι δ' ἀμφ' ἄλλῃσι μάχην ἐμάχοντο πύλῃσιν·
ἀργαλέον δέ με ταῦτα θεὸν ὣς πάντ' ἀγορεῦσαι·
π̲ά̲ν̲τ̲ῃ̲ γὰρ περὶ τεῖχος ὀρώρει θεσπιδαὲς πῦρ

(*Il.* 12.175–77)

Some warriors were fighting at one gate, some at another;
It is very difficult for me to tell all this as if I were a god.
For e̲v̲e̲r̲y̲w̲h̲e̲r̲e̲ around the wall the god-kindled fire flared up.

A divine narrator like the Muse could process and say it all, presenting a
faithful and natural verbal icon, which would reflect the chaotic battle in all
the minute details that happen all over the battlefield, along the entire
perimeter of the Greek wall at the same time. A human narrator, on the
other hand, cannot handle this, nor can his human audience. He has to
make a selection, a part that stands for the whole—not a natural icon,
which reproduces the vision of the battle as such, but a more arbitrary sign,
the transformation of the vision into speech. The epic story, in other
words, is not so much the unmediated mimesis of which the Muses would
be capable, as the mediated semiosis of speech.

Crucial in this signifying process, of course, is human consciousness,
which, as we saw in Chapter 3, can focus on no more than one thing at a
time, a property that is translated into the processual, sequential character of
speech. The succession of intonation units is in fact nowhere more clearly
articulated (and manipulated for rhetorical effect of various kinds, as we
will see in Part 3 below) than in battle narrative. Such narrative is more
stylized than some other Homeric speech genres, for example, the represented speech of characters,[12] and therefore, paradoxical though it may
seem, more typically speech: the verbalization of what is least amenable to
representation in speech makes the properties of speech, in particular its
progression in cognitively determined intonational chunks, stand out all
the more clearly. Or in different terms, battle narrative, with its multitude
of names and their attached associations, is less easily activated in the mind
of the performer than other parts of the epic story, and this requires, in
terminology borrowed from the cognitive psychologist, a reinforcement of
the constraints that facilitate the activation: intonation units in Homeric

---

[12] Note the higher incidence of epic correption in character speech, as observed by Kelly
(1974), which I take as a phonetic property of unmetered, ordinary speech.

discourse, after all, are not only a sign of its production, but also a prerequisite for its re-production.[13]

To give a full account of something in speech that is subject to human limitations is *katalégein* in Homeric parlance. This verb is frequently used by Homeric speakers, in a variety of situations and in a wider sense than our "catalogue." Consider the words of Odysseus at the beginning of the report of his wanderings at the Phaiacean banquet:

τί πρῶτόν τοι ἔπειτα τί δ' ὑστάτιον καταλέξω;

What shall I then tell you first, and what last?

(*Od.* 9.14)

The phrasing of this question is reminiscent of the questions posed to the Muses by the narrator of the *Iliad* at various stages of the battle before Troy, when lists of warriors slain are what seem to be uppermost in his mind, for example:[14]

ἔνθα τίνα πρῶτον, τίνα δ' ὕστατον ἐξενάριξεν
Ἕκτωρ Πριαμίδης, ὅτε οἱ Ζεὺς κῦδος ἔδωκεν;

There whom did he kill first, and whom last,
Hektor Priam's son, when Zeus granted him glory?

(*Il.* 11.299–300)

Both Odysseus and the narrator of the *Iliad* may be expressing themselves in unperiodic strung-on style, but that does not mean that their speech is aimless. They are concerned with a beginning and with an end to which they can direct their speech, the one verbalizing the activity of his own mind, and the other addressing an external divine source.[15]

One might object that the introductory words of the occasional dinner-table narrator grappling with the problem how to arrange his subject mat-

---

[13] See Rubin 1995: 101–8.

[14] Cf. also *Il.* 5.703; 16.692. See Beye 1964: 352, who discusses the τίνα δ' ὕστατον passages in connection with *Il.* 2.488, 12.176, cited above; see also De Jong 1987: 49–50.

[15] On poetic beginnings see Race 1992. On the use of πρῶτος 'first' and other superlatives in connection with questions to the Muses, see De Jong 1987: 47–49, as well as below. On beginnings and starting points see also the next chapter.

ter ("Where shall I begin?") are different from the request of a professional bard to the Muses, and that the former citation bears on how to organize a *story*, whereas the latter applies to a *list*, a common feature of epic battle narrative. But such a strict distinction between narrative information (story) and itemized information (list), natural as it may seem to us, is alien to the Homeric context. Turning things into speech, whatever those things are, and whether in bardic performance or in less formal situations, is to produce a catalogue in the full sense of *katalégein*, which Tilman Krischer, in a seminal discussion of the term and its importance for Homeric discourse in general, has glossed as "klassifizierend darstellen" 'represent as an exhaustive list'.[16] Speaking is by its very nature a classification, a pulling apart of what belongs together, and in spinning the thread of discourse the question of the beginning is paramount. Lists of warriors slain or contingents mustered are indeed more catalogic than other parts of Homeric narrative, but they are not opposed, as the catalogic, to the noncatalogic parts of the narrative. And the Muses are invoked or addressed before the poet engages in a catalogue, since where to begin in such cases is not as self-evident as it is in other situations. Speakers have to be crucially concerned with beginnings, starting points that set the mental process of activation in motion.

Time and Space

Thus far I have spoken of epic speech as a description of things seen, and so as a movement through time, but in the experience of epic singers and their audiences there is another dimension as well. For them epic narration is not only the time it takes to present a "catalogue," but also the movement that covers the distance between two points. The epic story line is like a hike, longer or shorter, along a trail that may be more readily visible or less at various places. The characterization of epic narrative as a path of song is of course well known, and in the light of the many excellent discussions of

[16] Krischer 1971: 158: "Wenn λέγειν generell das zusammenstellen einer Klasse bedeutet, das Präverb κατα- die Gründlichkeit oder Vollständigkeit des Vorgangs bezeichnet und der punktuelle Verbalaspekt andeutet, daß der Gegenstand vom ganzen her erfaßt wird, dann heißt καταλέγειν offenbar 'klassifizierend darstellen'." Krischer also makes the important point (1971: 132) that since καταλέγειν is only used of characters in the poem, and not of the activity of the poet himself, we have to assume that it was not confined to epic poetry, and "daß die Voraussetzungen des epischen Stils in gewissen Konventionen der Umgangssprache jener Zeit zu suchen sind." Such a remark is indeed close to the spirit of the argument of this book. On καταλέγειν, see also Kannicht 1988: 12–13.

the metapoetic statements in the *Odyssey* (involving such terms as *oímē* 'path', *metabaínō* 'shift paths', etc.) a new discussion here would be super-fluous.[17] What I think should be stressed, however, is that epic notions of path and space involve more than just a poetic metaphor. Path and space are realities in terms of which the presentation of the epic tale is viewed by the performers and their audiences; the epic story involves not only a continu-ously shifting present moment, but also a given location, not only a now but also a here.[18]

The ways in which the typically Homeric strategies of scanning scenes and of moving from scene to scene draw on the resources of the Greek language is the subject proper of this chapter and the next one. Limiting ourselves mainly to battle narrative, the speech genre in which the narrative trail is least visible, we shall see that, besides invoking or addressing the Muses, the Homeric narrator has other resources at his disposal. The Greek language provides a number of particles and other devices that enable speakers to let their listeners keep track of the flow of discourse in which they find themselves, by inviting them to make a step, or look forward, jointly with the speaker. The use of these devices is no doubt more stylized in Homeric special speech than in ordinary everyday speech, but the Ho-meric narrator, in spite of the special character of his idiom, can obviously not depart from the ways in which the language community at large struc-tures its discourses. The study of ancient Greek discourse markers, then, can shed light on this aspect of epic poetics.

The discussion below will focus in some detail on the cognitive and what I will call processual aspects of the speech units in Homeric discourse. My use of the term "process" and its cognates implies a deliberate departure from the predominantly referential practices of most (but not all) linguistic theory: often the design and organization of sentences is discussed in terms of their referential object.[19] We do not, however, have to contrast our own

---

[17] See, for example, Thornton 1984: 11, 26, 33–45, 148–49 (on the meaning of oímē 'path', on which see also Nagy 1996: 63 n. 20 for a different interpretation); Thalmann 1984: 124; Kannicht 1988: 10–12; Ford 1992: 40–48; Rubin 1995: 62. The notions of path and movement are of course not confined to Homer; see Hdt. 1.95.1, 117.2; 2.20.1, 22.1.

[18] Notice that the dimension of space has important implications for memory and recall that have been documented not in the context of the (re-)performance of epic but in the theory of classical rhetoric, in the form of the doctrine of the *loci* 'places'; see Yates 1966: 1–8. Rubin (1995: 57–59) makes a distinction between object (descriptive) imagery and spatial imagery, citing evidence for neurophysiological differences between the two. Rubin's distinction would seem to coincide with the opposition between time and space I am making here.

[19] Koch and Oesterreicher, in a fundamental discussion (1985: 23) of the parameters involved in the linguistic treatment of the differences between spoken and written language, speak of

cognitive and linguistic inadequacies with the mimetic perfection of the language of the Muses in Greek epic poetics to realize that human language, and human speech in particular, can never be a faithful verbal icon of its object, and that direct referentiality is no more than one aspect of what happens when people talk. No less important are the concepts in the mind of the speaker and listener as part of the jointly experienced cognitive process.

The presentation below focuses on what in stylistic terms has been called parataxis. This concept may be used, as we saw in Chapter 3, to distinguish Homeric style from the hypotactic and periodic style of later authors, but the discussion that follows will have a different orientation. Rather than constituting an allegedly primitive, preliterate type of syntax, the phenomena usually denoted by the term "parataxis" can be shown to serve a positive, deliberate purpose in the deployment of what might be called the syntax of movement. And since movement is action, we serve the restless, processual nature of Homeric discourse better when we replace "parataxis" with terms denoting not so much stylistic or syntactic *properties* of the text, as the narrator's *activities* on the path of speech. Hence the word "parataxis" may be reformulated as continuation or progression, a new step on the path of speech, with the markers of continuation (the particle *dé* in particular) constituting the engine of the syntax of movement.

Progression and Continuation

The Greek grammarian who called the particle *dé* a "step-over conjunction" (*súndesmos metabatikós*)[20] made a felicitous choice, for steps are exactly what *dé* marks, at least in Homeric discourse. The particle *dé* is the primary sign of continuation and progression in Homeric Greek, and the most widely used element in the syntax of movement.[21] In using *dé*, the epic

---

Prozeßhaftigkeit (of speech) vs. *Verdinglichung* (of writing). In modern linguistics, the distinction also lies at the basis of one of the more common differentiations of semantics (what a sentence means, is about, with "proposition" as crucial term) from pragmatics (the way in which a sentence is used, as utterance). See also the discussion of making, using, and doing in Chapter 7 below.

[20] Schol. ap. Dionysius Thrax, p. 62 H (cited by Ruijgh 1971: 135): καλεῖται (ὁ "δέ" σύνδεσμος) δὲ καὶ μεταβατικός· ἀπὸ προσώπου γὰρ εἰς πρόσωπον ἢ ἀπὸ πράγματος εἰς πρᾶγμα μεταβαίνοντες αὐτῷ κέχρηνται πάντες 'It (viz. the conjunction δέ) is also called stepping-over: it is commonly used when making a transition from character to character or from event to event.' Ruijgh (1971: 128–35) bases the "transitive value" which he assigns to δέ on this characterization.

[21] See the discussions in Bakker 1990b: 4–6; 1993b: 11–15; 1997b. In Bakker 1993c, Homeric

narrator covers distance, in the most general sense of the term; the poet has a goal in mind, but that has no bearing on his use of *dé*, which marks no more than a new step, a moment in time at which a new piece of information is activated in his consciousness. The particle *dé* is the most widely used linguistic *boundary marker* between foci of consciousness. And as an observable syntactic cue for such cognitive breaks in our text it is an important element for the study of how consciousness is turned into speech.

Our first example is the description of the Trojan rally and the arrangement of the two armies in battle order after Hektor has received a heartening message from Zeus by Iris:

a.	"Εκτωρ δ' ἐξ ὀχέων	and Hektor from his chariot,
b.	σὺν τεύχεσιν ἆλτο χαμᾶζε,	with his armor on he jumped to the ground,
c.	πάλλων δ' ὀξέα δοῦρα	and brandishing the sharp javelins,
d.	κατὰ στρατὸν ᾤχετο πάντῃ,	he went all over the army,
e.	ὀτρύνων μαχέσασθαι,	exhorting [his men] to fight;
f.	ἔγειρε δὲ φύλοπιν αἰνήν.	and he roused terrible battle,
g.	οἱ δ' ἐλελίχθησαν	and they, they rallied,
h.	καὶ ἐναντίοι ἔσταν Ἀχαιῶν,	and they took position opposite the Achaeans,
i.	Ἀργεῖοι δ' ἐτέρωθεν	and the Argives on the other side,
j.	ἐκαρτύναντο φάλαγγας.	they strengthened their rows,
k.	ἀρτύνθη δὲ μάχη,	and battle it was prepared,
l.	στὰν δ' ἀντίοι·	and they stood opposite each other,
m.	ἐν δ' Ἀγαμέμνων πρῶτος ὄρουσ',	and Agamemnon he was the first to rush forward
n.	ἔθελεν δὲ πολὺ προμάχεσθαι ἀπάντων.	and he wanted to fight far ahead of all.

(*Il.* 11.211–17)

We see here a remarkable case of discourse progression: out of thirteen units nine are linked to the previous discourse with *dé*, and if we see units b, d, and e as adding units belonging to a given nuclear clause (in ways that will be shown in the next chapter), then nine out of ten clauses are marked by *dé* (the exception being clause h, with the particle *kaí*, on which see

use of δέ is contrasted with the quite different (though not unrelated) functions and uses of the particle in later, Attic Greek. Klein 1992 is a corpus-based study of the conjunctives τε, καί, and δέ in *Iliad* 1, from an Indo-European perspective. Klein's findings, pointing to δέ as "the primary means of signaling discourse continuation in Homer" (26) and the cause of an idiom "nearly free of asyndeton" (49), is in agreement with the ideas put forward here.

below). Each unit marked by *dé* represents a separate detail which is suffi-ciently independent with respect to the previously verbalized focus of consciousness to be conceptualized as a separate event, a subpart of the total scene, and expressed as an independent clause, although details can also be phrased less independently, for which see below. The clauses, then, are successive steps in the narrator's verbalizing of the information of which the scene consists. The description, furthermore, is instructive in that it shows that the use of *dé* in Homer is so automatic and ubiquitous as to be insensi-tive to two considerations from the linguistic study of narrative that need to be briefly discussed: the continuity of topics and the movement of narrative time.

In the description of the rally a distinction can be made between the subjects of units a–f and units m–n on the one hand and the subjects of units g–l on the other. The latter are mere *subjects* of their clause, activated in the context of the subevent which the clause represents and replaced by the subject of the next clause; the former, Hektor and Agamemnon, are subjects in the role of *agents*. This role, possible in the scene as depicted by language, easily transcends the limits of a single sentence or clause.[22] The distinction between subject and agent is thus much more than the pos-sibility that the two do not coincide in a single passive sentence (e.g., "He was bitten terribly by that dog," where the subject of the sentence is not an agent but a patient).[23]

"Agent" is a word that applies to a discourse as a whole, whereas "sub-ject" is a syntactic term, a matter of the organization of sentences or clauses. The idea of an agent is therefore likely to last longer than one single focus of consciousness, and thus to have a certain history in the flow of speech.[24] An agent typically stays on the scene for a while as a protagonist, and in the flow of speech the agent must be introduced with some care, or reintro-

---

[22] Cf. Lambrecht's observations (1987) to the effect that in spoken French, lexical (i.e., nonpronominal) subjects tend to occur in nonagentive, intransitive sentences (cf. the example in the next note), whereas agentive clauses (featuring the activity of a topical protagonist, see below) tend to be expressed by means of pronouns.

[23] A clear instance of the distinction is also *Il.* 16.464–65, where the agent, Zeus, effects an event (he breaks the string of Teukros's bow) whose description requires descriptive clauses with their own subject ("and *the arrow* swerved off course, and *the bow* fell from his hands"). The narrative is not concerned with the arrow and the bow as such but only as grammatical subjects in clauses describing an event. Ammann (1922: 34–35) notes that such transient subjects tend to follow their verbs.

[24] See Chafe 1994: 66–67 on the difference between events and participants in the activation of a story. See also Chafe 1994: 53–56, on activation states; see also Chapter 5 below.

duced, as the topic with which the discourse is concerned at some point.[25] These operations involve the grammar of a language in characteristic ways. We shall see in the next chapter that the tracking and management of agents or topics in epic discourse is a rich source of addition and expansion phenomena (the addition of a name to an event, or of an event to a name, as a separate intonation unit); at this point we are concerned with the re-introduction, or reactivation of agents as moments of continuation. A characteristic and simple example of such a reintroduction is:

ὁ δὲ Κύπριν ἐπῴχετο νηλέϊ χαλκῷ,

and he, he went after Kupris with pitiless bronze

(Il. 5.330)

This is a reactivation of Diomedes as agent after the attention of the narra-tor has been directed elsewhere; the hero is restored in his role of protago-nist for the moment. In such cases, obviously too numerous for more examples to be needed, it is the pronoun *ho* that marks or objectifies the switch—since it signals a switch in topic, it is often called a topic in linguis-tics—and it is *dé* that marks the switch as a moment of continuation in the flow of discourse. In the following example, we see two such switches (units a and c), separated by a single step (unit b) that does not involve the switch of an agent. Yet the three units are equally marked by *dé* as moments of continuation:[26]

a. ὁ δ᾽ ἄρ᾽ ἀσπίδος ὀμφαλὸν οὖτα,   and he (=Aias), he hit the navel of the shield,
b. ὦσε δέ μιν σθένεϊ μεγάλῳ·   and he pushed him with mighty force,
c. ὁ δὲ χάσσατ᾽ ὀπίσσω   and he (=Hektor), he shrunk back to the rear.

(Il. 13.192–93)

[25] Topic is frequently described as that part of the sentence "about which" something is said, or the part of a sentence containing the old information, as opposed to the new information elsewhere in the sentence, which is called the focus (e.g., Dik 1989: 264–65; Slings 1992: 106). In keeping with the conception of speech presented here, I prefer a more processual, less sentence-bound account of topics, in which they tend to be more clearly marked if a switch or transition occurs in the flow of speech. See the discussion of the particle δέ as a topic or boundary marker in Bakker 1993c. See also Bakker 1993b: 12 and below. Extensive discussion of topic as a matter of greater or lesser continuity in a discourse in Givón, ed. 1983.

[26] See also the sustained series of ὁ δέ and αὐτὰρ ὁ in Il. 20.455–89 (456, 460, 469, 472, 474, 481, 484, 487) with which the narrator tracks Achilles as the agent in this scene, returning to him after the description of each new killing.

In still other cases, there is no switch whatsoever, either in agent or in subject; the subject, applying to one and the same agent or topic, stays the same through a number of clauses:

Ἕκτωρ δ᾿ ὦκ᾿ ἀπέλεθρον ἀνέδραμε,	and Hektor, swiftly away he sprang up
μίκτο δ᾿ ὁμίλῳ,	and he merged with the crowd,
στῆ δὲ γνὺξ ἐριπὼν	and he stayed dropping on one knee

(Il. 11.354–55)

The use of dé in Homeric discourse is so general and ubiquitous as to bridge the very real difference between the continuity of a topic or agent (when successive clauses may or may not have different subjects) and its discontinuity (or the reintroduction of an agent): in either case, what is marked is just a step forward in the deployment of the discourse.[27]

The second consideration is the movement of narrative time. In the examples just given, one might think of the temporal relation between two events as the motivating factor in the use of dé, whereby a step on the path of speech, a moment in performance time, would correspond with the time of the scene depicted, a moment in story time. Yet even this general characterization is too specific for the function of dé in Greek speech. In itself this is clear already from the simple fact that dé is not confined to narrative contexts, in which the speaker is concerned with the creation of story events by means of speech (performance events): it also freely occurs in nonnarrative speech, where a sequential ordering of events is obviously not what the speaker aims to achieve. Consider, for example, the following fragment from the prayer of Glaukos to Zeus:

ἀμφὶ δέ μοι χεὶρ	and on both sides my arm,
ὀξείῃς ὀδύνῃσιν ἐλήλαται,	by sharp pains it is struck,
οὐδέ μοι αἷμα τερσῆναι δύναται,	and my blood, it cannot dry,
βαρύθει δέ μοι ὦμος ὑπ᾿ αὐτοῦ·	and it aches, my shoulder under it,
ἔγχος δ᾿ οὐ δύναμαι σχεῖν ἔμπεδον,	and my spear I cannot hold fast,
οὐδὲ μάχεσθαι	and not fight either,
ἐλθὼν δυσμενέεσσιν.	going against enemy men,
ἀνὴρ δ᾿ ὥριστος ὄλωλε,	and the best man, he is dead,
Σαρπηδών, Διὸς υἱός·	Sarpedon, Zeus's son,
ὁ δ᾿ οὐδ᾿ οὗ παιδὸς ἀμύνει.	and he, he does not even protect his son.

(Il. 16.517–22)

---

[27] Notice that in post-Homeric Greek the use of δέ tends to be more and more confined to discontinuous topic situations; the particle develops an increasingly tight bond with the demon-

But, more important for our purpose, the movement of story time is not a factor of primary importance for the way in which the Homeric narrator presents his speech, and this sets Homeric discourse apart from modern narrative, or rather, from what constitutes the essence of narrative in the modern linguistic study of it. In discussions of tense, verbal aspect, and other linguistic features of stories, foregrounded portions of a narrative are usually distinguished from its background.[28] In these studies the foreground is characterized by a sequential ordering of events, as the backbone of the narration or the story line, whereas the background is what explains or motivates the events of the story line.[29] In other words, on this view foreground narrates, whereas background describes.

Yet such a distinction, ascribing to texts the unmediated quality of visual representation (see my remarks on *akríbeia* 'sharpness' above), seems less appropriate for the syntax of movement in Homeric discourse, in which allegedly backgrounded explanatory or descriptive passages are just as much movement along the path of speech as their foregrounded counterparts,[30] and conversely, where foregrounded action-packed narrative passages have the descriptive visual quality that is commonly ascribed to background.

In the study of epic speech, the foreground should not be treated exclusively as the narrative representation of action or events, as opposed to a nonnarrative, descriptive background. Foregrounding is just as dynamic as the speech process itself, and this quality can be emphasized by replacing the static notion of representation by a visual concept of dynamic perception. We may say that a portion of narrative is in the foreground if it is "in focus," or coming into focus. This distinction applies not to specific parts of a text as opposed to others, but to any part of a spoken text *at the moment of its utterance.*[31] And rather than representing events directly, we may say that epic narration frequently freezes the action and its time frame, in order to make possible the action and time of speech. In other words, movement and activity on the battlefield is stalled into a tableau, and the way in which

---

strative ὁ (which virtually does not occur on its own anymore, as it still does in Homer). The particle δέ thus tends to become a topic marker; see Bakker 1993c: 293–95.

[28] See, for example, Labov 1972; Hopper 1979; Hopper and Thompson 1980; Dry 1983; Thompson 1987; Fleischman 1989. See also Bakker 1991.

[29] A particularly clear statement of this is Hopper 1979: 215–16.

[30] See also the discussion of the allegedly backgrounding particle γάρ in Chapter 5.

[31] Compare this formulation with Auerbach's analysis of Homeric style (1953: 3–7) as backgroundless, continuously in foreground. The difference between the two accounts lies in my stressing the medial aspects of the narration, the act of observing and verbalizing, whereas Auerbach is concerned with the objective representation of the phenomena described.

the epic narrator finds his way through areas of fighting on his path resembles the way people look at pictures.

We shall see in the next chapter that there are regular and recurrent patterns in the narrator's visual scanning of the battlefield, patterns that in their connection with memory and cognitive production seem to be a better criterion for orality than formulaic style as such. For the moment, what interests me is the use of *dé* to mark the steps in the scanning of the picture, and the projection of it onto the time frame of speech. The particle *dé*, whose use is automatic and unmarked, indicates the shifting focus in the speaker's field of vision, rather than any inherent temporal quality of events in the narrative. Its marking of performance time, not story time, can be clearly seen in the following description of a killing event:

a. Ἀντίλοχος δὲ Μύδωνα βάλ᾽,   and Antilokhos he hit Mudon,
b. ἡνίοχον θεράποντα,   charioteer servant,
c. ἐσθλὸν Ἀτυμνιάδην—   valiant son of Atumnios,
d. ὁ δ᾽ ὑπέστρεφε μώνυχας ἵππους—   and he, he turned his one-hoofed horses,
e. χερμαδίῳ ἀγκῶνα τυχὼν μέσον·   with a stone striking [him] on the middle of
                                     the elbow.

(*Il.* 5.580–82)

The clausal unit d, a brief switch to the victim (*ho d'* 'and he') describes an event that seems to be out of temporal sequence.[32] Instead of a moment in the scene depicted, the clause constitutes a moment in its description, and rather than a sentence, the passage as a whole is a short catalogue of temporally ordered descriptive items, two of which (units b and c) are expansions triggered by the idea of Mudon.[33] Consider also the following description of the grisly details of a slaying:

τὸ δ᾽ ἀντικρὺ   and right through,
δόρυ χάλκεον ἐξεπέρησε   the bronze spear, it pierced
νέρθεν ὑπ᾽ ἐγκεφάλοιο,   from below under the brain,
κέασσε δ᾽ ἄρ᾽ ὀστέα λευκά·   and it splintered the white bones,
ἐκ δὲ τίναχθεν ὀδόντες,   and the teeth, they were shaken out,

---

[32] One could point to the use of the imperfect here, as the verbal form that is appropriate to actions that are off the time line (see, e.g., Hopper 1979).

[33] Kirk's treatment (1990: 117) of ἀγκῶνα ... μέσον in unit e as the object of βάλ᾽ in unit a is a clear example of the sentential analysis of Homeric discourse that I am arguing against. On the problems with treating nouns in Homer as the object or subject of their verb, see Chapter 5 below.

ἐνέπλησθεν δέ οἱ ἄμφω	and they were filled, the both
αἵματος ὀφθαλμοί·	eyes with blood,
τὸ δ' ἀνὰ στόμα καὶ κατὰ ῥῖνας	and through the mouth and the nostrils
πρῆσε χανών·	he blew gaping
θανάτου δὲ μέλαν νέφος ἀμφεκάλυψεν.	and the black cloud of death covered [him] round.

(Il. 16.346–50)

What we have here are not so much narrative statements asserting temporal sequence as descriptive visual details as they pass through the speaker's consciousness.[34] In fact, not even the scene as a whole is an event with its own place in story time; it is presented as the description of one out of a number of simultaneous killing-events, a complex scene of mass fighting over an extended area in which Trojans are killed in the flight. One edge of the tableau is framed in the following way:[35]

ἔνθα δ' ἀνὴρ ἕλεν ἄνδρα	and there man he took man,
κεδασθείσης ὑσμίνης	in the spreading battle
ἡγεμόνων.	of the leaders.

(Il. 16.306–7)

The catalogue of nine killings that follows is thus a selection on the part of a consciousness that is watching the scene, zooming in as if it were a camera lens on items of particular salience and interest.[36] Transitions from one selection to the next are marked by dé, as is the movement from detail to detail within a selected catalogue item. The movement of story time is halted throughout to make possible the movement through performance

[34] Cf. Fleischman's analysis (1990a: 273) of the description of a similar though less realistic slaying in *Chanson de Roland*: "Passages describing the epic blow, like those describing many of the conventionalized gestures of epic action, are not intended to advance story time but to reveal the *qualities* of an agent."

[35] Notice the indication of the undifferentiated substance of the narrative (ἀνὴρ ἕλεν ἄνδρα 'man took man', cf. *Il.* 4.472) as well as the indication of spatial dimension (κεδασθείσης 'had spread out'). The closure of this fighting catalogue at 16.351 (οὗτοι ἄρ' ἡγεμόνες Δαναῶν | ἕλεν ἄνδρα ἕκαστος 'so these leaders of the Danaans | each took his man') has phraseology strongly reminiscent of the closure of the Catalogue of Ships (2.760).

[36] On the epic poet as camera user see also Latacz 1977: 78. Latacz's term *Selektionssignale* is instructive: a good example is the demonstrative adverb ἔνθα 'there', a marker frequently used in the movement from one killing-scene as selected item to the other. In Homeric discourse this element is often just as nonreferential and processual as δέ, with which it frequently combines. Cf. *Il.* 4.223, 473, 517; 5.1, 144, 159; 16.306, 337, etc. Some referential cases: *Il.* 2.724; 3.185, 426.

time, in which "first" (*prôtos*) typically has the processual, nonreferential meaning "first in my account," rather than "first in the reality depicted."[37]

From the point of view of writing and sentential syntax, *dé* and similar elements in other languages are likely to be misinterpreted. Their sheer frequency looks primitive and crudely repetitive when rendered on paper. Converted to the syntactic categories of the written page, the relation between clauses marked by *dé* becomes a matter of indiscriminately prolonged coordination (the formation of complex sentences from simple sentences arranged on one syntactic plane) and a potential sign of the simplicity of a given text.[38] The processual nature of *dé*, however, belongs to a different domain. A speaker using the particle in Homeric discourse is not concerned with what is for us syntactic correctness, as is clear, for example, from the frequent cases of apodotic *dé* in a main clause following a subclause:[39]

αὐτὰρ ἐπεὶ Λυκόοργος	but when Lukoörgos
ἐνὶ μεγάροισιν ἐγήρα,	he grew old in the hall,
δῶκε δ᾽ Ἐρευθαλίωνι	(and) he gave [it] to Ereuthalion.

(*Il.* 7.148–49)

Such cases are anomalous only if the syntactic articulation of the hierarchy between clauses is taken as a (later) norm to which Homer does not conform. But rather than locating Homeric discourse on a scale running from primitive to sophisticated, it would be well to consider the goals and strategies of speech, suppressing the written framework for a moment. In so doing we place ourselves in a position to see that the main concern of the Homeric narrator is movement, an activity that requires a continuous channeling and monitoring of the speech flow through time. It is this factor, overriding any aesthetic judgment one might make from a stylistic

[37] See also Beye 1964 and above all Latacz (1977: 83–84), who discusses πρῶτος as another *Selektionssignal*. As to the sequential ordering of events, if one wants to state unambiguously that there is a temporal sequence in story time, one has to introduce the clause in question with ἔπειτα δέ 'and then': ἕλε δ᾽ ἄνδρα Βιήνορα, | ποιμένα λαῶν, ‖ αὐτόν, | ἔπειτα δ᾽ ἑταῖρον, | Ὀϊλῆα πλήξιππον 'and he took a man, Bienor, | herdsman of the people, ‖ himself, | and thereafter his comrade, | Oïleus the horse-whipper (*Il.* 11.92–93; cf. *Il.* 5.164; 16.229, 532–34; 17.64).

[38] In fact, the prime marker of coordination in Greek (on any level: word, word group, clause, sentence) is καί, a particle that can be used in Attic Greek to lend a purposive simplicity and naiveté to written texts (see Trenkner 1958). On the difference between δέ and καί, see below.

[39] Cf. *Il.* 1.58; 7.314; *Od.* 5.366; Hes. *Theog.* 60. See also Bakker 1997b.

point of view, that explains the sustained repetition of *dé* in our Homer text as one of the prime signs of speech, and one of the elements that best survive the transcription of speech into text.[40]

Inclusion

If there is a coordinative particle in Greek, it is not *dé* but *kaí*, and before we continue the discussion of progression and continuation in Homeric discourse, a brief confrontation of *dé* with this particle may be in order.[41] Even though under certain circumstances the difference between these two words for "and" may be neutralized,[42] in principle there is a clear distinction. Owing to its origins,[43] *kaí* is the particle not of progression but of inclusion: it is the particle used to coordinate two elements into a single idea that may (but need not) be expressed as one intonation unit.

When *dé* cannot occur (i.e., when the two items linked are not clauses), the expansion effected by *kaí* is unit-internal in most cases: the two elements linked by *kaí* may be nouns of any case or syntactic function (e.g., *phónon kaì kêra mélainan* 'murder and black death'); prepositional phrases (e.g., *katà phréna kaì katà thumón* 'in mind and in spirit'); verbs in any form (e.g., *agorḗsato kaì metéeipen* 'spoke forth and addressed them'); or other elements (e.g., *éntha kaì éntha* 'there and there').[44] Thus whereas *dé* discretizes (presenting two ideas as two different steps in a speech or as two items

[40] Beaman (1984: 47, 59, 60–61, 79) does not speak of continuation, but opposes the use of "and" in spoken English as a "filler word" to its use for sentential coordination; Halliday and Hassan (1976: 233–38) distinguish an additive use of "and" from a coordinative use, and state (244) that additive "and" is derivable from coordination proper (I would reverse this relation). On "and" in spoken English, see also Schiffrin 1987: 128–52; Chafe 1988: 10–12.

[41] On δέ and καί, see Ruijgh 1971: 130–33; Klein 1992; Bakker 1990b: 5–6; 1993c: 280, 288–92. Notice that unlike δέ, καί is not a postpositive particle that signals an intonational boundary: it can equally well occur within units and at the boundary between units.

[42] Neutralization of linguistic elements which are otherwise different is discussed in Bakker 1988: 14–18. In the case of δέ and καί, neutralization may occur when the need to use μέν (on which see below) prevents the automatic use of δέ, and καί is used instead (e.g., *Il.* 5.344; 11.99; 22.274).

[43] The connection between καί and κάς, and the derivation of καί from *κάς (< *κασί < *κατί 'together') is uncontroversial among historical linguists. See Ruijgh 1971: 180–82; Lüttel 1981. Furthermore, the original and central function of καί is that of an adverb with the inclusive meaning "also/too" or "even" (called a focus particle in Bakker 1988: 40–43).

[44] On such doublets see O'Nolan 1978.

in a catalogue), *kaí* is the particle of integration: rather than shifting the focus to a new idea as part of the ongoing flow of speech, *kaí* prolongs the focus.[45]

When *dé* can in principle occur instead of *kaí* (i.e., when the two linked items are clauses), we note that *kaí* can be used to introduce a unit in which a given idea is rephrased in order to highlight a different aspect of it, marking not so much that something new is coming into focus as that what was already in focus continues to be so and is being expanded at the present moment. Consider the following examples, in which *dé* marks the step to a new idea and *kaí* introduces a unit that verbalizes the idea in different words and from a different angle:

ὣς ἔφατ',	thus he spoke,
ἔδεισεν δ' ὁ γέρων	and the old man, he got scared,
καὶ ἐπείθετο μύθῳ·	and obeyed his word.

(*Il.* 1.33)

ἵετο δ' αἰεὶ Αἰνείαν κτεῖναι	and he was striving all the time to kill Aineias,
καὶ ἀπὸ κλυτὰ τεύχεα δῦσαι.	and to strip his renowned armor.

(*Il.* 5.434–35)

From the perspective of a Homeric warrior, killing an opponent and stripping him of his armor are such closely related ideas as to allow of an integrative linkage with *kaí*. In terminology that will be more fully developed in Chapter 8 below, "kill" is in certain contexts a nuclear or core idea, and "strip" a possible expansion of it.[46] Sometimes the idea of inclusion seems to convey a simultaneity of two or more actions that contrasts with the indeterminacy of *dé* in that regard:[47]

ἦ ῥα, καὶ ἀμπεπαλὼν	he spoke and balancing [it] above his head,
προΐει δολιχόσκιον ἔγχος	he threw the far-shadowing spear,

[45] Note that this characterization does not apply to καί as scalar particle (in the adverbial sense "even" or "also"), a use that is not unrelated to the basic value of inclusion, but which has no direct bearing on speech as flow and process. On inclusive scalar particles, see Bakker 1988: 40–48, 75, 84.

[46] See also the discussion of close-up in Chapter 5.

[47] Cf. Ruijgh (1971: 134), who assigns to δέ the status of unmarked and to καί that of marked term in a privative opposition. The phrasing προΐει δολιχόσκιον ἔγχος (unit b of the following extract) occurs eleven times in the *Iliad*, only once (5.15) *not* followed by καί. See also 5.97–98 and 11.375–76, where καί integrates the pulling of the bow and the subsequent hit.

καὶ βάλε Τυδείδαο κατ᾽ ἀσπίδα.   and hit Tudeus's son in the shield.

(Il. 5.280–81)

Speaking (the taunting of an opponent on the battlefield), calibrating the spear, throwing it, and hitting the target are really one complex event, and the poet uses the integrative, noncatalogic particle *kaí* to bring out that wholeness. It is true that due to its own time-consuming nature, speech can never represent simultaneity of two events as such, since it takes at least two temporally ordered speech events to name them: as we have seen, speech as such is no unmediated mimesis. But a speaker can assert the simultaneity, using the less processual and more referent-oriented particle *kaí* instead of *dé*.[48] In terms of vision this would mean that he stresses less the process of perception than the qualities of the object perceived.

One context in which *kaí* invariably occurs is the reversal passage, in which a god or hero intervenes at the last moment to prevent the untimely death of a major epic character. In this scene, Diomedes has hit Aineias with a stone and is about to kill him:[49]

a.	ἀμφὶ δὲ ὄσσε	and both his eyes
b.	κελαινὴ νὺξ ἐκάλυψε.	black night, it covered,
c.	καί νύ κεν ἔνθ᾽ ἀπόλοιτο	and now he would have died there,
d.	ἄναξ ἀνδρῶν Αἰνείας,	leader of men Aineias,
e.	εἰ μὴ ἄρ᾽ ὀξὺ νόησε	if she had not looked sharply,
f.	Διὸς θυγάτηρ Ἀφροδίτη,	Aphrodite daughter of Zeus.

(Il. 5.310–12)

The near-disastrous event is expressed positively in units a–b and is repeated as a nonrealized event in unit c, which is linked to the preceding discourse with *kaí*. The particle marks its clause as a negative rephrasing or counterpart of the preceding description. Instead of being merely included within the scope of what precedes, however, the negative statement of the nonevent explicitly points forward to the next unit after the addition (in unit d) of the name: because unit c is marked as unreal by the modal particle *ken*, it creates a strong anticipation as to the next real event, thus serving as narrative bridge between the description of danger and the rescue, enhanc-

---

[48] See also the frequent expression στῆ δὲ μαλ᾽ ἐγγὺς ἰὼν καὶ ἀκόντισε δουρὶ φαεινῷ 'stood close and threw the shining javelin' (e.g., Il.4.496).

[49] See the discussion of this type of passage in Chapter 7 below, with the literature cited there.

ing the saliency of the latter. The function of the *kaí* clause in "if not" situations thus testifies to the double nature of speech units in the ongoing flow of discourse through time: they have a meaningful relation both with their past and with their future, a double nature that will crucially concern us below and in the next chapter.

The inclusive nature of *kaí*, finally, can be exploited to convey meaning that transcends the significance of a given epic moment, as when Hektor's death is foreshadowed at the moment of his greatest glory:

a.	μινυνθάδιος γὰρ	short-lived indeed
b.	ἔμελλεν ἔσσεσθ'·	he was to be,
c.	ἤδη γάρ οἱ ἐπόρνυε	for already she was rousing against him
d.	μόρσιμον ἦμαρ	the day of doom,
e.	Παλλὰς 'Αθηναίη	Pallas Athene,
f.	ὑπὸ Πηλεΐδαο βίηφιν.	through the might of Peleus's son,
g.	<u>καί</u> ῥ' ἔθελεν ῥῆξαι	<u>and</u> he wanted to break
h.	στίχας ἀνδρῶν πειρητίζων,	the ranks of men, probing them.

(*Il.* 15.612–15)

The *kaí* statement, in comparison with which *dé* would have been weak and colorless, integrates Hektor's present prowess into the foreshadowing, linking death and glory into one indissoluble whole.[50]

Progression, Dialogism, and *Enargeia*

In the discussion of discourse progression by means of *dé*, we saw that there is nothing in the structure of the clauses as such that either causes or prohibits the linkage with *dé*. But that does not mean that continuation and linkage with *dé* is unconstrained or unchecked. Rather than grammar, structure, or syntax, however, it is the interactive nature of the speech situation or performance itself and the availability of time that puts constraints on continuative connection in discourse, and this brings us to the interactive and dialogic potential of the connective particle *dé*, or how continuation in Homer is marked in such a way as to reflect an imaginary interaction with an addressee.

---

[50] See also *Il.* 12.10–11, where καί links Hektor's life, Achilles's wrath, and Troy's safety into one complex fact: "So long as Hektor was alive and (καί) Achilles was angry and (καί) Priam's city was undestroyed."

It is commonplace to state that *dé* (δέ) is etymologically connected with *dḗ* (δή) as a phonetically shortened and weakened version of this latter particle.[51] What is less often mentioned is that this similarity in form, weakening with the passage of time, might well be connected with a parallel similarity in meaning, *dé* being a weaker, "bleached" version of *dḗ* semantically as well as morphologically. *Dḗ* is often called a confirmative particle,[52] but is better characterized as a marker of evidentiality.[53] *Dḗ* conveys that the consciousness verbalized receives its input from the speaker's immediate environment, from what is perceptually clear and evident. The verbalization of the perception, however, is not simply an evidential statement; the *dḗ* clause, being directed to an addressee, signals that the speaker assumes that the hearer is capable of witnessing the same evidence, and in uttering the *dḗ* clause the speaker wants to convey that the addressee shares the same evident environment. The particle *dḗ* in conversation is thus no less socializing than evidential: speakers using *dḗ* assume that their addressees are "with them", that they share their physical situation (or by an easy extension, the same emotional and intellectual situation). The use of *dḗ*, then, can be seen as a symptom of this involvement. Examples of this shared situation are frequent in the discourse of Homeric speakers:

Τεῦκρε πέπον,	dear Teukros,
δὴ νῶϊν ἀπέκτατο	see, he has died on us two,
πιστὸς ἑταῖρος	our trustworthy comrade.

(Il. 15.437)

ὄρσεο, διογενὲς Πατρόκλεες,	rise up, Patroklos born of Zeus
ἱπποκέλευθε·	horseman,
λεύσσω δὴ παρὰ νηυσὶ	I see there at the ships
πυρὸς δηΐοιο ἰωήν·	the glow of destructive fire.

(Il. 16.126–27)

In the first example the speaker is Aias, who addresses his half-brother Teukros in a situation in which both are witnessing the death of Luko-phron, Aias's *therápōn* 'henchman', a charioteer who is accidentally hit and

---

[51] See Risch 1969; Ruijgh 1971: 646. We may add that the suffix -δε in the proximal demonstrative ὅδε 'this one here' is probably also related to δή.

[52] See, for example, Denniston 1954: 203–4: "The essential meaning seems clearly to be 'verily,' 'actually,' 'indeed.' δή denotes that a thing really and truly is so: or that it is very much so."

[53] So already the accounts in the German grammarians (Kühner and Gerth 1904: 126–27; Brugmann and Thumb 1913: 630). Previous discussion on Homeric δή in Bakker 1993b: 11–12. See also the discussion in Van Ophuijsen 1993: 140–51, based on examples from Plato's *Phaedo*.

killed by Hektor. Aias's statement presupposes the situational as well as emotional involvement of Teukros, and his phrasing thus testifies to his judgment as to the similarity of the idea in his consciousness to that of the idea in his addressee's consciousness: both share the same present experience (notice also the involvement dative *nōïn* 'for the two of us').[54] In the second example Achilles verbalizes a perception which he is sure he shares with Patroklos; the verbalization is thus not so much an assertion that he "sees" something as a verbalization of a common ground, a starting point for action on which both agree. The presupposed common basis for conducting discourse can thus be exploited for rhetorical purposes, as in the following case, in which Poseidon, in the shape of Kalkhas the seer, is exhorting the Greeks to make a stand against Hektor and the Trojans:

a.	ὦ πέπονες,	you weaklings,
b.	τάχα δή τι κακὸν ποιήσετε μεῖζον	soon you'll be doing something bad, worse than this,
c.	τῇδε μεθημοσύνῃ·	by this slackening of yours,
d.	ἀλλ᾽ ἐν φρεσὶ θέσθε ἕκαστος	but each of you, put it in your mind,
e.	αἰδῶ καὶ νέμεσιν·	shame and outrage,[55]
f.	δὴ γὰρ μέγα νεῖκος ὄρωρεν.	for see, a great quarrel it has erupted,
g.	Ἕκτωρ δὴ παρὰ νηυσὶ	see, Hektor at the ships,
h.	βοὴν ἀγαθὸς πολεμίζει	good at the cry he makes war.

(*Il.* 13.120–23)

The instances of *dé* in units f and g, as in the example just discussed, derive from the speaker's assumption that the addressees are *able* to see for themselves what drives the speaker's consciousness: the evidence marked by the particle is a matter of shared environment and perception. The instance of *dé* in unit b, on the other hand, derives from the assumption that the addressees are *willing* to see what the speaker has in mind. The involvement of the speaker and the addressees is less a matter of actually *sharing an environment* than a matter of *cooperation*: the speaker assumes that the listeners are willing to see the evidence produced, so that conducting the discourse becomes an activity aimed at a shared seeing, a being together in the situation created by the speaker's phrasing.[56]

Shared seeing is the aim of any discourse that mediates between two

---

[54] See Denniston 1954: 208 for two examples of the collocation of δή and νῶϊν.

[55] Notice the linkage by καί of two closely related concepts. On αἰδώς and νέμεσις, see Redfield 1994: 115–19 (on αἰδώς and ἔλεος see Chapter 8 below).

[56] On involvement see also Tannen 1985; 1989: 9–35.

consciousnesses, and very few utterances are made for their own sake or just as statements of certainty, belief, or opinion. The actual use of language transcends the abstraction of it offered by the philosophers or logicians. Most speech is necessarily directed to someone, a consciousness other than the speaker's, and response from this other consciousness, even if it remains implicit in the form of cooperation assumed in the mind of the speaker, is essential for the presentation of discourse and its continuation. Speech must be at least implicitly dialogic, presupposing reaction of some sort, whether overt or covert, even when no one is required or expected to give an explicit answer.[57]

With this dialogism and involvement as a background, let us return to the visual quality of Homeric discourse. I argued above that speech, whether it is Homeric or not, cannot convey the properties of its referent in the way a visual icon can represent them. But that does not mean that Homeric speech cannot effect the visualization of its referent in the mind of its hearer, given a willingness to participate in the scene depicted. In fact, ever since antiquity, critics of Homer have been struck by the graphic quality of Homeric discourse, its power to put events and their participants before the hearers' eyes and to involve them in the epic action.[58] Ford is probably right that "we should not reduce . . . to an aesthetic notion" what he calls Homeric "vividness" (translating Greek enárgeia), because its background is "magical and epiphanic."[59] Yet the means by which the Homeric narrator achieves the immediate presence of the epic events in performance are often not different from those used by speakers in general when they want to talk in an engaging way about things that are not physically present in the speech situation.

In a recent discussion, stating obvious facts in an illuminating way, Chafe has drawn attention to the capacity of the human mind to be activated not only by sensory input from the immediate environment, but also by what is not in the here and now.[60] In the latter case, which Chafe calls "displace-

---

[57] See Bakhtin 1986: 68–70; Morson and Emerson 1990: 127–35. In linguistics the interaction implicit in a discourse is sometimes referred to as diaphony; see Kroon 1994: 111–15.

[58] Gorgias, *Hel.* 9; Plato, *Ion* 535b–e; Longinus, *De subl.* 15; Quintilian, *Inst. or.* 6.2.29; as well as the scholia on Homer about ἐνάργεια 'graphic vividness' (on which see Zanker 1981). See, for example, *schol.* bT in *Il.* 6.467: ταῦτα δὲ τὰ ἔπη οὕτως ἐστὶν ἐναργείας μεστά, ὅτι οὐ μόνον ἀκούεται τὰ πράγματα, ἀλλὰ καὶ ὁρᾶται. λαβὼν δὲ τοῦτο ἐκ τοῦ βίου ὁ ποιητὴς ἄκρως περιεγένετο τῇ μιμήσει 'these words are so full of *enargeia* that one not only hears the events but also sees them; taking this scene from life itself the poet brilliantly succeeds in his *mimesis*'.

[59] Ford 1992: 55.

[60] Chafe 1994: 32, 195–211. An earlier significant treatment of these matters is Bühler's 1934 discussion of *deixis*, in terms of what he calls *demonstratio ad oculos* and *deixis ad phantasma*.

ment" (as opposed to the "immediacy" of our physical environment), the speech-producing consciousness receives its input, by way of remembering or imagining, from another consciousness that is either the speaker's own or belongs to someone else. This remote consciousness is located in another time and/or place in which it does the actual seeing. The human mind appears to have a natural inclination to turn away from the physical present and to create a mental here and now, either by producing speech or listening to it. The obvious sign of this imaging potential in human discourse is the ubiquitous use of evidentiality markers and other linguistic devices pertaining to the here and now—the pretence is that what is remembered or imagined is actually *seen*, and the devices are deployed on the assumption that the listener is willing to play along with the pretence.[61]

The distal consciousness that feeds the verbalizing consciousness of the Homeric narrator may be in the last resort the remote authoritative perception of the Muse, a relation that turns memory and remembering into something quite special, a mediation between the human and the divine;[62] yet the means by which the poet locates the remote evidence of his tale in the immediacy of the present cannot have been very different from the strategies used by speakers whose consciousness receives input from a nearer and more readily accessible source. Homeric narrative abounds with evidentiality markers, whose use has to be seen in connection with the use made of them by the characters in the epic.[63] Returning to the discussion of *dé*,[64] we may now say that the use of this particle draws the hearer into the story by marking the narration as deriving from a shared basis, a common

[61] Among the devices commonly used are the historical present as a conversational strategy, spatial *deixis*, and above all the mimetic strategy of direct speech (impersonation).

[62] See Vernant 1959; Détienne 1967: 9; Thalmann 1984: 147; Ford 1992: 53; Bakker 1993b: 17–19; 1997a. The nature of memory as discussed by these authors accords with the discussion of remembering (considered as an activity, not a thing) in Bartlett 1932. See the use made of him by Treitler (1974: 344–47) and Chafe (1994: 53, 145): remembering is not a mere reproduction of something past, the management of a mental archive, but an imaginative reconstruction of the past in the present. Bartlett's insistence on the similarity between memory and perception amounts to an experimental underpinning of the *enargeia* of Homeric discourse. See also the remarks above on imagery and perception.

[63] Conforming to Martin's insight (1989) that the speech of the poet is no less a *muthos*-speech act than that of the characters in the poem (where μῦθος is understood as "authoritative speech act").

[64] Other important evidentiality markers in Homer include the particle ἄρα and the verb μέλλειν, both marking conclusions of a speaker based on the evidence of the physical surroundings, and thus characterizing Homeric discourse as activated, realized in the present (see Bakker 1993b: 16–25; 1997a).

experience that binds the narrator and the listeners together as if they were actually jointly witnessing a given scene.

Seeing jointly and drawing the listener into the scene described are pervasive features of epic narration, but these features are particularly common when significant events or breaks in the story are marked by *hóte* 'when', *tóte* 'then', or both. It is at such moments that the narrator most needs the participation of the listener: the poet assumes that participation and hence overtly expresses it. Consider, for example, how the scene of Hektor's death is introduced:[65]

ἀλλ᾽ ὅτε δὴ	but when
τὸ τέταρτον ἐπὶ κρουνοὺς ἀφίκοντο,	for the fourth time they arrived at the spring,
καὶ τότε δὴ	(and) then,
χρύσεια πατὴρ ἐτίταινε τάλαντα,	father [Zeus] held up the golden scales.

(Il. 22.208–9)

Speaking as if the events are present in the here and now of the narration is a ubiquitous and natural strategy of the epic narrator, but the importance of evidentiality and vividness is not confined to it. In a weakened and attenuated form it constitutes the basis, not only of the participation of the listener in the story, but also of the very continuation of the epic tale. If *dé* is a weak form of *dḗ*, then its meaning is similar but weaker; *dé* is more often and more routinely used than *dḗ*, and it reduces participatory cooperation and joint seeing to jointly making a new step in the movement of discourse through time.[66] Continuation in meaningful discourse, after all, is not a monologic decision on the part of the speaker; it makes sense only when there is common ground, when the listener is prepared to "stay with" the speaker.

Conducting a discourse, and thereby performing what may be called the

[65] The passage is an example of the three-times motif (τρὶς μέν), a sure sign of impending failure and doom and therefore an effective suspense-creating device. See Bannert 1988: 41–57; Fenik 1968: 46–48. Notice the remarkable and recurrent use of apodotic καί in this kind of passage (see also, e.g., *Il.* 1.494; 16.780; 18.350). In the extract cited, the segmentation amounts to the alternation of what Chafe (1994: 63–64) calls "regulatory intonation units" (ἀλλ᾽ ὅτε δή, καὶ τότε δή) with two "substantive intonation units," resulting in two balancing pairs. Units like καὶ τότε δή 'and then' or αὐτὰρ ἔπειτα 'and thereafter' regulate the flow of discourse or interaction rather than being part of it. As Chafe notes (1994: 64), regulatory intonation units are shorter than substantive ones, but may also be expressed as parts of larger units.

[66] Sometimes (e.g., Leaf 1900–1902 on *Il.* 1.340 and 13.260) δέ as a weak form of δή is distinguished from the real δέ, an entirely gratuitous practice resulting from the interpretation of cases in which it is hard for *us* to translate δέ with "and" or "but."

act of continuation—the making of assertions that presuppose cooperation on the part of the addressee—entails the manipulation and ongoing extension of such a common ground. Willingness on the part of the hearer, therefore, is something the speaker has to take for granted in order to speak with any confidence at all. It is *dé* that marks this assumption. As such, the particle is a reflex of the communicative side of continuation, making even the most monologic discourse an implicit dialogue with a listener whose reactions—even if only assumed on the part of the speaker—shape the verbalization of the speaker's consciousness. But *dé* is at the same time a sign of the authority of epic discourse and of its speaker, who holds the floor longer and more thoroughly than any ordinary speaker would do, and who assumes that this stance, typical of the special speech of the performance, has the listener's consent.[67]

Progression and Negotiation

Continuation in the ongoing speech process means that each moment in the duration of the process results from the previous moment, and in its turn serves as basis or context for the next moment. Any speech unit, therefore, is a stepping-stone to the next one. But a speech unit can also be marked explicitly as a stepping-stone, a basis from which to continue, and this brings us to the particle *mén*. It is commonly assumed that *mén* (μέν) can be used as an emphatic or affirmative adverb, in which case it is seen as a weak, bleached form of *mén* (μήν). It can also be used as a preparatory coordinator, the counterpart of *dé* in the correlative pair *mén . . . dé*.[68] Owing to the general function of this pair in Attic Greek texts, the particle *mén* is usually seen to mark a referent in the text, one that is opposed to the referent marked by *dé* (e.g., *ho mén . . . ho dé* 'the one . . . the other'). A textual account like this, however, will hardly do in a discussion of Homeric discourse. Like *dé*, the particle *mén* in Homer is best considered from a speech perspective. Both have processual functions. The particle *mén* has its proper place in the flow of speech through time, rather than in a text that is meant or thought to be a static artifact representing the entities about

---

[67] Cooperation is always implicit in the presentation of epic narrative in the performer's assessment of the audience's attention, and the ensuing decision either to continue or to break off the performance session. The sensitivity of Demodokos's performance to social context in *Odyssey* 8 comes to mind here. See also Radlov in Chadwick and Chadwick 1932–40: 3:184–85; Lord 1960: 16–17. See also Chapter 6 on the performance of American folk preachers.

[68] See Denniston 1954: 359, 369; Ruijgh 1971: 197–99, 741; Bakker 1993c: 298–305; 1996b.

which it speaks. And the fact that the affirmative use is more common in Homer, while the preparatory use is not fully developed,[69] suggests that the processual use of *mén* (. . . *dé*) cannot be seen in isolation from the use of the particle as an affirmative adverb.

The usual textbook distinction between the two uses of *mén*, in fact, seems to be motivated by Attic usage and projected backward in time onto Homeric discourse. Freeing ourselves from this preconception and searching for more specific descriptions than emphatic or affirmative, we note that *mén* is often used to mark a statement that clears the ground, establishing a framework for discourse to come, and as such it tends to be used at the beginning of a speech. An example is Hektor's angry response to Poludamas in the second nocturnal assembly of the Trojans:

Πουλυδάμα,	Poludamas,
σὺ μὲν οὐκέτ᾽ ἐμοὶ φίλα ταῦτ᾽ ἀγορεύεις,	you, you no longer say things that please me.

(Il. 18.285)

This is not so much an assertion in its own right as the preparation for more salient assertions to come, and it seems that *mén* marks the statement as performing this function. In the quotation just given, the particle marks the statement as a whole, rather than the single pronoun (*sù* 'you').[70] When a statement with *dé* follows, it has normally been anticipated by the speaker in uttering the *mén* clause. But when *mén* . . . *dé* is used in Attic texts, the anticipatory *mén* clause states the first member of an antithetical or contrastive pair, whereas the use of *mén* . . . *dé* in Homer testifies to the earlier function of these particles as the markers of assertions in an ongoing and always at least implicitly interactive flow of discourse. A speaker using *mén*, looking forward to an upcoming statement with *dé*, does not so much *presuppose* a common basis for conducting discourse as *establish* one.[71] Thus *mén* marks the prerequisite of continuation, the indication of a point from which to start.

In overtly interactive and dialogic discourse, the establishment of a basis

[69] Ruijgh 1971: 741; 1981; Klein 1992.

[70] As Denniston (1954: 360) thinks. Other cases of μέν at the beginning of speeches include *Il.* 13.47; 9.308–10 (Achilles' great speech to the embassy): χρὴ μὲν δὴ τὸν μῦθον ἀπηλεγέως ἀποειπεῖν 'clearly this speech of yours has to be rejected outright'. Cf. also Hes. *W&D* 109, 111 (the beginning of the Five Ages of Man); notice also the category of inceptive μέν at the beginning of tragedies or of speeches in tragedy (Denniston 1954: 382–84).

[71] See also Bakker 1993b: 12–15.

for discourse yet to come often takes the form of a concession, as in English "true" or "it is true that," by which a point is conceded not so much to weaken the speaker's position as to create an environment in which another point can be presented. Such a negotiation is what happens in the following words of Odysseus to Sokos, who has just wounded him:

a. ἆ δείλ᾽, ἦ μάλα δή   ah wretch, <u>yes</u> clearly so
b. σε κιχάνεται αἰπὺς ὄλεθρος.   steep destruction, it overtakes you
c. ἤτοι μέν ῥ᾽ ἔμ᾽ ἔπαυσας   <u>yes indeed</u>, you may have stopped me
d. ἐπὶ Τρώεσσι μάχεσθαι·   fighting against the Trojans,
e. σοὶ δ᾽ ἐγὼ ἐνθάδε φημὶ   <u>and/but</u> for you I say here
f. φόνον καὶ κῆρα μέλαιναν   murder and black death
g. ἤματι τῷδ᾽ ἔσσεσθαι,   there will be on this very same day,
h. ἐμῷ δ᾽ ὑπὸ δουρὶ δαμέντα   <u>and/but</u> subdued by my spear [you]
i. εὖχος ἐμοὶ δώσειν,   will give fame to me
j. ψυχὴν δ᾽ Ἄϊδι κλυτοπώλῳ·   <u>and</u> [your] soul to Hades with the noble steeds.

(*Il.* 11.441–45)

After stating in units a and b the general character of the situation, a statement that involves both the physical environment (*dé*) and a strong commitment both to the situation and the words spoken therein, the speaker proceeds to particulars (a common Homeric strategy, as we shall see in the next chapter). The fact that his addressee has incapacitated him is conceded in unit c and marked (*mén*), not for its own sake or as a step in an ongoing series of verbalizations, but to create an environment in which the next phrasings (marked by *dé*, beginning with unit e) will be maximally effective. The speaker, in other words, negotiates a framework within which the attention (if not the cooperation) of the interlocutor can be presupposed, and the subsequent phrasings can be marked accordingly.[72]

In monologic discourse, like that of the Homeric narrator, the dialogic negotiation that is characteristic of the use of *mén* turns from explicit to implicit, but the general force of a *mén* statement remains: it clears the ground for later statements, providing a basis from which further continuation is possible, and thus establishes the common ground that is necessary for this continuation to be meaningful and successful. There are various

---

[72] Notice that the dialogic nature of μέν is confirmed by its frequent collocation and virtual interchangeability (Ruijgh 1981) with ἤτοι (displaying a transparent etymology in ἦ + τοι: affirmative particle + dative of the second person pronoun). For a particularly clear example of the collocation, see Hes. *Theog.* 116: ἤτοι μὲν πρώτιστα Χάος γένετ᾽ 'well then, first of all there was Khaos', the beginning of the theogony proper, after the proem. Visser (1987: 146–48) shows that the semantic affinity between the two particles can be exploited for purposes of versification.

ways in which this happens. One of these is a recurrent feature of the Iliadic battle, in which the major opponents of heroes are frequently missed with a spear throw, and something else often accidentally hit:

a. Σαρπηδὼν δ᾽	and Sarpedon,
b. αὐτοῦ μὲν ἀπήμβροτε	he missed <u>him</u> (=Patroklos)
c. δουρὶ φαεινῷ	with the shining spear,
d. δεύτερον ὁρμηθείς,	charging for the second time,
e. ὁ δὲ Πήδασον οὔτασεν ἵππον	and he, he wounded the horse Pedasos,
f. ἔγχεϊ δεξιὸν ὦμον·	with the spear in the right shoulder.

(*Il.* 16.466–68)

From the point of view of classical Attic Greek the use of *mén . . . dé* in this example is anomalous: *dè* in unit e seems misplaced, for one expects the particle to go with Pedasos the horse, thus marking a contrast (*autoû mèn . . . Pédason dè* 'him [he missed] but Pedasos [he hit]').[73] Instead, *dé* seems to mark a constituent (*ho* 'he', i.e., Sarpedon) that cannot be construed as contrastive with the *mén* constituent (*autoû* 'him', i.e., Patroklos). An opposition between two referents, however, is not what the speaker here intends. Rather, the two particles mark specific moments in the flow of discourse. In other words, *mèn* applies not to the warrior aimed at and referred to by the pronoun (*autoû* in unit b), but to the clause as a whole, or better, to its preparatory relation with what follows. And *ho dè*, for its part, is not what answers *autoû mèn* in an opposition of two referents represented by the text; it marks a new start, the reinstatement of the agent of the scene described (see this chapter's earlier discussion of *ho dè* in *Il.* 5.330), a description that takes off from the platform provided by the *mén* clause.[74]

The processual function of *mén* is equally clear when the function of the *mén* statement as stepping-stone is combined with its function of rounding off a previous description. In this scene, Diomedes has just killed Astunoös and Hupeiron:

a. τοὺς μὲν ἔασ᾽,	<u>them</u> he left lying,
b. ὁ δ᾽ Ἄβαντα μετῴχετο	<u>and he</u>, he went after Abas
c. καὶ Πολύιδον,	as well as Poluidos,
d. υἱέας Εὐρυδάμαντος,	sons of Eurudamas
e. ὀνειροπόλοιο γέροντος·	old man dream-reader.

(*Il.* 5.148–49)

[73] This is the treatment proposed in Kühner and Gerth 1904: 268 for such cases.

[74] See also *Il.* 1.191; 4.491; 8.119, 302; 15.430, 521–23; 17.609–10; 20.321–22; 21.171. The usage is not confined to Homer: see Hdt. 9.111.1.

Again, *dé* in unit b seems misplaced if one expects an opposition between Diomedes' previous victims and the new ones.[75] But the poet is not
concerned with this referential opposition. His language reflects movement, the transition not from one killing to the next, but from the *verbalization* of the first killing to that of the next: *mén* and *dé* mark events in
performance time, not in story time. The *mén* unit verbalizes the end of a
scene not as a new step but as the basis from which to make a new step, the
observation of the next killing.

The basis for further discourse which is provided by *mén* may also be a
moment that is explicitly marked as *not* a switch to the other participant on
the scene. In such cases the *mén* unit is uttered in order to convey that the
attention of the listener should remain focused on whoever was already in
focus. We have just been told that no one was quicker than Diomedes to
cross the ditch and make a stand against the Trojans:[76]

a. ἀλλὰ πολὺ πρῶτος	No, by far the first
b. Τρώων ἕλεν ἄνδρα κορυστήν,	he (=Diomedes) took a helmeted man of the Trojans,
c. Φραδμονίδην Ἀγέλαον·	Agelaos the son of Phradmon,
d. <u>ὁ μὲν</u> φύγαδ᾽ ἔτραπεν ἵππους·	<u>and he</u> (=Agelaos), he turned his horses to flight:
e. τῷ δὲ μεταστρεφθέντι	<u>and in him</u> (=Agelaos) wheeling around
f. μεταφρένῳ ἐν δόρυ πῆξεν	in his back he (=Diomedes) fastened his spear.

(*Il.* 8.256–58)

Nothing could be farther removed from the alleged norm in the use of
mén . . . dé, distilled from Attic Greek texts, in which the two particles mark
an antithesis in style or an opposition between two referents.[77] In units d–e
there is only one referent, marked in turn by *mén* and then *dé*. But more
importantly, the use of *ho mèn* in unit d amounts to a specific processing
instruction to the listener: it conveys the information "*not* the other participant, continue with the one already in focus," whereas *ho dé* would have

---

[75] See *Il.* 8.125–26; 11.426; 20.458–60 (with αὐτὰρ ὁ instead of ὁ δέ). On such cases, see also
Bakker 1993b: 12–13; 1993c: 304–5.

[76] Similar digressive cases are *Il.* 2.101; 14.446–47; 16.402–4 (discussed in Bakker 1993b: 4–
13); 16.789 (see Chapter 5 below); 20.463 (see Chapter 5).

[77] To be sure, contrasts that are coordinated by μέν . . . δέ are not absent in Homer (e.g., *Il.*
20.462: <u>τὸν μὲν</u> δουρὶ βαλών, <u>τὸν δὲ</u> σχεδὸν ἄορι τύψας 'hitting <u>the one</u> with the spear, stabbing
<u>the other</u> from nearby with the sword'), but such examples are not so much the central use of the
particles as a special case of the wider phenomenon described here.

conveyed a switch to the other participant, as we saw above. The oblique pronoun marked by *dé* (*tôi dè*) then takes up the participant already in focus as a starting point to move to the other one. Instead of a referential or stylistic contrast, then, *mén* in unit d marks a *moment at which a switch is withheld*, a moment consciously marked as something other than a new step with a new item coming into focus, and a characteristic way of guiding the listener's consciousness through the flow of speech.

The discussion of *mén* just presented leaves us with an important observation: speech units in the Homeric spoken medium, the unperiodic strung-on style of the stylisticians, may be uttered, not just as an addition to what precedes or as a step forward on the path of speech, but with an eye on what lies ahead. In this regard the syntax of movement is but a subpart of the wider strategies of Homeric speechmaking, and of the specific aesthetic of Homeric discourse, to which we turn in the next chapter.

CHAPTER 5

Homeric Framings

The feat of extricating a particular element from a pattern shows intelligence at work within perception itself. Quite in general, intelligence is often the ability to wrest a hidden feature or disguised relation from an averse context. It is an ability that can lead to important discoveries. At the same time, the resistance of the context to such an operation raises a peculiar problem. After all, there is good sense in the warning that "one must never take things out of context." They may be falsified, distorted, and even destroyed by the isolation. At the very least they may be changed.
—Rudolph Arnheim, *Visual Thinking*

If telling the epic story may be seen in terms of translational movement, then the act of narration and its syntactic articulation not only involve movement but also a knowledge of where to move. The very selection of a path implies orientation and a sense of direction, and the act of movement typically presupposes that one has found one's bearings. This aspect of epic narrative has been well described and documented in various ways. For example, in his discussion of Homeric catalogic style, Krischer has pointed out a pervasive tendency to state the general character of a scene or sequence of scenes, by way of orientation, and only then to state the particulars.[1]

A simple but instructive example of this phenomenon is the beginning of battle in the fourth book of the *Iliad*: a general picture is presented of the two opposed armies, the din of battle, the cries of victors and vanquished, and blood streaming over the earth (*Il.* 4.446–56). Only then do we hear that Antilokhos was "the first" to kill a Trojan warrior (457), a statement

---

[1] Krischer 1971: 132. Krischer's demonstration involves such topics as the organization of *aristeiai* (traditional description of a hero's finest hour in battle), and a reassessment of Zielinski's Law (see Zielinski 1899–1901), which, as Krischer points out, is based on moments of branching (*Verzweigung*) of two action strings—particulars that are preceded by a general, orienting statement.

that sounds odd in the light of the mayhem that has already been de-scribed.[2] It becomes understandable, however, when one realizes that the preceding description was an orienting preview, a look ahead along the narrative track, rather than a narrative, referential statement in its own right.

A natural consequence of speaking about the speech process in spatial terms is that orientation in speech may be seen, quite literally, in terms of awareness of one's surroundings. Chafe, whose ideas on consciousness and speech were introduced in Chapter 3, notes that the human mind needs a general sense of time and place in order to "be in" a given situation.[3] A moment of focal vision, for example, needs a certain amount of back-ground awareness in order to be meaningful and enlightening, and in general terms, any piece of active information or moment of consciousness requires a certain amount of information, of which one is half-conscious, to serve as its background.[4]

When a consciousness is engaged in remembering and imagining, as in the case of most narrators and their audiences, actual vision turns into visualization, but the need for orientation remains. One's surroundings and relative position on the path of speech will be determined vis-à-vis a given scene, a mental picture. Such a scene is too substantial to be grasped in its entirety in one focus of consciousness, however, and has to be broken down into its constitutive parts during its mental scanning, while it is being verbalized into a series of speech units. This process benefits, in many cases, from a global, orienting unit, which precedes the description of the scene and provides context for it. Consider, for example, what one of Chafe's subjects in the Pear Film project does in the verbalization of a scene:[5]

a. [1.15] A—nd [.1] then a boy comes by,
b. [.1] on a bicycle,
c. the man is in the tree,
d. [.9] and the boy gets off the bicycle,
e. and . . looks at the man,

---

[2] Krischer 1971: 134; see also Latacz 1977: 83. See also the remarks on πρῶτος as a processual, rather than referential sign in Chapter 4 above.

[3] Chafe 1980: 26–49; 1987: 42–45; 1990: 93–96; 1994: 30, 128–29.

[4] Chafe speaks of "peripheral consciousness" here and "semi-active" information (1987: 25, 28–31; 1994: 53, 72). More on "active" and "semi-active" (as well as "inactive") later on in this chapter.

[5] See Chafe, ed. 1980: 307; Chafe 1980: 27. On orientation in storytelling see also Labov 1972: 363–65.

    f. and then [.9] uh looks at the bushels,

    g. and he . . starts to just take a few,

    h. and then he decides to take the whole bushel.

This speaker is visualizing a scene in his head: in units a–c, he orients himself by giving the general character of the scene, which in this case consists of the participants and their relative locations. Once this background has been established as context and direction for the narrative, the speaker can proceed by giving the little story of which the scene consists. As a Homeric speaker would do with *dé*, he marks the successive steps with the continuative particle "and."[6]

A unit verbalized after an orienting statement may be said to be added to it, which leads us back to the philological notion of adding style discussed in Chapter 3. Just as in the case of parataxis as movement, I propose to replace the stylistic concepts of adding style or appositional style with one that emphasizes agency. In terms that are less metaphorical than they may seem, we might speak then of a *close-up*: the speaker stands still for a moment on the path of speech to look more closely at the scene, or the speaker focuses on how the scene came about, explaining it and thus providing a basis for what is next in the story. This activity finds its expression in loose, fragmented syntax, the addition of speech units of any kind (from nouns or noun-epithet phrases to participial or prepositional phrases to whole clauses). Such loose syntactic addition, however, is very different from mere random cumulation, as we shall see. The addition of a detail or piece of explanation crucially presupposes a context in which the detail falls into place. And this context more often than not has been set up explicitly in order to accommodate the detail verbalized in the addition.

Rather than being unplanned, then, added units in the adding style are at the heart of strategies that involve planning and looking ahead. This is especially the case when the unit(s) serving as background (I shall speak of "starting point") is (are) a preliminary, global preview of an event to be described more fully in the narrative. Such a preview serves as a guidepost indicating the course and direction to be taken on the path of speech. "Orientation" is the term that I have been using; another term, pertaining less to movement than to vision, is "framing."[7] This word is often used in linguistics and cognitive science in ways that are so professionalized that

---

[6] See above, Chapters 3 and 4.

[7] "Frame" is a key term in the discussion of knowledge representation as conducted since the

even the metaphor behind it has been lost. My use of the term below will be quite literal and graphic: I define it as the demarcation of a frame limiting one's field of vision for the next moments or speech units, the area within which addition of detail can meaningfully take place. Orientation and framing have a wide range of syntactic manifestations in Homeric discourse, from thematic noun phrases staging the participants in a given event to the proleptic mentioning of events before they are due in chronological order. But whatever their nature, all these grammatical elements testify to the general movement of Homeric discourse, syntactically or suprasyntactically, from the global to the specific, and from the framing to the framed.

Close-Up and Addition

In the discussion of *mén* at the end of the previous chapter, we saw that progression and continuation may require a looking ahead in the flow of discourse: a speaker may verbalize a clause not so much as a statement in its own right as to provide a stepping-stone for statements to be verbalized shortly thereafter. In the same way, an adding unit that provides a second, closer look at a given scene may be prepared and staged by a preceding unit that serves as its frame (in visual terms) or starting point (in terms of movement). The relation between framing discourse on the one hand and detail within the frame on the other appears to be quite fundamental for Homeric discourse. In what follows I shall discuss some of the syntactic aspects and possibilities of framing and close-up, keeping an eye open for the same or similar phenomena on the suprasyntactic levels of the organization and flow of Homeric narrative. The following may serve as typical examples of moments of addition in which a close-up is verbalized:

a. ὁ δ᾽ ἔγχεϊ νύξε παραστὰς   and with the spear he hit [him] from nearby,
b. γναθμὸν δεξιτερόν,   on the right jaw.

(Il. 16.404–5)

---

mid-1970s within the context of cognitive science and artificial intelligence (e.g., Winograd 1975), in which the word denotes "cluster of knowledge," "interconnected network of information," or the like. Closely related concepts are goals, plans, and scripts (culturally determined mental scenarios for certain action sequences directed at performing a given task). See Schank and Abelson 1977. The application of these concepts to Homer (Miller 1987; Minchin 1992) is anticipated in the work of Nagler (1974).

a. τόν ῥ᾽ ἔβαλε πρῶτος   he first hit him,
b. κόρυθος φάλον ἱπποδασείης,   on the crest of his horse-haired helmet.

(*Il.* 4.459)

The b-units are, in syntactic terms, additions to the a-units. In terms of the underlying cognitive activity that propels verbalization and syntax, the speaker uses the b-units to focus on a detail selected from what had been visualized a moment before. The b-units narrow down the field of vision and zoom in on the scene, which is itself already a selection. The more detailed second shot is entirely dependent for its meaning on the more global first one, and so is its verbalization. Syntactically, the adding unit has no independent status; it leans on the preceding one which serves as its frame.

The notion of syntactic dependence and apposition might seem to imply that the adding unit is less important than the previous unit: an appendix or optional afterthought to something already complete. But whatever the value of this characterization may be for other discourses, it surely does not apply to Homer. When a unit is added, a detail within a frame has been singled out for verbalization. Nothing compels us to say that the detail is any less important than the frame, and in fact the detail may be the very reason why the frame has been set up at all. We begin to see, then, that between addition and framing a reciprocal relation may exist: if a given unit y is adding to the preceding unit x, then the function of unit x, conversely, may be the framing of unit y.

Units uttered within a frame, considered not in the dimension of vision but as a matter of performance time, can be seen as expansions of the framing unit. The way in which framing units provide context for units to come, in fact, is a major aspect of the aesthetics of Homeric discourse that emerges when the unperiodic strung-on style is studied as a phenomenon in its own right, rather than with reference to periodic style. In a recent article, Joseph Russo has discussed the pervasive Homeric tendency toward repetition and fullness and has characterized it as "Item Plus," the "master trope of traditional epic verse-making."[8] According to this principle, a given basic idea can be supplemented by material that is either an appositional, an explanatory, or a metonymic extension, according to whether it rephrases or widens the basic idea, or links it to what follows. This phenomenon is indeed pervasive in Homeric discourse. In Chapter 8 we shall deal with the implications of the expansion aesthetic for the way in which

[8] Russo 1994: 374.

meter and formulas are deployed; in the present chapter we are concerned with how expansion involves the resources of ordinary language.

The detail added to a preceding framing unit need not be visual. Often the mentioning of a name, the verbalization of the theme of a hero, activates concepts and facts associated with this hero. The peripheral notions are added to the name appositionally in the form of epithets, patronymics, or other qualifications. Accumulation of such details takes time and is thus the usual strategy in the full, catalogic introduction of heroes, as in the following example:[9]

Ἐλεφήνωρ,	Elephenor,
ὄζος Ἄρηος,	scion of Ares,
Χαλκωδοντιάδης,	son of Khalkodon,
μεγαθύμων ἀρχὸς Ἀβάντων.	lord of the great-hearted Abantes.

(*Il.* 2.540–41)

Whenever one of the qualifications associated with a name involves the relation between two items (e.g., the bearer of the name and someone else or his place of birth) and accordingly needs a verb, the consequence will be an appositional (digressive) relative clause.[10] Such appositive relative clauses are the usual introduction to the biography of the hero slain in the battle, on which see below. The relative clause may occur at any moment during the list of qualifications and is not bound to the slot immediately following the name. Consider, for example, the first appearance of Kalkhas the seer in the *Iliad*:

Κάλχας Θεστορίδης,	Kalkhas son of Thestor,
οἰωνοπόλων ὄχ᾽ ἄριστος,	of the bird-watchers by far the best,
ὃς ᾔδη τά τ᾽ ἐόντα	who saw what is,
τά τ᾽ ἐσσόμενα πρό τ᾽ ἐόντα,	what will be and what came before.

(*Il.* 1.69–70)

Very often, the situation is reversed and the name itself is added to what precedes, rather than specifying the theme to which subsequent additions

[9] The same sequence, except for the insertion of ὄζος Ἄρηος, occurs not very much later, at 4.463–64, and Elephenor is not mentioned again in the *Iliad*. Has the second mention been triggered by the presence of the first? See Beye 1964: 363 on the influence of the Catalogue on the earlier stages of the *Iliad* battle and Hainsworth 1976 on clustering as a feature of Homeric discourse in general, a phenomenon that is amenable to cognitive analysis.

[10] Appositive relatives are hardly subordinate clauses (Lehmann 1984: 270–72), and the dividing line in Homer between relatives and anaphoric pronouns is sometimes hard to draw.

conform. Typically, what precedes the added name is a clause consisting minimally of an anaphoric pronoun in the nominative case and a verb; the pronoun is most often marked by *dé* as a moment of continuation in the narrative (*ho dé* 'and he'). Sometimes the addition of the name takes place within the confines of a recognizable speech unit;[11]

ὁ δέ οἱ σχεδὸν ἦλθεν Ἀχιλλεὺς.   and he, Achilles came close to him.

(*Il.* 22.131)

But more frequently, the name constitutes a speech unit on its own, and epithets are often involved. Consider, for example:[12]

ὁ δ᾽ ἅμα πρότερος καὶ ἀρείων   but he [was] both older and braver,
ἥρως Πρωτεσίλαος ἀρήϊος·   hero Protesilaos the warrior.

(*Il.* 2.707–8)

αὐτὰρ ὁ δεύτατος ἦλθεν   but he, he came last,
ἄναξ ἀνδρῶν Ἀγαμέμνων,   lord of men Agamemnon.

(*Il.* 19.51)

Such added names are in agreement with a pronoun in the nominative case in the preceding clause, and thus the pronoun and the name denote one and the same person. In other cases the pronoun is in an oblique case and denotes a character other than the character to whom the name belongs. These cases include the well-known answering formulas discussed by Parry in his study of the noun-epithet formula in Homer.[13] Rather than considering them predicate formulas followed by subject formulas I treat them here as two stylized intonation units: a separate naming unit added to a preceding clause:

---

[11] Cf. *Il.* 6.390: ὁ δ᾽ ἀπέσσυτο δώματος Ἕκτωρ 'and he rushed from the house, Hektor'; *Od.* 6.141; 17.235: ὁ δὲ μερμήριξεν Ὀδυσσεύς 'and he pondered, Odysseus'. On these cases see also Chapter 8 below. Cases in which a name-epithet formula is added to a verb within the confines of a metrical unit include *Il.* 5.617, 859; 12.462; 13.823; 20.388; 21.161; 22.330; 23.218, 779; *Od.* 6.117; 7.21; 13.187; 17.506; 22.81.

[12] Almost any page in Homer yields instances of this phenomenon. See, for example, *Il.* 1.488–89; 2.105; 2.402; 3.81, 118, 328–29; 4.329, 502–3; 5.17–18, 133, 449; 8.355–56; 10.148; 15.520–21; 16.317–18, 339–40, 479–80; 19.40; 20.502–3; 21.67, 162–3; *Od.* 1.125, 319; 5.94, 354; 6.1, 41, 224, 249; 7.1, 139, 177, 230, 344; 8.7; 14.413; 18.311–12; 19.1 (=51); 20.1, 242; 21.359; 22.1; 23.344; 24.176.

[13] Parry 1971: 11–16.

τὸν δ᾽ αὖτε προσέειπε   <u>and him</u> then he addressed,
πολύτλας δῖος Ὀδυσσεύς·   <u>much-suffering godlike Odysseus.</u>

(*Il.* 9.676)

The use of a noun-epithet formula as an addition to a clause has many aspects: stylistic, poetic, and metrical. These will be discussed in Chapters 7 and 8 below. But features like style, formulas, and meter are not aesthetic features in and of themselves, or features that separate poetry from prose. Rather, they derive from the properties of ordinary language and should, accordingly, be studied from the point of view of speech before we assign poetic functions to them. Segmentation into speech units is due to cognitive factors and properties of the human mind, and the way in which those units are added to each other in the linear progression of the epic tale also has its source in the workings of the conscious mind. What then is the function of names or nouns that are added, as separate intonation units, to a preceding clause in the flow of speech?

To answer this question we have to return to the notion of topic or agent introduced in the previous chapter. Mentioning a name may evoke a set of associations (to be emphasized by an epithet, for example), but that does not exhaust the functions of names in the epic story. Names denote concepts that are likely to last longer than a single act of perception and its verbalization: instead of being a passing moment experienced on the path of speech, names often denote concepts that are active through time, in the speech flow of the performance. A hero or god who is an agent through a sequence of events is at the same time an active concept through the series of events that constitutes the representation of the epic events in speech, that is, in the consciousness of the speaker and his audience. Such a concept is not merely something experienced on the path of speech, but a companion on that path, sometimes for short distances, sometimes for longer stretches, or even all the way through.

Such longer-lasting concepts need a certain amount of management to serve their purpose in the epic story: there are always other characters on the scene with whose actions the activities of a given protagonist interact; or the concept of a protagonist may have to be reactivated in the minds of the audience. Often a mere topic switch (verbalized as *ho dé* 'and he') suffices to keep track of the concept of a given character and identify him with respect to others. This happens in the example given in the previous chapter, where the narrator returns to Diomedes after some time has elapsed, or rather, he reactivates the idea of this hero in his mind:

a. ὁ δὲ Κύπριν ἐπῴχετο   and he, he went after Kupris
b. νηλέϊ χαλκῷ,   with pitiless bronze.

(*Il.* 5.330)

But sometimes the narrator judges that more is necessary. In the example just given, the poet could have said *Tudéos huiós* 'Tudeus's son' instead of *nēléï khalkôi* 'with pitiless bronze' in unit b, loosely inserting a name that might have been redundant for some listeners but not for others. Names, then, may be used in Homeric narrative, not as subjects to any clause, but as tracking devices, reminders of who is active at a given point. And in uttering them, the speaker is not so much concerned with new information as with channeling the flow of speech and making sure that a given event is seen in the right perspective—again I stress the processual over the referential. Such additions may often seem redundant and unnecessary to us as readers, but then we are outside the flow of speech, being in a position to look back in our text and to see, in the two-dimensional, timeless space of the printed page, what was meant to be experienced along a track on which returning is impossible.

The addition of names or nouns is often called "right-dislocation" in linguistics; this infelicitous term not only introduces a two-dimensional visual opposition (left vs. right) that derives from the printed page and is of no concern to Homer (or to any other speaker for that matter), it also implies a deviation from a sentential norm, a movement of a word or phrase out of its proper place.[14] Such a characterization, which is also apparent in terms like "afterthought" or "repair,"[15] amounts to the ancient "strung-on" verdict in modern guise. All this nomenclature describes speech in terms of writing: it starts from the ideal of an integrated sentence and treats what is most natural to speech as a deviation from this norm.

Speech occurs in time and proceeds by addition. In this process, additions are not "right-dislocations" that "repair" the previous clause; that clause is a starting point, the context set up for the proper mention of a

---

[14] The term "right-dislocation" derives from transformational linguistics, but is also being used by functional linguists. See, for example, Givón 1984–91: 760–62; Geluykens 1994: 89. I have also used this terminology in an earlier effort dealing with these matters (Bakker 1990b: 10–11). On the complementary phenomenon of left-dislocation, see below.

[15] Compare also the notion of "tail" in Dik 1989: 135, 265, 358, defined as a "final constituent which falls outside the clause proper" (358).

name and other pieces of detail.[16] Such a starting point may consist of a clause in its most simple form, the pairing of a verb with an object, and it may serve the purpose of indicating an event in a global and preliminary way, as a frame accommodating pieces of detail to be supplied shortly, or as a kind of checklist, containing items in embryonic form to be worked out later. As an example of this phenomenon, consider the following passage:[17]

αὐτὰρ ὁ βοῦν ἱέρευσεν ἄναξ ἀνδρῶν Ἀγαμέμνων
πίονα πενταέτηρον ὑπερμενέϊ Κρονίωνι,

(Il. 2.402–3)

What we have here, within the reception conventions of our reading culture, are two hexameter lines in which a sentence is expressed: "But leader of men Agamemnon sacrificed a fat, five-year-old bull to the all-mighty son of Kronos." In the translated sentence, the subject, direct object, and indirect object are all integrated within an overarching construction, held together by the verb "sacrificed." Such a sentence, however, would be unlikely to occur in speech, whether ordinary or special; its conglomeration of detail would be too complex to be grasped by the verbalizing consciousness as an integrated whole. An alternative is to conceive of the Greek as a short track (which is part, of course, of the ongoing narrative track), consisting of a starting point that verbalizes the event in the most general way (*boûn hiéreusen* 'sacrificed a bull'), to which detail is added in three installments, each being a separate intonation unit and representing a separate focus of consciousness, and one of them being the loose addition of the name of the agent in the event:

a. αὐτὰρ ὁ βοῦν ἱέρευσεν   but he, he sacrificed a bull,
b. ἄναξ ἀνδρῶν Ἀγαμέμνων   ruler of men Agamemnon,
c. πίονα πενταέτηρον   fat, five years old,
d. ὑπερμενέϊ Κρονίωνι,   to the all-mighty son of Kronos.

[16] Notice that the notion of "starting point and added information" also figures prominently in the work of Chafe. See, for example, Chafe 1987: 36–38; 1994: 82–85. But whereas for Chafe the relation between starting point and addition pertains to the internal constituency of a clause (the starting point being the subject of the clause, in speech mostly a personal pronoun), in the argument presented here it applies to the relation between the clause as a whole and what follows it.

[17] See also the analysis of *Il.* 1.1–7 in Bakker 1997b.

The nominative noun-epithet phrase in unit b is not the subject of the clause, nor is the dative noun-epithet phrase in unit d its indirect object. Both are additions, appositions to the clause in unit a, details filling in the picture. The nominative phrase in unit b agrees with the pronoun *ho* in unit a, just as the accusative phrase in unit c agrees with the object *boûn* 'bull' in unit a. But whereas *boûn* is necessary as an object, owing to the fact that "bull" is an integral part of the idea verbalized in unit a, the pronoun *ho* is surely not necessary as a subject. Its function is to indicate a topic switch, a shift in attention, and the reestablishment of Agamemnon as agent or protagonist after the concept of this hero has been out of focus for a few moments (2.394–401). In the previous chapter we have discussed such switches as moments of continuation marked by the particle *dé*; in unit a the particle *autár* appears instead. This particle has an original meaning that is perhaps more specifically adversative than that of *dé* (whose meaning, as we saw, amounts to a weakened version of the evidential particle).[18] For the purpose of marking switches and other transitions in Homeric discourse, however, the two particles are equivalent and serve as metrical alternatives for one another. In what follows I will treat them indiscriminately.[19]

The degree of naturalness with which nominal units can be added to a clausal core in Homeric discourse is connected with a peculiarity of the Greek verb which is obvious but often underestimated in our sentential perception of Homer and other Greek texts. The Greek verb does not need an overt nominal or pronominal subject: it expresses person and number by its own morphology and is thus more autonomous than the English verb. And if the verb is more autonomous, so are the noun phrases following it (or preceding it, as we shall see in the next section). This fact is presented as follows in one of the handbooks of comparative grammar: "The verb *phâsi* 'they say' does not need a subject to be plural. And it is not the apposition *egṓ te kaì sú* ['both I and you'] that ensures that the verb *sunomologḗsōmen* ['let us come to agreement'] is first person plural in Plato's phrase at *Thg.* 122B, but the fact that the phrase is about "you and me"; the verbal form would be the same if the pronouns did not occur in the phrase. This is the

---

[18] The particle αὐτάρ probably goes back, as Ruijgh (1971: 716) suggests, to a petrified collocation of the adverb αὖτις (αὖθις 'again', 'on the other hand') and the evidential particle ἄρα, and serves as synonymous metrical doublet of the particle ἀτάρ. But cf. Denniston (1954: 55), who derives αὐτάρ from αὖτε 'then'. Diachronically, dialect fluctuation seems a plausible explanation of the coexistence of the two allomorphs (ἀτάρ being the Ionian, and αὐτάρ the older Aeolic or even Mycenaean form): αὐτάρ does not occur frequently outside epic discourse.

[19] Cf. also the collocation of both particles with ἔπειτα 'then', 'thereafter' (αὐτὰρ ἔπειτα, ἔπειτα δέ) and more important, the frequent use of αὐτάρ in clauses following a preparatory μέν (e.g., *Il.* 11.99–101; 17.609–10; 20.458–60). See Chapter 4.

consequence of the autonomy of the Indo-European word: each element in a phrase has in and of itself the form called for by the sense to be expressed."[20]

Therefore, any overtly expressed subject in Greek, whether nominal or pronominal, is an addition to its verb, and especially a longer phrasing, with its rhythmical momentum and an intonational contour of its own, has a good chance of being realized as a separate unit, the verbalization of a single focus of consciousness. Thus a noun-epithet formula, like unit b in the example just cited, remains a loosely added unit even when the pronoun is absent, as in the following case:

οἱ δ' ὅτε δὴ	and they, when
κλισίῃσιν ἐν Ἀτρεΐδαο γένοντο,	they were in the tent of Atreus's son
τοῖσι δὲ βοῦν ἱέρευσεν	(and) for them a bull he sacrificed,
ἄναξ ἀνδρῶν Ἀγαμέμνων	leader of men Agamemnon,
ἄρσενα πενταέτηρον	male, five years old,
ὑπερμενέϊ Κρονίωνι.	to the all-mighty son of Kronos.

(Il. 7.313–15)

The same principle applies when the noun-epithet phrase offers new information, verbalizing the first appearance of a hero in a given situation.[21] In the following example, the phrasing for Agamemnon in unit b is not the subject of the preceding clause, any more than the following accusative phrase (unit c) is its object; both are items in a chain of additions supplementing the preliminary statement made in the preceding core clause:[22]

[20] "Il n'y a pas besoin d'un sujet pour que φᾶσι 'on dit' soit au pluriel. Ce n'est pas l'apposition ἐγώ τε καὶ σύ qui fait que le verbe συνομολογήσωμεν est à la première personne du pluriel dans la phrase de Platon, Théag. 122 B, c'est le fait qu'il est question de 'toi et moi'; la forme verbale serait la même si les pronoms ne figuraient pas dans la phrase. Cela résulte toujours du caractère d'autonomie du mot indo-européen: chaque élément de la phrase a par lui-même la forme qu'appelle le sens à exprimer," Meillet and Vendryes 1968: 598. In the same passage the authors reject the notion of accord or syntactic agreement: the "subject" to a plural verb is necessarily plural itself, but independently of the verb, without there being any grammatical agreement. The general heading under which Meillet and Vendryes discuss these matters is "apposition"—a specific characteristic of Homeric Greek and early Indo-European—as opposed to the "rection" or "government" of later Greek styles and Indo-European languages. The opposition between apposition and rection states in the diachronic dimension what the opposition between fragmentation and integration (see Chapter 3) states in the context of the medial difference between speech and writing.

[21] On the poetic and ritual potential of noun-epithet formulas denoting first appearances, see Chapter 7 below.

[22] See Meillet, who states (1937: 358–59) that any genitive, dative or accusative expression in a Greek sentence is no more governed by its verb than is an instrumental or locative phrase. The following passage is also discussed by Higbie (1990: 34) and was athetized by Zenodotus.

a. αὐτὸς γάρ σφιν δῶκεν   for he himself to them he had given [it],
b. ἄναξ ἀνδρῶν Ἀγαμέμνων   leader of men Agamemnon,
c. νῆας ἐϋσσέλμους   the well-benched ships,
d. περάαν ἐπὶ οἴνοπα πόντον   to cross the wine-blue sea,
e. Ἀτρείδης,   the son of Atreus,
f. ἐπεὶ οὔ σφι θαλάσσια ἔργα μεμήλει.   since works of the sea, they were not on
                                        their mind.

(*Il.* 2.612–14)

One might consider some of these additions, especially the formulaic accusative phrase in unit c,[23] and the remarkable second mention of Agamemnon in unit e, to be metrically motivated. This may be true, but meter, as I shall argue in Chapter 6, is the stylization of ordinary speech and not an artificial poetic construct. An analysis of formulaic elements as "metrically motivated" must therefore be handled with some circumspection: the final consideration, for the poet as well as for the researcher, must remain the function of these phrases in the stylized speech, which is the loose addition of detail to a preliminary core. Thus even if a phrase like unit e, which does not contribute as much to the flow of information as do the surrounding units, has been inserted primarily for metrical purposes, its status is still not that of a mere metrical stopgap that is inevitable in rapidly composed oral poetry. More precisely, it has that feature *too*, but phrases with a primarily vocal function and a diminished cognitive load are not confined to oral composition in performance; they are characteristic of speech in general. And the stylization of such phrases is just as important for the poet and his audience as is redundancy in general for ordinary speakers and their listeners.[24]

[23] The Greek language can leave objects unexpressed when they are understood from the preceding context, where English has to use dummy objects like "him" or "it." See for example *Il.* 2.102–8, where the sceptre is understood as object after its mention in 101 but not expressed (see also Bakker 1990b: 12). On this basis, I see the full-length metrical phrases Ἕκτορα Πριαμίδην at *Il.* 15.604 and ποδώκεα Πηλείωνα at *Il.* 20.27 as added accusative namings rather than as direct objects governed by the verb in the clause before. Sometimes, however, the object in the core clause is expressed by a pronoun, μιν or τόν (e.g., *Il.* 13.315–16: οἵ μιν ἅδην ἐλόωσι | καὶ ἐσσυμένον πολέμοιο, ‖ Ἕκτορα Πριαμίδην, | καὶ εἰ μάλα καρτερός ἐστιν 'they will give him enough war to swallow | fierce though he is ‖ Hektor Priam's son | even though he is very strong'). See also *Il.* 13.765–66; 16.142–43 (=19.388–90); 21.249–50; *Od.* 1.194–95: δὴ γάρ μιν ἔφαντ' ἐπιδήμιον εἶναι, | σὸν πατέρ' 'they were saying he was here in this country, your father'; Hes. *Theog.* 696–97. Dative examples are *Il.* 20.321–22; Hes. *Theog.* 485–86.

[24] See also Bakker 1990b: 8–10, and Chapter 8 below, where I make a distinction between units as additions and addition *within* units. Against meter as the ultimate artistic and communicative constraint on epic discourse see also Nagler 1974: xxi–xxii.

Properties inherited from Indo-European syntax, then, facilitate the loose and fragmented speech that is in accordance with the processes of the human mind in general. Frequently, a piece of information, or cluster of interrelated ideas, is simply too large to be conceived of in consciousness as one synthetic, integrated whole; it has to be broken down into its component parts, by a principle that has been called by Chafe the "one new idea constraint": due to the limits of human consciousness no linguistic unit can contain two separate ideas, or distinct items of information.[25] If a given complex idea contains two items of new information, these are most likely to be presented as two separate intonation units. The question what constitutes an idea, finally, will depend on the context within which something is focused on and verbalized. The idea of Agamemnon or of Atreus's son, for example, will be verbalized as a separate unit in a context in which the poet is concerned with tracking this character, as in units b and e in the extract last cited; but it will be part of a unit when the description of an event is called for, as in the case of "they were in the tent of Atreus's son" in unit b of the example cited before.[26]

The wider implication of the observation that units can be added as details to a general picture is that the typical Homeric strategy, noticed by Krischer and others, of moving from the general to the particular has a clear function in the Homeric syntax of movement and close-up. The general orienting previews, which precede more detailed descriptions of scenes or sequences of scenes, are paralleled at the level of single scenes or events and their articulation in syntax, where we see a catalogue of additions to a clausal core. The core clause functions not as a flawed sentence to be repaired by subsequent additions, but as a starting point, a direction from which the detail added in later units is approached. The notion of a starting point or preview will remain central in our discussion: not only does it bind the syntactic and the suprasyntactic movement of Homeric discourse together, it also has more aspects to it than the preceding discussion has revealed.

[25] Chafe 1994: 108–19, from which I borrow the term "one new idea constraint." See also Givón 1984–91: 258–63, for the "one chunk per clause principle," and DuBois 1987: 826, for the "one new argument constraint" ("argument" being a linguistic term applying to the complements of the verb: subject, object, indirect object).

[26] Another factor determining whether or not a given idea will be verbalized as a single phrase is the phonetic contour or informational richness of the words involved. See for example Chafe 1994: 146–60; Devine and Stephens 1994: 414. There is also the rate or delivery of speech as the cause of the distribution of information across two units, where another speech style would result in one unit (see Chapter 6 below).

Frames and Goals

Names, as we have seen, frequently follow clauses in the flow of speech, acting as additions to a clausal core unit. But the reverse is also true, and this arrangement is no less frequent or important. The name itself may act as a frame, preceding instead of following its clause. For this use, which involves another aspect of the tracking of participants in the epic story, the simple name, rather than the noun-epithet formula, tends to be used. The name is marked by the particle *dé* or *autár* as a new step in the progression of the narrative, a step signaling that the god or hero in question will be the frame, or theme, for the moment or moments to come.[27] The study of such preceding names, as long as it does not mistake them for the subjects of their clauses, may lead to a change in view that is similar to that of the added, right-dislocated names discussed above. Instead of being left-dislocated elements, false starts, or otherwise deviations from a sentential norm, such names are units in their own right that are uttered for a purpose. One common function for a framing, preposed unit is contrast, as in the following simple example:

a.	ὡς ὁ μὲν ἔνθα καθεῦδε	so he, he slept there,
b.	πολύτλας δῖος Ὀδυσσεὺς	much-suffering godlike Odysseus,
c.	ὕπνῳ καὶ καμάτῳ ἀρημένος·	worn out with sleep and fatigue,
d.	αὐτὰρ Ἀθήνη	but [as for] Athene,
e.	βῆ ῥ' ἐς Φαιήκων ἀνδρῶν	she went to the Phaeaceans'
f.	δῆμόν τε πόλιν τε,	people and city.

$$(Od. 6.1-3)$$

Examples like this provide evidence that such verbal figures as chiasmus (the arrangement of two pairs of elements in an order *abba*) and hysteron proteron (the reversal of a natural order) are not by themselves a matter of style in the sense of literary embellishment used by philologists; they are

---

[27] Notice that for this reason such elements have themselves been called themes (e.g., Dik 1989: 135; Halliday 1967), by a metonymy not unrelated to that of topic, as discussed above. Geluykens (1992: 33–81) offers extensive discussion of preposed constituents (a phenomenon he calls left-dislocation). The concept of framing used in the present discussion covers the three main functions attributed to left-dislocation by Geluykens: referent introduction, recoverability (function with respect to the preceding discourse), and topicality (function with respect to subsequent discourse). Geluykens (1992: 100–108) discusses left-dislocated elements as separate tone groups (intonation units, in the terminology used here), dealing with the phenomenon that serves as the basis for stylization in Homeric discourse.

quite normal in living speech, where they result from a natural sequence in the flow of ideas and their verbalization. The mention of Odysseus's name (unit b) triggers the name of the other participant from previous scenes, and that name is verbalized (unit d) in direct contrast with what precedes, and so must come before its own clause. The example deserves special notice, furthermore, in that it contains a feature pertaining to the framing function of unit d that survives the recording of speech into text: the particle *rh(a)* in unit e. This enclitic is postpositive and it marks an intonational boundary; as such it is restricted, according to Wackernagel's Law, to the second place in the clause; the analysis of the preceding name as a separate unit reveals that instead of constituting an exception (fourth place in a sentence beginning with *autàr Athênê* as its subject), the enclitic is used in accordance with the law, in the second position of a clausal unit uttered within the frame of the previous one that is prosodically distinct.[28]

The following example is a more complicated case of chiasmus. The chiastic structure involves two pairs of items, two agents and two patients in a particularly complex killing-scene. The two pairs are arranged in the order $A^1p^1p^2A^2$ and the whole stretch of discourse is under the scope of one preposed, framing unit:

a.	Νεστορίδαι δ'	and the sons of Nestor,
b.	ὁ μὲν οὔτασ' Ἀτύμνιον	he, he wounded Atumnios,
c.	ὀξέϊ δουρὶ	with the sharp spear,
d.	Ἀντίλοχος,	Antilokhos,
e.	λαπάρης δὲ διήλασε	and he drove it through his flank
f.	χάλκεον ἔγχος·	the bronze spear,
g.	ἤριπε δὲ προπάροιθε.	and he fell before him,
h.	Μάρις δ' αὐτοσχεδὰ δουρὶ	and Maris from nearby with the spear,
i.	Ἀντιλόχῳ ἐπόρουσε	he rushed at Antilokhos,
j.	κασιγνήτοιο χολωθείς,	angry because of his brother,
k.	στὰς πρόσθεν νέκυος·	putting himself before the body,
l.	τοῦ δ' ἀντίθεος Θρασυμήδης	and him godlike Thrasumedes,

---

[28] See Ruijgh 1990: 229–31. In addition to the examples he cites (*Il.* 5.748; 16.220–21 [see below]; *Od.* 8.55–56, 449–50; 10.241–42) and the example in the text, cf. also: *Il.* 2.310; 5.849; 10.73; 11.101; 14.462; 16.307–8, 466; 20.484; 21.17, 205; *Od.* 18.66–67; 19.209–10; Hes. *Theog.* 226, 551. See also Bakker 1990b: 12–14. Another recorded feature pointing to the extraclausal, framing status of units is the modal particle κε(ν) or ἄν, equally enclitic (Ruijgh 1990: 232; Devine and Stephens 1994: 422–23). See for example *Il.* 5.85: Τυδείδην δ' | οὐκ ἄν γνοίης | ποτέροισι μετείη 'And Tydeus's son | you could not have known | among whom he was', a case of prolepsis, on which see Panhuis 1984; more literature on prolepsis is cited in Slings 1992: 105 n. 46.

m. ἔφθη ὀρεξάμενος   he was beforehand in reaching,

n. πρὶν οὐτάσαι,   before [he could] wound [him],

o. οὐδ' ἀφάμαρτεν,   and he did not miss,

p. ὦμον ἄφαρ·   the shoulder from nearby.

(*Il.* 16.317–23)

Three times a frame is opened here by a preposed name (units a, h, and l), and each time that moment is marked as one of continuation (notice the particle *dé*). The joint action of the two sons of Nestor is appropriately framed by the a-unit *Nestorídai d'* 'and the sons of Nestor'. Traditional grammar would call this phrase a pending nominative or dislocated subject, which is cut loose from the network of the syntactic construction and causes an anacoluthon.[29] It would be better to see this phrase as establishing the theme of the upcoming description: the joint slaying of one pair of brothers by another. Unit a is a new step (marked by *dé*) not only in the sense that it verbalizes a new detail coming into focus but also because it accommodates such detail. The unit marks a new item in a catalogue of killings and at the same time holds together the catalogue of details pertaining to this particular double killing.

The first of these details verbalized in the space opened up by *Nestorídai d'* is a statement with the particle *mén*, of the type that we discussed at the end of the previous chapter. Its processual force is particularly clear: rather than being referential ("the one," antithetically opposed to "the other"), the phrase is a starting point at the onset of the narrator's movement along the narrative track previewed by the a-unit.[30] The first stage of this "Nestorid track" is the pairing of the first brother with his victim. It consists of three steps that verbalize new detail coming into focus (units b, e,

---

[29] E.g., Kühner and Gerth 1898–1904: 1:47. A particularly clear example of this phenomenon is *Il.* 6.510–11; ὁ δ' ἀγλαΐηφι πεποιθώς ‖ ῥίμφα ἑ γοῦνα φέρει | μετά τ' ἤθεα καὶ νομὸν ἵππων 'and he, confident in his splendor ‖ lightly his legs carry him | along the abodes and pasture of horses', cited and discussed by Slings 1992: 96–100. The cognitive complexity of "lightly his feet carry him who is confident in his splendor" would violate the one idea per unit constraint; the result is a division into two foci of consciousness, whereby the verbalization of the first contains an "ungrammatical" dangling nominative and participle. For another pending nominative and an "ungrammatical" change of subject, see *Il.* 5. 27–29.

[30] Of course, the use of ὁ μέν in unit b is similar to classical Greek's referential use of μέν . . . δέ, in that the mentioning of "the one" brother creates the anticipation that "the other" will be mentioned. The point is, however, that the two sons of Nestor are not opposed to each other as two referential objects.

and g), and three adding units that either zoom in on this detail (units c and f) or serve the disambiguating function that we discussed above (unit d).[31]

Instead of continuing with "And the other brother, Thrasumedes, he killed Maris, who rushed at Antilokhos . . . ," the narrator proceeds with the brother of the *victim*, set up as frame (unit h) triggered by the idea of the victim just verbalized. This new frame is a subframe within the encompassing frame. It establishes Maris for four units as the new agent or protagonist in this complex scene. One might want to consider *Máris* as the subject of the verb *epórouse* 'rushed at' in the next unit. As noted above, however, in the appositional syntax of Homeric Greek this verb and its clause do not need an overt name for them to be "complete"; moreover, when additional adverbial detail is involved that situates Maris vis-à-vis the killer of his brother (*autoskhedà dourì* 'from nearby with his spear'), the total amount of information becomes simply too much for one unit: introducing a character on the scene and telling what he did requires at least two units by the "one idea constraint" mentioned above.

In the third subframe (unit l), the idea of Maris, the agent of the previous subframe, expressed as a pronoun in an oblique case (*toû d'*) serves as stepping-stone for the appearance of Thrasumedes, linking this new agent to the previous discourse. The naming of Thrasumedes, serving as frame for the four units to follow, is itself directly linked to the overarching frame in unit a. Because he is one of the Nestorids, the idea of Thrasumedes was already partly activated by the activation of the Nestorid track in unit a.[32] In such cases, Chafe speaks of a semiactive state, in which one is "peripherally aware" of something within the context of something else.[33] The overall structure or movement of the whole passage as framed by unit a is thus $A^1p^1p^2A^2$: the activation of Antilokhos (A^1) is a starting point: it raises the expectation as to "the other brother" (A^2) and so indicates a goal. This goal is then reached via the intervening description of the two victims (p^1p^2). We shall see later in this chapter that the indications of goals and the

---

[31] Notice that the *naming* of the first agent (A^1 in the chiastic arrangement $A^1p^1p^2A^2$) actually *follows* the naming of the first patient in unit b.

[32] The literature on pragmatics abounds in mentions of this phenomenon, the activation of concepts in association with a theme or set of expectations. See Schank and Abelson 1977: 41; Tannen 1979; Prince 1981; Chafe 1987: 29. Frames often create a context in which the use of definite pronouns is possible or appropriate (e.g., talk about "wheels" within the context of a given car set up as frame).

[33] Chafe 1987: 28–31; 1994: 53, 71–76.

movement toward them through intervening space is a wide-ranging feature in the speech syntax of Homeric discourse.

As further illustration that our idea of sentential syntax is irrelevant for what the epic narrator wants or needs to achieve, consider the way in which Circe presents the dangers of Skulla and Kharubdis to Odysseus:

a.	οἱ δὲ δύω σκόπελοι	and the two peaks,
b.	ὁ μὲν οὐρανὸν εὐρὺν ἱκάνει	the one, it reaches into the sky,
c.	ὀξείῃ κορυφῇ,	with sharp summit,
d.	νεφέλη δέ μιν ἀμφιβέβηκε	and a cloud, it stands around it
e.	κυανέη·	a black one

(*Od.* 12.73–75)

x.	τὸν δ᾽ ἕτερον σκόπελον	and [as for] the other peak
y.	χθαμαλώτερον ὄψει, Ὀδυσσεῦ,	you'll see it lower, Odysseus,
z.	πλησίον ἀλλήλων·	[they are] close to each other.

(*Od.* 12.101–2)

With unit a the speaker does *not* start a sentence that goes awry and loses itself in anacoluthic confusion (*mén* being separated from "its" *dé* by 28 metrical lines). Nor would a genitive phrase for unit a ("and of the two peaks the one . . . , the other") have been grammatically more "correct."[34] The a-unit is an orienting frame and unit b a clausal unit uttered within it. Unit b looks ahead to the other rock and places the description of Skulla and her abode in the right perspective. Again, we see a strategy of framing and goal-seeking in which the specific detail selected for verbalization is framed and accommodated by a global preview. In the following example, Tros the son of Alastor beseeches Achilles not to kill him. Here the initial frame (unit a) is an accusative phrase:

a.	Τρῶα δ᾽ Ἀλαστορίδην,—	Tros the son of Alastor (acc.),
b.	ὁ μὲν ἀντίος ἤλυθε γούνων,	he, he came up against his knees,
c.	εἴ πώς εὖ πεφίδοιτο λαβὼν	in the hope that he would spare him taking him prisoner,
d.	καὶ ζωὸν ἀφείη,	and let him go alive,
e.	μηδὲ κατακτείνειεν	and not kill him,
f.	ὁμηλικίην ἐλεήσας,	taking pity on a man his own age,
g.	νήπιος, οὐδὲ τὸ ἤδη,	misguided soul, and he did not know this

---

[34] Cf. Russo 1994: 382–83.

h. ὃ οὐ πείσεσθαι ἔμελλεν·   that he was not going to persuade him
i. οὐ γάρ τι γλυκύθυμος ἀνὴρ ἦν   for this was not a sweet-hearted man
j. οὐδ᾽ ἀγανόφρων,   nor kind-spirited,
k. ἀλλὰ μάλ᾽ ἐμμεμαώς·   but one in a rage,
l. ὃ μὲν ἥπτετο χείρεσι γούνων   <u>he</u>, he touched his knees with his hands
m. ἱέμενος λίσσεσθ᾽,   eager to supplicate,
n. ὃ δὲ φασγάνῳ οὖτα καθ᾽ ἧπαρ·   <u>and he</u>, he thrust his sword in the liver.

(Il. 20.463–69)

When we view this passage as a sentential structure, we would have to say that the accusative of unit a is dislocated from a verb which does not occur until unit n (*oúta* 'stabbed'). More in line with the flow of the passage, however, is to take the a-unit as a frame within which other units are uttered, one of them containing the logically central verb. This is not to say that *Trôa d' Alastorídēn* 'Tros the son of Alastor' is complete as it stands: the phrase obviously needs complementation of some sort. The important point, however, is that judging phrases by their syntactic completeness or incompleteness is a practice betraying the literate bias discussed in previous chapters. Linguistic expressions, as I will propose more fully in Chapter 7 below, are not so much "things" as *behaviors* that have no meaning outside the context in which they are performed. In the present context (a description of Achilles wreaking havoc among the Trojans) an accusative phrase marked off by intonational boundaries can mean only one thing: a new victim of Achilles is coming into focus. And this contextually determined activation will ensure that the hearer is sufficiently oriented in the upcoming description.[35] Within the frame we witness a series of additions held together by the repeated *ho mén* (units b and l), keeping the attention of the hearer focused on the participant activated by the framing unit, until finally in unit n (marked by *ho dé*) the jump can be made to the agent and the details of the killing.[36] Note that the description of the killing of Tros comes in three parts: the frame (unit a); a focusing on detail pertaining to the victim (units b–m); and the killer and the killing (unit n and beyond). As we shall see later in the chapter, this tripartite structure appears to be a constant in the deployment of Homeric narrative.

Scenes such as the ones framed by the names of the Nestorid brothers

---

[35] Notice the accusatives in the preceding line (*Il.* 20.462: τὸν μὲν δουρὶ βαλών, τὸν δὲ σχεδὸν ἄορι τύψας 'hitting <u>the one</u> with the spear, stabbing <u>the other</u> from nearby with the sword', after which unit a in the text can be read "and as for Tros son of Alastor").

[36] For this use of μέν, see Chapter 4.

and Tros in the preceding examples are killing scenes involving two participants or parties: a victor and a victim. Accordingly, the framing unit may
also consist of two names. Consider, for example:[37]

a. Μηριόνης δ᾽ Ἀκάμαντα	And Meriones (nom.) Akamas (acc.)
b. κιχεὶς ποσὶ καρπαλίμοισι	overtaking (=Meriones) with swift feet,
c. νύξ᾽ ἵππων ἐπιβησόμενον	he (=Meriones) struck [Akamas] mounting the chariot
d. κατὰ δεξιὸν ὦμον·	in the right shoulder

(*Il.* 16.342–43)

a. Ἕκτορα δ᾽ Ἰδομενεὺς	And Hektor (acc.) Idomeneus (nom.)
b. μετὰ Λήϊτον ὁρμηθέντα	rushing (=Hektor) after Leïtos:
c. βεβλήκει θώρηκα	· he (=Idomeneus) hit [Hektor] on the corslet,
d. κατὰ στῆθος παρὰ μαζόν·	on the chest near the nipple.

(*Il.* 17.605–6)

In these cases, a–units frame the passages and orient the listener, providing global indications of the scene, and then added units of familiar types
and functions offer close-ups: participial phrases (b–units) with detail pertaining to the target or victor; prepositional phrases (d–units) zooming in
on the place of the blow; and clausal c–units that verbalize the event proper.
Like the verb of wounding (*oúta*) in the description of the killing of Tros
that we discussed above, the verbs in the c–units here, *núks'* and *beblḗkei*, are
not the "verb" of their sentences, governing a subject and an object from
which they are separated by the end of the metrical line. As we saw above,
the noun phrase in Homeric Greek is more autonomous than in later
Greek or in English, having a tendency to contract a relationship of *agreement* with a verb (sometimes across a unit boundary), rather than one of
government (within a linguistic unit, such as the sentence).[38]

Thus the a–units, even though they are "incomplete" from a strictly
syntactic point of view, are perfectly intelligible in this particular context;
they stage the two participants, along with their roles (agent or patient) as
marked by inflectional morphology, in the upcoming killing-scene. In the

[37] See also Bakker 1990b: 14–16. Notice that the examples differ in that in the second case
"Hektor" is active or given information and "Idomeneus" is new information.

[38] Lehmann 1993: 216, building on Meillet's observations (1937: 358–59), relates this autonomy of the word in the phrase to his own argument that Proto-Indo-European was an "active-
passive language," a language with nominal inflection that codes not grammatical roles (subject,
object) but semantic roles (agent, patient).

terminology developed here, the names in each a-unit serve as starting points for the transformation of the scene into language. The verbs in the c-units, conversely, do not need the names as "complementation": after all, what seems to us a single verb (*núkse*) can represent an utterance on its own with a subject and an object ("[he] struck [him]"), given the appropriate context. Such a context is in this case, of course, provided by the a-units, which in their turn are uttered within a context that determines their meaning and serves as an interpretive frame: the context of catalogic battle narrative, in which pairs of warriors are staged and indicated as frames for the scenes to come.[39] As always in the flow of speech through time, any unit is uttered within the context of its immediate past and provides, in its turn, context for its immediate future.

If one accepts that the a-units in these passages function not as subjects and objects of a sentence, but as frames for a scene, one's reading of the following passage might be altered accordingly:[40]

a.	ἔνθ᾽ ἤτοι Πάτροκλος	there, you know, Patroklos (nom.),
b.	ἀγακλειτὸν Θρασύμηλον,	much-famed Thrasumelos (acc.),
c.	ὅς ῥ᾽ ἠὺς θεράπων	who the strong servant
d.	Σαρπηδόνος ἦεν ἄνακτος,	of lord Sarpedon he was,
e.	τὸν βάλε νείαιραν	him (=Thrasumelos) he (=Patroklos) hit in the belly,
f.	κατὰ γαστέρα,	in the stomach,
g.	λῦσε δὲ γυῖα.	and he loosened [his] limbs.

(*Il*. 16.463–65)

In such cases, the temptation is to see the verb (*bále* in unit e) as postponed. The result is a reading of the passage as an anacoluthon, a deviation from a sentential norm that is either condemned or accepted by calling it an oral

[39] In catalogic battle narrative, the idea of killing, in other words, is given: present and active in the performer's consciousness and assumed to be present and active in the audience's mind as well. Concepts that are given and active will need only attenuated expression, or no expression at all, in the phrasing of the focus of consciousness in question. On "given" in the sense of "active," see Chafe 1980: 10; 1987: 26–31; 1994: 72. On the given status of verbs of killing in battle narrative, see also Chapter 8.

[40] See also *Il*. 5.76–83; 11.122–27, 321–22; 13.427–35; 14.409–12; 15.430–34; 16.401–10 (see Bakker 1993b: 4–12); 17.306–9, 610–17 (the most complex case). Notice that in many cases the victim is a charioteer hit accidentally, a frequent incident in Iliadic battle (Fenik 1968: 204). On processual ἔνθ(α) 'there' and ἤτοι in unit a, see the relevant notes in Chapter 4. Only here and in the nearby *Il*. 16.399 (a good case of clustering, cf. 16.314, 322) do we find the collocation of these two particles.

anacoluthon.[41] The anacoluthon in this passage disappears when considered in light of the two previous examples. Notice, first of all, the structural similarities. After the two participants are named, detail pertaining to the victim is added, but as an appositive relative clause (units c–d) this time, not in the form of a participial phrase. It is this syntactic difference that makes the pronoun *tòn* in unit e necessary to avoid confusion. Rather than a change in construction or a repair strategy, however, the relational demonstrative clause *tòn bále neíairan* reflects a purposeful strategy, situating the verbalization of the present moment within the context of the immediately previous discourse. In other words, the verbalization of detail pertaining to Thrasumelos has created a second frame, a subframe within the confines of the first, encompassing frame. It is the pronoun that acknowledges the second frame as such; its function is not so much to mark the transition to a new frame (note the absence of *dé*) as to signal the moment that was anticipated when the narrator set the first frame: a close-up, rather than a new step. The details of the killing proper, then, can be seen as the final stage in a three-stage process: frame (or starting point), subframe, and a goal to which both frames are aiming. This characterization has the merit of bringing out the common element in many seemingly unconnected phenomena in the syntax of Homeric speech and composition. Before we continue our discussion of frames and goals, however, one more function of framing-names in Homeric discourse has to be briefly discussed.

The Syntax of Activation

The framing-name in lists of warriors slaying and slain in the battle typically sets up a character who is new to the stage as theme for discourse to come, the agent or patient in a killing-scene. But framing-names may also verbalize a return to a character, a reactivation of the concept of a character. Since we have already applied this concept to added names, a brief differentiation of the various possibilities might be useful here. The simplest and easiest transition from one protagonist to another, as we saw in the previous chapter, is a simple topic switch without names (*ho dé* 'and he'). In this case, both characters are present on the scene currently in focus

---

[41] For instance, Janko 1992: 276. Kirk (1962: 169) calls the similar passage *Il.* 17.610–17 "some of the weakest battle-narrative in the Iliad."

and are fully active in the minds of the narrator and the audience, so they need not be explicitly named. When the second character has been out of sight for a short while, without the scene in question having been changed, that character's name may be added to the *ho dé* clause. In such cases we might say that the second character has become near-active in the minds of speaker and audience. The added name, signaling the transition to the active state, is meant as a reminder, to keep the narrative on the right track. When more time has elapsed since the last mention of a character, and when different scenes have been described in the meantime, we may say that the character is returning, and that in the minds of the narrator and the audience the idea of the character is activated from a semiactive state, the status of an idea of which one is peripherally aware. The verbalization of such a moment typically involves a framing-name that functions as signpost on the narrative track.[42] The name is normally without an epithet, and marked by *dé* or *autár* as a moment of continuation. In the examples that follow, both the return of Odysseus to the narrative after Thetis's visit to Achilles and the return of Achilles after a description of the Myrmidons marching into battle are marked by *autár*.

a. τὸν δὲ λίπ᾽ αὐτοῦ   and him she left there,
b. χωόμενον κατὰ θυμὸν   raging in his heart,
c. ἐϋζώνοιο γυναικός,   about the fair-girdled woman,
d. τήν ῥα βίῃ ἀέκοντος ἀπηύρων·   her they had taken by force against his will,
e. αὐτὰρ Ὀδυσσεὺς   but Odysseus,
f. ἐς Χρύσην ἵκανεν   he reached Khruse,
g. ἄγων ἱερὴν ἑκατόμβην.   leading the sacred hecatomb.

(*Il.* 1.428–31)

a. πάντων δὲ προπάροιθε   and ahead of all of them,
b. δύ᾽ ἀνέρε θωρήσσοντο,   two men, they marched in armor,
c. Πάτροκλός τε καὶ Αὐτομέδων,   Patroklos and Automedon,
d. ἕνα θυμὸν ἔχοντες,   being one in their fury,
e. πρόσθεν Μυρμιδόνων πολεμιζέμεν.   to fight in front of the Myrmidons,
f. αὐτὰρ Ἀχιλλεὺς   but Achilles,
g. βῆ ῥ᾽ ἴμεν ἐς κλισίην,   he went to his tent.

(*Il.* 16.218–21)

[42] Lambrecht (1987: 231–35) uses a similar distinction between framing and added names (topics and antitopics in his terminology), considered in terms of recoverability (the participant being less recoverable in the case of framing).

In these examples we see a switch back to a major character, who is thus once more set up as protagonist after a given interval. The switch moment is constituted by *autár* and the name of the returning hero (unit e in the first passage and unit f in the second). Rather than being the subjects of an enjambing clause (they occur at the end of the metrical line), these units serve as frames for what lies ahead.[43] In the first example, the narrator resumes the thread (the return of Khruseïs to her father by the embassy of Odysseus) that was left at *Il.* 1.312, before the attention was directed to Thetis's visit to Achilles. In the second example Achilles is set up, after scenes describing the preparation of the Myrmidons for battle, as the agent in a brief scene setting the perspective for the following *Patrokleia*. In both cases a separate unit is devoted to the narrative act of returning to Odysseus and Achilles, reflecting the cognitive effort that is involved in the reactivation.[44]

Finally, characters may also make an entirely new appearance on the stage, coming out of absence into presence, or in cognitive terms, becoming an active concept in the minds of the narrator and his audience out of an inactive state. In the specific context of catalogic battle narrative, as we have seen, the normal method of verbalization is the simple framing-name, serving as label: the name of either the agent or the patient, or both names combined within one unit. Another frequently used method for effecting the new appearance of a hero is the noun-epithet formula, preceded by a unit in which the relation of the new character vis-à-vis the character already present is specified, most often a relation of seeing;

a. τὸν δ' ὡς οὖν ἐνόησε   and him (=Diomedes) when he (=Pandaros) saw,
b. Λυκάονος ἀγλαὸς υἱὸς   the radiant son (=Pandaros) of Lukaon

(*Il.* 5.95)

The new character, named in unit b, sees somebody who is currently in focus. But rather than reporting an act of perception, the a-unit serves as link or transition between the new character and the one already present, who is verbalized as a demonstrative pronoun in an oblique case. In Chapter 7 we will discuss in detail the pragmatics and poetics of such moments, which are of prime importance in the epic tale. Here we simply observe

---

[43] Notice the particle ῥ(α) in unit g of the second example, confirming that unit f is intonationally independent.

[44] Chafe (1994: 71–81) speaks of "activation cost" in this connection.

that noun-epithet formulas preceded by such a relational clause are an important way of introducing new characters on the scene.

We have discussed various ways of making transitions to a character in the Homeric narrative. The different methods available for verbalizing such transitions reflect both the status of the character in the narrative and the way in which poet and audience conceptualize the character. For example, if s/he is present in the narrative, a character will be active in the consciousness, and a transition to the character will be verbalized in a certain way; a returning character will be semiactive in the consciousness, and the transition will be verbalized accordingly. The four possibilities may be schematically summarized as follows:[45]

Character in the narrative	Character in the consciousness of poet and listeners	Verbalization
present	active	• ὁ δέ or αὐτὰρ ὁ clause without name
copresent	near-active	• ὁ δέ clause + name in same unit • ὁ δέ clause + noun-epithet phrase in next unit • answering-formula + noun-epithet phrase in next unit
returning	semiactive	• simple name with δέ or αὐτάρ + clause in next unit
appearing	inactive	• simple name with δέ + clause in next unit • τοῦ/τῷ/τὸν δέ clause + noun-epithet phrase in next unit

This schema is merely meant to represent the findings of the preceding pages. It is approximate and does not pretend to predict the precise way in which a given transition to or (re)appearance of a character is articulated in speech syntax. In the end, living discourse defies neat categorization and always produces exceptions for which no special explanation or justification seems available.[46] But that should not keep us from making some generalizations.

---

[45] Note that the category "near-active" in the second column has been added to Chafe's categories of "active," "semiactive," and "inactive." Chafe (1987: 25–36; 1994: 71–76) relates these terms to "given," "accessible," and "new" information, respectively.

[46] For example, in *Il.* 1.488–89 the reappearance of Achilles after Odysseus's trip to Khruse (see the example above) is not verbalized as a framing name but as an amplified noun-epithet

Explanation and Epic Regression

As the last step in our overview of framing phenomena in Homeric speech syntax, we turn from preposed names to the particle *gár*. This element of Homeric discourse is seemingly quite unrelated to the framing phenomena discussed thus far, yet it will yield a discussion that leads to the same goal as many of the demonstrations above. J. D. Denniston describes what he calls confirmatory and causal *gár* as "commoner in writers whose mode of thought is simple than in those whose logical faculties are more fully developed. The former tend to state a fact before investigating its reason, while the latter more frequently follow the logical order, cause and effect."[47] And indeed we frequently find *gár* in Homer (one of the "writers" meant), though not as the marker of a "cause" after its "effect," and even less as the reflex of a prelogical, primitive mind. Rather than marking causes or reasons, *gár* is an important element in the flow of speech itself, where it is used to mark moments at which looking more closely at the point reached so far on the path of speech (i.e., movement into a frame) may take the form of an explanation added to what precedes. And far from being illogical, such added explanations are a key part in the logic of movement in speech: the purposeful exploration of a well-chosen, strategic starting point from which the narrator and the audience orient themselves.

A clause marked by *gár* may be no more than additional visual detail pertaining to the picture verbalized in a preceding unit. In such cases the explanation is a detail added to a frame, and not very different from the adding units verbalized to zoom in on the scene before the speaker's eyes, which we discussed earlier.

a. ὁ μὲν εὐξέστῳ ἐνὶ δίφρῳ	he in his well-polished chariot,
b. ἧστο ἀλείς·	he sat crouching,
c. ἐκ γὰρ πλήγη φρένας,	for he was knocked out of his wits,
d. ἐκ δ' ἄρα χειρῶν	and from his hands,
e. ἡνία ἠίχθησαν.	the reins they had slipped.

(*Il.* 16.402–4)

---

formula staged by a preceding αὐτὰρ ὁ clause: αὐτὰρ ὁ μήνιε νηυσὶ παρήμενος ὠκυπόροισι, ‖ διογενὴς Πηλῆος υἱός, πόδας ὠκὺς Ἀχιλλεύς 'but he clung to his wrath, sitting beside the swift ships, divinely born son of Peleus, swift-footed Achilles'. Similarly, the return to Odysseus and Eumaios at *Od.* 15.301, after 300 lines of intervening scenes, is verbalized as an added, not as a framing name.

[47] Denniston 1954: 58.

The *gár* clause in unit c verbalizes a closer look at the scene depicted in units a–b and thereby explains that earlier perception.[48] Clauses with *gár* may be used to complement the general picture, filling in the frame presented by the previous clause. We have seen how an earlier clause often serves that purpose, offering a global preview of the scene in question. The death of Patroklos provides an instructive example:[49]

a.	ἔνθ᾽ ἄρα τοι, Πάτροκλε,	there for you, Patroklos,
b.	φάνη βιότοιο τελευτή·	the end of your life, it appeared,
c.	ἤντετο γάρ τοι Φοῖβος	for Phoibos came face to face with you,
d.	ἐνὶ κρατερῇ ὑσμίνῃ	in the strong battle,
e.	δεινός·	terrible,
f.	ὁ μὲν τὸν ἰόντα κατὰ κλόνον	and he (=Patroklos) him moving (=Phoibos) through the crowd
g.	οὐκ ἐνόησεν·	he did not see
h.	ἠέρι γὰρ πολλῇ	for in thick mist
i.	κεκαλυμμένος ἀντεβόλησε·	covered he (=Phoibos) came against him:
j.	στῆ δ᾽ ὄπιθεν,	and he stood behind
k.	πλῆξεν δὲ μετάφρενον	and he struck his back.

(*Il.* 16.787–91)

After a general indication of the scene in units a and b, the participants are staged in units c–i, with two *gár* statements (units c and h) filling in the picture, along with a preparatory *mén* clause (unit f). Only at the point reached in unit j does the description of the event itself begin, and it is this moment that the narrator anticipates when uttering units a and b. Those units, then, are not merely a starting point; they are at the same time pointers to a goal, indications of the direction the discourse is taking. And far from being mere explanations, loosely added to a fact that would otherwise remain unclear, the *gár* statements are entirely bound up with the syntax of movement: they cover the narrative space between the near-distance goal and the point from which it begins to come into focus.[50] The

---

[48] One could imagine the c-clause expressed as a participle, adding detail to the participle in the previous clause. Notice the presence of μέν in unit a. For another combination of μέν and γάρ see *Il.* 17.366–68.

[49] For the "apostrophe" in units a–c, see Bakker 1993c: 23, focusing on the use of the evidential particle ἄρα in unit a. Note that the scene in which Patroklos dies is preceded by an evidential subclause marked by δή, which in turn is preceded by an instance of the three-times motif. This whole climactic and pivotal event is marked throughout by a clustering of evidentiality phenomena.

[50] Cf. Lang's remarks (1984: 5–12) on digressions in Herodotus. It is customary in the

passage, then, could be called a three-stage process, just as the deaths of Tros and Thrasumelos discussed above: it consists of a starting point, a goal, and the movement from the one to the other.

Often this movement implies the reversal of temporal sequence: the *gár* statement may involve events that took place, chronologically, before the event that has been set up as goal in the initial, framing unit. This phenomenon has been called, in a discussion not dealing with speech syntax but clearly relevant for our present purpose, epic regression, the presentation of events in reverse chronological order.[51] What is not reversed, however, is the attention of the narrator, who is really looking forward rather than back; rather than dealing with a historical digression, a swerving off the narrative track, the narrator is engaged in a purposeful strategy for better approaching the highlights on the track.

Given these considerations, it is not surprising that *gár* is particularly at home in the vicinity of the starting point of all starting points, the very beginning of the epic tale. It is here that choosing the right vantage point, sufficiently global but also sufficiently relevant and specific, is particularly important, if one wants to avoid a presentation of events *ab ovo* that is not only dull but often also impossible, as the Homeric narrator and most other storytellers realize. Explanatory goal-seeking statements with *gár* are a natural consequence of the fact that at the beginning, when the story has not yet acquired the momentum it will have later on, looking ahead at goals to be reached in due course is as yet more important than the covering of actual distances.

Thus during the first moments of the *Iliad*, after the preliminary statement that it was Apollo who brought about the harmful encounter between Achilles and Agamemnon (*Il.* 1.8–9), it is a *gár* statement (9) that leads the way in the direction of the goal set up by that preliminary statement: the description of the plague sent by Apollo (51–52) and the reason for Achilles to call the army to the assembly (53), an event that is, again, previewed and approached by a presentation of events in reverse order:

a.	τῇ δεκάτῃ δ' ἀγορήνδε	and on the tenth day to the assembly
b.	καλέσσατο λαὸν Ἀχιλλεύς·	Achilles, he had the people called,
c.	τῷ γὰρ ἐπὶ φρεσὶ θῆκε	for on his mind she put [it],

---

modern literature on grammar and discourse (e.g., Hopper 1979: 215–16) to treat digressive material in a story (marked by γάρ in Greek) as explanatory background, as against the foreground of the main line of the narrative. The use of γάρ in Homer runs counter to such a conception. See also Chapter 4 above.

[51] Krischer 1971: 136–40.

d. θεὰ λευκώλενος Ἥρη·   goddess white-armed Hera,
e. κήδετο γὰρ Δαναῶν,   for she cared about the Danaans
f. ὅτι ῥα θνῄσκοντας ὁρᾶτο.   since she saw [them] dying,
g. οἳ δ᾽ ἐπεὶ οὖν ἤγερθεν   and they, when they were then assembled

(Il. 1.54–57)

Again, we see a movement in three stages: starting point and orienting preview (units a–b), goal (unit g), and movement from the one to the other (units c–f). The last-mentioned stage is not a twofold statement of a cause after its effect but reflects a deliberate strategy of moving from the global to the specific as a means of making headway in speech.[52] Notice, finally, that the particle *oûn* (unit g) frequently signals the moment at which the goal is reached. This particle thus forms with *gár* a correlative pair ("goal sought . . . goal reached"), a relation not unlike that between *mén* and *dé* in their processual, Homeric function.[53]

Ring Composition and the Grammar of Discourse

In the preceding discussion of addition and framing I aimed to show that adding style or parataxis in Homeric discourse is not just random cumulation. More often than not a unit is not only connected with what precedes but also leads to what follows, and this relation of any given present moment to its past and its future is what gives the listener an orientation and the discourse its meaning. But Homeric discourse would not be special speech if it did not systematize and enhance these strategies. Two aspects of the enhancement of framing and orientation concern us in the remainder of this chapter: the explicit articulation of orienting steps in ring composition, and their grammatical fixity in the case of the most frequently recurring scene in Iliadic narrative, the catalogic description of the epic *androktasia*, of which we have seen already some examples. Let us start with the latter case.

[52] See also the γάρ statements in Nestor's narrative (*Il.* 11.688, 690, 692, 698, 700). An extreme case is Hdt. 4.1.1–3, where we see no less than six statements with γάρ in the buildup to the Scythian tale, all of which are regressive. See also Hes. *Theog.* 535 (first step in Prometheus story, cf. 521 and 615–16), 571 (first step in Pandora story, cf. 570 and 585); *W&D* 42, 43, 90 (marking the steps in the Pandora story, as indicated by Thalmann 1984: 19).

[53] For γάρ . . . οὖν, see *Il.* 2.319–21; 4.376–82. For μέν . . . οὖν, see *Il.* 2.657–61; 3.2–4, 16–21, 330–40. On οὖν alone as coming to the narrative point, see *Il.* 3.154; 5.95; 10.272; 11.642; 16.394 (after a simile); 22.475; 24.329. The correlation of γάρ and οὖν is also common in post-Homeric Greek; see Van Ophuijsen (1993: 93–96) on Plato.

In the preceding discussions we met a number of times with the scanning of a scene in the form of a three-stage process, consisting of a preview, a goal, and narrative space in between. This type of movement agrees with the tripartite structure that Charles Beye assigns as common property to the two most catalogic context types in Homeric discourse: the heroic *androktasia* in battle narrative and the entries in the Catalogue of Ships in the second book of the *Iliad*.[54] Beye observes that such catalogic progressions (which he calls items) typically consist of an A-part, giving the "basic information" (the names of the victor and the victim in the *androktasia*, or the name of the town and its leader(s) in the Catalogue); a B-part consisting of an "anecdote" (biographical or genealogical detail about the victim or the leader of the contingent); and a C-part, consisting of "contextual information" (detail that is relevant to the context of the list, that is, the actual fighting).[55] The following passage is presented by Beye as a prime instance of what has become known as the ABC-scheme:

a.	υἱὸν δὲ Στροφίοιο	And the son (acc.) of Strophios,
b.	Σκαμάνδριον, αἴμονα θήρης,	Skamandrios skillful in the chase,
c.	Ἀτρεΐδης Μενέλαος	Atreus's son Menelaos (nom.),
d.	ἕλ᾽ ἔγχεϊ ὀξυόεντι,	he took [him] with the sharp spear,
e.	ἐσθλὸν θηρητῆρα·	the valiant hunter (=Skamandrios),
f.	δίδαξε γὰρ Ἄρτεμις αὐτὴ	for Artemis herself had taught [him],
g.	βάλλειν ἄγρια πάντα,	to strike at all the wild animals,
h.	τά τε τρέφει οὔρεσιν ὕλη·	that the forest nourishes in the mountains;
i.	ἀλλ᾽ οὔ οἱ τότε γε χραῖσμ᾽	but not then did she help him,
j.	Ἄρτεμις ἰοχέαιρα,	Artemis of the showering arrows,
k.	οὐδὲ ἐκηβολίαι,	nor did the far shootings,
l.	ᾗσιν τὸ πρίν γ᾽ ἐκέκαστο·	in which earlier he excelled:
m.	ἀλλά μιν Ἀτρεΐδης	but him Atreus's son (nom.),
n.	δουρικλειτὸς Μενέλαος	Menelaos famed for the spear,
o.	πρόσθεν ἕθεν φεύγοντα	[him] fleeing before him (=Menelaos),
p.	μετάφρενον οὔτασε δουρὶ	he (=Menelaos) stabbed in the back with the spear,
q.	ὤμων μεσσηγύς,	between the shoulders,
r.	διὰ δὲ στήθεσφιν ἔλασσεν,	and he drove [it] through the chest,
s.	ἤριπε δὲ πρηνής,	and he fell forward on his face,
t.	ἀράβησε δὲ τεύχε᾽ ἐπ᾽ αὐτῷ.	and his armor clattered upon him.

(*Il.* 5.49–58)

---

54 Beye 1964; cf. Fenik 1968: 16–17.
55 Beye 1964: 346–47.

The basic information is given in units a–d; unit e provides a transition to the anecdote, which comprises units f–h; units i–l provide a link between the anecdote and the contextual information, which runs from unit m to the end of the passage.[56]

To consider the *androktasia* as conforming to a structure that pertains to this particular narrative context or task might obscure the fact that what motivates the pattern is also common to the framing and orientation strategies discussed in the previous section. And to call this type of scene an item (as if it were a record in a database, consisting of three fields) might likewise obscure the dynamic nature of Homeric catalogues; for the management of this database remains a matter of movement, in which the narrator makes use of the same framing and movement techniques that we discussed earlier. In the example just presented, for example, the anecdote is introduced by the particle *gár* in unit f, which, as often in Homer, signals the first step into the frame, toward the goal indicated. The frame, in this case, is set by unit e, *esthlòn thērētêra* 'valiant hunter', which leads up to units o–p: the hunter has become hunted.[57] The transition from the anecdote to the contextual information is made in unit m by the adversative particle *allá* 'but', which underlines the double irony of the protégé being abandoned by his divine patron in the hour of need, and of the warrior slain being the patient in an activity in which he himself excels.

In other cases it is not the particle *gár* but an appositional relative clause that introduces the anecdote, signaling movement into the frame; and instead of *allá* it is the relational demonstrative that marks the transition to the contextual information, or the moment previewed by the orientation;

a. τὼ δὲ πεσόντ᾽ ἐλέησε   and the two falling he pitied,
b. μέγας Τελαμώνιος Αἴας·   huge Aias son of Telamon,

---

[56] Units p–t closely resemble the details of a killing described a few moments earlier in the narrative (5.40–42), a killing without an anecdote, in which γάρ does not mark the step from A to B, but from A to C, as the zooming in on detail discussed above (*Il.* 5.39–40: ἔκβαλε δίφρου· ‖ πρώτῳ γὰρ στρεφθέντι | μεταφρένῳ ἐν δόρυ πῆξεν 'threw him out of the chariot ‖ for him the first as he turned | he planted the spear in his back'). See also Beye 1964: 347; Visser 1987: 50. Other killings without a B-part, not mentioned by Beye, are the examples discussed above, in which the unit with the names of the victor and the victim can be seen as a condensed version of the A-part, and the unit with the verb as the C-part (Bakker 1990b: 15 n. 45). For a typology of killing-scenes, see Visser 1987: 44–57.

[57] The killing occurs in the context of a major rout in the battle, in which victims are mounting their chariots in order to escape and are killed from behind. See such formulas as νύξ᾽ ἵππων ἐπιβησόμενον 'he struck him as he was mounting his chariot' (*Il.* 5.46; 16.343). For more details see Latacz 1977: 212–23.

c.	στῆ δὲ μάλ᾽ ἐγγὺς ἰών,	and he stood coming quite close in,
d.	καὶ ἀκόντισε δουρὶ φαεινῷ,	and made a cast with the shining spear,
e.	καὶ βάλεν Ἄμφιον,	and hit Amphios,
f.	Σελάγου υἱόν,	the son of Selagos,
g.	ὅς ῥ᾽ ἐνὶ Παισῷ ναῖε	who lived in Paisos,
h.	πολυκτήμων πολυλήϊος·	rich in possessions rich in harvest,
i.	ἀλλά ἑ μοῖρα ἦγ᾽ ἐπικουρήσοντα	but his fate brought him as an ally,
j.	μετὰ Πρίαμόν τε καὶ υἷας.	for Priam and [his] sons,
k.	τόν ῥα κατὰ ζωστῆρα βάλεν	so him in the girdle he hit,
l.	Τελαμώνιος Αἴας,	Aias Telamon's son (nom.),
m.	νειαίρῃ δ᾽ ἐν γαστρὶ	and in the lower belly,
n.	πάγη δολιχόσκιον ἔγχος,	it stuck, the far-shadowing spear
o.	δούπησεν δὲ πεσών·	and he fell with a thud,
p.	ὁ δ᾽ ἐπέδραμε	and he rushed forward,
q.	φαίδιμος Αἴας,	shining Aias,
r.	τεύχεα συλήσων·	to strip the armor.

(*Il.* 5.610–18)

The A-part in this case (units a–f) is not the mere pairing of two names in order to frame a catalogic entry, but involves an appearance of Aias by way of a noun-epithet formula in unit b, in a typical way that will concern us in Chapters 7 and 8. What follows is an example of the throw-and-hit sequence discussed in Chapter 4, involving the particle *kaí*, and revealing the name of the victim. The B-part (units g–j), which is introduced by an appositional relative clause, gives depth to the killing by situating it within the interrelated network of the heroic world and its inhabitants; far from being a digression containing detail that is not immediately relevant for the context at hand, it constitutes an important moment in the movement of epic discourse in more than one temporal dimension: the killing proper (the C-part, units k–r) can now take place within the context of the victim's tradition.[58]

---

[58] This poetics of the *androktasia*, in which the *kleos* of the warrior slain serves as context for the *kleos* of the victorious hero, is grounded in the mentality and point of view of the epic heroes themselves. See the passage (*Il.* 7.81–91) in which Hektor imagines the σῆμα 'tomb' of the warrior slain by him as what activates his own *kleos* in the minds and speech of men to come. Note, furthermore, that the appositional relative clause introducing the victim's tradition is frequently, as here, marked by the evidential particle ἄρα (ὅς ῥ᾽ or ὅς ῥα), stressing the validity of the present speech as based on previous speech. Likewise, the relational pronoun introducing the description of the killing proper is often marked by the same particle (τόν ῥα), emphasizing that the description is prompted by evidence produced by the present discourse itself; for more details, see Bakker 1993b: 15–23; 1997a.

Rather than a fixed structure, then, to be inserted as a stereotyped item in a given context, the ABC-pattern is a case in which the usual presentation and orientation strategies of epic discourse are directed at a specific goal. And what structural fixity there is in the scheme derives from the recurrent nature of this goal, which may lead, as often in human linguistic behavior, to routinization. In fact, we might view the ABC-scheme as the kind of grammar that will be discussed in more detail below (see Chapter 8): it displays the regularity that results from the recurrence of a given situation, in this case the need to have one warrior killed by another. Yet just as with all manifestations of grammar in live speech, this is not regularity for its own sake: fixity in battle catalogues is the result of recurrence, rather than vice versa.[59]

The ABC-scheme is but one of the possible directions from which ring composition can be approached; other directions include epic regression, the proleptic mentioning of an event before it is due in the chronology of a narrative; the natural order of chiasmus or hysteron proteron; and in general the relation between a frame and a goal. The common denominator of these strategies is the reciprocal relation between units in a sequence. In a simple case, unit a serves as a frame for unit b. This moment of framing is actually an instance of reciprocity: when unit a frames unit b, this means that unit b provides detail for unit a.

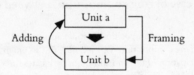

In more complex cases, the relationships and reciprocities are not merely confined to contiguous units.

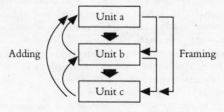

[59] The criticism of the ABC-scheme in Tsagarakis 1982: 127–33 does not really apply, because fixity and regularity are a natural *result* of the use of the ABC-pattern as a recurrent discourse strategy (without implying either lack of freedom or formulaic necessity) rather than its *purpose*.

Here the initial framing unit a (called the starting point in the discussions above) serves as frame for what is added to it (unit b), but at the same time looks ahead to what lies beyond (unit c). When this latter strategy is tightened and formalized by means of the devices mentioned above, or by similarities in phraseology between units a and c, we may speak of ring composition, which involves the explicit presentation of speech as uttered within a frame and the precise monitoring of the speech process by the speech itself. This is achieved by marking the end of the frame and indicating how a present moment relates to the past moment at which it was prepared.

Ring composition, then, is less a feature of archaic style as such (in opposition to other styles) than an index of the ways in which this style, as special speech, draws on the resources of ordinary speech.[60] Yet the formalization is never so total that the ring becomes a structure for its own sake in which the end is a return to the beginning, a structure that finds its fulfillment in a symmetrical array on paper.[61] The term "ring," in fact, might invoke the wrong image, in that speech, which proceeds through time, does not and cannot go back to an earlier point; it has to move forward and in so doing cannot but be uttered within the context of previous speech and provide context for speech to come. The principle that repetition in speech is impossible insofar as no two contexts are exactly identical appears to apply quite strongly in the case of ring composition: between the indication of the

---

[60] The fullest account of ring composition is still Van Otterlo's, who makes the insightful suggestion (1944: 48) that ring composition is concerned, not so much with the repetition of the beginning as with the anticipation of the end, although he locates this observation in the climate characteristic of the time: "Auf diese Weise wurde ja in der früheren Periode der Stilgeschichte, da der menschliche Geist sich selbstverständlich noch nicht an längere Gedankenkomplexe gewohnt hatte, sowohl dem Autor für die Entfaltung der Gedanken, wie dem Publikum für das Verständnis derselben sofort ein Anhaltspunkt gewährt." See also Gaisser 1969; Thalmann 1984: 8–21; Edwards 1991: 44–48. The present discussion is indebted to Lang 1984: 5–12. For a discussion of hysteron proteron and chiasmus as figures of style related to ring composition, see Bassett 1938: 120–25. Bassett rightly stresses the primacy of these phenomena as Homeric speech strategies over their status as recognized rhetorical figures in later times (on rhetoric and figures of style, see also Chapter 6 below). Minchin 1995, an approach congenial to my own, came to my attention too late to be of use in the preparation of this chapter.

[61] Note in this connection the difference between my use of framing and Thalmann's (1984) (whose emphasis on oral reception and the function of ring composition therein is otherwise consistent with my approach). Thalmann uses the term "framing" for the way in which a statement "surrounds" a given core. The term "ring composition," in fact, tends to be used by many scholars in a much wider sense than meant here, as any mirroring of segments on either side of a given center; the present discussion has focused on cases where such repetition can be more functionally accounted for in terms of starting points and goals.

goal and its achievement, the world has changed.[62] The global framing-statement, uttered during a moment of orientation, has become a specific, fully contextualized concept by the time the speaker reaches the goal.

The change is due, of course, to what lies between the two statements. Rather than a digression or an object inserted in the discourse, in-between speech is an integral part of its flow, approaching one of the salient moments of the discourse in a purposeful way. The section framed by the ring-composition device is uttered to provide the context for what follows, enhancing the previewed moment (at the opening of the ring) by locating it within a temporal or conceptual perspective other than that which prevails at the moment of previewing. In the discussion of the ABC-scheme we saw that the killing proper may be described within the context of the tradition of the victim, which lifts the narrative out of the time and place of the present moment. In other cases, such as similes (also a recurrent case of ring composition in Homer), the context provided is a realm of experience other than the one active at the present moment, but one that lends depth and significance to whatever is in the mind of the performer and the audience at the moment in question.[63]

Viewed in this light, the second mention of the previewed event is not so much the closing of the ring or the rounding off of a digression—and as such the transition of a backgrounded portion of the text back to the narrative foreground[64]—as a statement made in the reality produced by the discourse itself, a reality that has been explicitly established for the purpose of accommodating the previewed moment. In other words, the reciprocity between framing and adding (adding being the utterance of a unit or series of units within a frame) is nowhere more explicit than in the case of ring composition, a characteristic moment of Homeric discourse experienced as a flow of speech through time.

Syntax and Suprasyntax: Some Conclusions

In this chapter we have reviewed a number of phenomena in Homeric discourse that are likely to escape our notice within the perspective of

---

[62] This point is repeatedly made by writers on ring composition. See Gaisser 1969: 4; Thalmann 1984: 22.

[63] See Edwards 1987: 102–10; 1991: 24–41.

[64] On background and foreground, see Chapter 4.

sentential syntax, but that are of importance for an understanding of how Homeric poetry is organized as a process. The discussion of framing has enabled us to establish a common denominator of phenomena that remain separate and disconnected in an approach less sensitive to the strategies specifically pertaining to the medium of speech. In particular, I have argued that some stylistic phenomena, such as chiasmus and ring composition, are not so much aesthetic features in their own right as natural consequences of the medium of speech as process.

Of central interest in this regard is the finding that one and the same phenomenon may be observed in various ways and in various degrees of grammatical fixity. We saw that Beye's ABC-pattern for killing-scenes and many ring-compositional phenomena are not so much schemes in their own right as tighter and more explicit versions of what happens elsewhere in a less structured way. In Chapter 8 we will study even tighter forms of the same phenomenon: framing and addition on the level of the verse in the metrical grammar of poetry. But we can also move to the opposite end of the scale: framing is not confined to syntax in the more narrow sense of the articulation of clauses and phrases at the local level. Syntax and suprasyntax, the grammar of the story as a whole, are manifestations at different levels of one and the same phenomenon. In other words, the goal indicated by a given framing speech unit, or series of units, may be farther ahead than in the examples discussed; yet the strategy of moving from the one to the other is not different from the syntax of framing that we have studied.[65]

In this way the *Iliad* begins with a preview. Not only the first speech unit of the *Iliad*, but also the proem and indeed the whole first book, look ahead to the moment at which the action of the wrath of Achilles really takes off, much later in the poem. This much lauded quality of *in medias res*, however, appears much less the virtue by which a poem and its poet can be distinguished from other poems and their authors—Homer having emancipated himself from the paratactic composition style and compulsory sequentiality of his forebears—than an effective way of drawing on the specific properties of the spoken medium. No speech is meaningful out of context, and in framing the narrative, locally as well as globally, the epic narrator opens up narrative space, provides direction, and intensifies the experience of those who move along the path by creating anticipation of what lies ahead.

---

[65] See Lang 1984: 7–8, on "hooks"; Thornton 1984: 67–72, on "goals" and "signposting"; Thalmann 1984: 13–14, on the proleptic introduction of the Cyclopes and Hundred-handers in Hes. *Theog.* 139–53.

PART THREE

SPECIAL SPEECH

CHAPTER 6

Rhythm and Rhetoric

All of poetry I consider to be and refer to as discourse with meter.
—Gorgias of Leontini, *In Defense of Helen*

It is strange how long it has taken the European literatures to learn that style is not an absolute, a something that is to be imposed on the language from Greek or Latin models, but merely the language itself, running in its natural grooves.
—Edward Sapir, *Language*

In the preceding chapters we have been concerned with what it means for language to be spoken, a question that presupposes the one which will occupy us in the remaining chapters of this book: what does it mean for speech to be special? In order to discuss the special, poetic features of Homeric discourse, we must first discuss the features of Homeric discourse as speech, in particular its segmentation into basic speech units that are cognitively determined.[1] Accordingly, in the discussions to be presented in this third part of the study, we shall start each time from the cognitively determined intonation unit as it is observable in Homer. In the present chapter the subject approached in this way is meter; formulas in their semantic and metrical quality will be discussed in Chapters 7 and 8. The task will be to determine each time how one of the most basic properties of language in the spoken medium is enhanced, or stylized, into a poetic feature belonging to special speech, the discourse of the special occasion.

Distinguishing the two questions, the one pertaining to speech and the other to special speech, is useful as a method preventing us from approaching such matters as style and meter too early, and so assigning to them qualifications that apply only with hindsight, within a perspective of what

[1] See Chapter 3.

is for us poetry. The boundary line between speech features and special speech features, however, cannot be drawn sharply: poetic features of Homeric style can be reduced to speech features precisely because speech features can easily become poetic.[2] In the previous chapter we saw for example how framing, a common relation between intonation units, can result in ring composition and other "poetic" phenomena; in the present chapter we are concerned with how meter can result from the rhythmical regularization and streamlining of speech units.

The discussion of Homeric metrics along these lines does not take issue with the existing accounts of the dactylic hexameter or question their findings. Rather, it differs from them in the perspective chosen, in the direction from which some unquestionable metrical facts are approached. We are accustomed, whether consciously or not, to regard meter as a structure imposed on a discourse, a metrical form used for conveying the poetic message. We tend to view discourse units in a poetic text in terms of the metrical structure of the poem (verses, cola, and so forth). In the discussions that follow we shall try to reverse this perspective, not viewing discourse in terms of meter, but meter in terms of discourse. I propose to see meter not as a poetic form in itself but as emergent from spoken discourse with its typical spoken articulation. This argument will give us an opportunity to rethink some of the implications of the contrast between poetry and prose, and to search in everyday speech for the stylistic foundations of Greek literary texts.

Meter, Number, and Periodic Style

To start our discussion of rhythm and meter in Homeric speech, I return to the passage from the third book of Aristotle's *Rhetoric* with which I began Part 2: the discussion of unperiodic and periodic style. Whereas our subject earlier was unperiodic style and the later versions of that concept (adding or paratactic style), we are now primarily concerned with periodic style, and the properties that Aristotle assigns to this mode of discourse (emphasis added):

[2] In fact, some authors argue that ordinary language is inherently poetic (Friedrich 1986: 24–27) or that ordinary language is not something that can be isolated from poetic language (Fish 1980: 97–111).

λέγω δὲ περίοδον λέξιν ἔχουσαν ἀρχὴν καὶ τελευτὴν αὐτὴν καθ' αὑτὴν καὶ μέγεθος εὐσύνοπτον. ἡδεῖα δ' ἡ τοιαύτη καὶ εὐμαθής, ἡδεῖα μὲν διὰ τὸ ἐναντίως ἔχειν τῷ ἀπεράντῳ, καὶ ὅτι αἰεί τι οἴεται ἔχειν ὁ ἀκροατὴς τῷ ἀεὶ πεπεράνθαι τι αὑτῷ· τὸ δὲ μηδὲν προνοεῖν εἶναι μηδὲ ἀνύειν ἀηδές. εὐμαθὴς δέ, ὅτι εὐμνημόνευτος. τοῦτο δέ, ὅτι <u>ἀριθμὸν</u> ἔχει ἡ ἐν περιόδοις λέξις, ὃ πάντων εὐμνημονευτότατον. διὸ καὶ τὰ μέτρα πάντες μνημονεύουσι μᾶλλον τῶν χύδην· ἀριθμὸν γὰρ ἔχει ᾧ μετρεῖται. (*Rh.* 1409ᵃ35–1409ᵇ8, ed. Kassel)

I call "period" an utterance with an inherent beginning and end as well as a length that can be beheld at a single glance. Such a type of discourse is not only pleasant, but also easy to learn. It is pleasant by the fact that it is the opposite of what is unbounded, and because the listener at every moment has the idea of having hold of something, by the fact that every moment is bounded in itself. For having no anticipation of what is to come or not completing anything is unpleasant. It is easy to learn because it is easy to recall. This is because periodic discourse has <u>number</u>, which of all things is easiest to recall. This is why all people memorize metrical discourse more easily than language that is poured forth. For it has number by which it can be measured.

We usually discuss periodic style in terms of the balanced syntax and stylistic subtlety that come with hypotactic construction, defined in opposition to parataxis. Aristotle, however, appears to have a quite different conception of periods.[3] Using the term "period" to designate what are for us parts of periods, he assigns to these smaller units properties that do not seem to be directly applicable to our syntactic conception of period. The periodic style is "pleasant," according to Aristotle, because of its boundedness, which is a matter of hearer's anticipation: periodic style, as opposed to unperiodic style, gives the hearer a sense of what will come next. From Aristotle's wording it is not immediately clear whether this anticipation is a matter of the relation between periods or of the period internally. In any case, the second property mentioned, that something in periodic style is "easy to learn," applies to the latter possibility. Aristotle says of periodic style that "it is easy to learn because it is easy to recall" (*eumathès dé, hóti eumnēmóneutos*), the reason being that periodic discourse has number,

---

[3] For a discussion of the differences between Aristotle's use of the term περίοδος and later uses (Demetrius, Cicero), see Siebenborn 1987 (with more literature), who argues for an origin of the term in the sphere of dance and music. My metrical understanding of "period" in this chapter is in agreement with Siebenborn's discussion.

which is "of all things easiest to recall" (*pántōn eumnēmoneutótaton*). For Aristotle, number is another kind of pleasant limitation,[4] and hence the pleasures of the periodic style, which derive from the style's boundedness, are related to the ease with which periodic speech is remembered, for that ease comes from the bounded nature of its rhythm or number.

Metered poetry also belongs to this category of number, as Aristotle mentions in passing. This move may be unexpected for us in a discussion of what is for us prose, but it becomes less surprising when we realize that rhetorical prose in antiquity is less a mode of written communication than a specific speech genre that is continuously defined with respect to poetry: while the poetic speech genres have number and rhythm to such a degree of fixity that one can speak of meter, the periodic style of rhetorical prose is periodic in its being less strict and fixed than poetic meter, but rhythmical and numbered all the same. For Aristotle, then, periodic style seems to be less a matter of syntactic composition and production than of the experience of rhythm—and therefore a matter of delivery and performance. Aristotle actually uses terminology that for us, paradoxically, seems more appropriate for the constraints under which oral composition and / or recall in performance has to take place.[5] But if periodic discourse is discussed in terms suggesting rhythmical anticipation and memorization, what are we to do with the allegedly unperiodic style of Homeric metered poetry, where rhythm and number are, if anything, even stronger?

Is Homeric style periodic? The question seems a contradiction in terms when we define period in the modern way. As we saw in the previous chapters, Homeric discourse is by no means simply paratactic, but that is not to say that Homeric syntax is hypotactic. The question becomes more interesting, however, when we adopt Aristotle's different perspective and elaborate on it, viewing rhetorical periodic discourse not in terms of syntax or style but in terms of speech, as a special discourse for a special occasion. The opposition between Homeric poetry and classical rhetoric then becomes not so much a matter of style, of the *Kunstsprache* of Homeric epic as opposed to the *Kunstprosa* of the classical period, as of different per-

---

[4]   Cf. ibid. 1408ᵇ28–30, another mention of the boundedness of number and the unpleasantness of the unbounded. The Greek terms ἀριθμός 'number' and ῥυθμός 'rhythm' may have been connected by folk etymology; in Latin, a single term *numerus* is used (see below).

[5]   For detailed discussion of multiple constraints (including rhythm) in the composition and recall of epic and other oral genres, see Rubin 1995, the work of a cognitive psychologist. On rhythm and memorability see also Turner 1992: 93.

formance genres, each departing in its own way from ordinary everyday discourse.

In this chapter I explore some of the possibilities of viewing Homeric discourse within this rhetorical framework. Taking the categories poetry and prose somewhat less for granted than they are usually taken, I will argue that both Homeric poetry and classical rhetorical prose are, each in their own specific and very different ways, the rhetorical enhancement and manipulation of the basic properties of ordinary speech.[6] Both are special speech, based on strategies that are reserved for special performance occasions and meant, in a truly rhetorical sense, to have a special effect on an audience. The main thrust of the argument is that the stylistic opposition between periodic and unperiodic may not be the most meaningful way to bring out the differences between Homeric poetry and classical rhetorical prose. Rather, we might say that both are periodic in their own very different ways.

The periodic nature of Homeric discourse, I will argue, lies in the interaction between the speech units and meter. In this kind of discourse, in which periods are defined in terms of meter, the number quality of the discourse units is so strong that it determines not only the units as such, but also the way in which they are related to each other as rhythmical units. This genre of special speech will be opposed to the prose type of discourse, in which number is merely a matter of the rhythm of speech units taken by themselves: an important property, but still subordinate to the way in which the speech units follow each other in the flow of rhetorical discourse. Let us now consider how both types of periodicity can be best described and how they achieve their specific rhetorical effects.

Rhythm in Speech

We saw that for Aristotle number, or rhythm, is an important factor in the learning or recall of a discourse. But rhythm, as a constraint that facilitates memorization, would not be effective if it did not operate in concert with the general possibilities and limitations of human consciousness that we discussed in the previous chapters. On this basis we can view the in-

---

[6] For discussion of rhetorical strategies in Homer, see also Mueller 1984: 11–13; Hainsworth 1993: 92–93 (focusing more on τάξις 'structure, ordering' than on λέξις 'style').

tonation unit of ordinary spoken discourse as the proper locus for rhythm, and approach Homeric meter from the vantage point of speech. In doing so we are encouraged by the general observation that rhythm is not an external factor, superimposed on language from outside; language has its own rhythm, which can be strengthened, regularized, and standardized to the point at which we can speak of meter. Rather than separating poetry from language as art from life, then, the metrical factor integrates poetry within speech, in ways that turn the discussion of meter in the present chapter into a complement of the discussion of consciousness and cognition in the previous ones.

No speaker is entirely at the mercy of the cognitive limitations that I described in Chapter 3, and cognition is not the only factor that makes speech what it is, at least speech as the object of stylization in the form of special speech. It is true that spoken discourse may be best described as a process, revealing some of the properties of consciousness as a process or flow; but that does not mean that this process is involuntary, having only the limitations of the processing consciousness as its constitutive features. In fact, speech is purposeful behavior no less than it is constrained by cognition, frequently involving deliberate choices as to presentation and effect. To bring out this important aspect of speech, I will speak of rhetoric in this chapter, as the necessary counterpart of the cognition that I examined in Part 2. Cognition and rhetoric, the latter concept to be understood in a broad, pretheoretical sense, can be seen as opposite but interrelated forces.[7] It is the interplay of cognitive and rhetorical features, in varying ratios, that defines the style of most ordinary spoken discourse. And a discourse is rhetorically more sophisticated to the degree that the intonation units of ordinary speech are consciously and deliberately manipulated, in various ways, but without their losing their cognitive role in the production and reception of the discourse in question.

Even the most casual, unpremeditated discourse displays rhetorical features that are revealing for the strategies that we will see later on in more rehearsed and sophisticated discourses. Consider the following example

---

[7] The concepts "rhetoric" and "rhetorical" are often (e.g., Cole 1990: 12; Ford 1992: 17) taken to imply professional reflection on language, and hence a distinction between form and content. My understanding of the concepts in this chapter is purposely wider and "pretheoretical," covering any purposeful enhancement of speech in whatever situation. Rhetoric comes thus close to pragmatics; see Leech 1983: 15.

from Chafe's corpus of data on spoken discourse, the climax of a conversational narrative:[8]

a. . . . And there were these two women,
b. . . hiking up ahead of us.
c. . . . [1.5] And you sort of got,
d. to a rise,
e. and then the lake,
f. was kind of right there,
g. where we were gonna . . . camp.
h. . . . And the two of them,
i. . . got to the rise,
j. . . and the next minute,
k. . . . [0.9] they just . . fell over.
l. . . Totally.

This highly informal fragment, consisting of twelve intonation units, is a curious mix of cognitive and rhetorical features. The rhetorical features, which concern us here, occur at the end of the passage, in the last three units.[9] There are two long pauses in the fragment, one before unit c and the other between units j and k. The two breaks are similar in length, but of an altogether different nature. Unit c, along with units d–g, is framing and orienting: it sets the scene for the event to be narrated. The pause preceding unit c seems to reflect the mental effort connected with the activation, the visualization of the scene; it is followed by four swiftly delivered units, as if the substance of those units had been "booted" during the pause. For this reason we may call the pause cognitive. The pause after unit j, on the other hand, can be called rhetorical: instead of merely reflecting mental effort, it is used as a device to create suspense at the climax of this little narrative. In fact, the pause is part of a presentation strategy which also involves

---

[8] From Chafe 1990: 85, presented and analyzed again in Chafe 1994: 130–31 to illustrate "climax" in conversational narrative. In this method of transcription the pauses between intonation units are shown by dots: two dots indicate brief breaks up to one-half-second long and three dots mark longer pauses (up to one second). Numbers in brackets indicate measured pauses (in seconds); see Chafe 1994: xiii. The pauses within units g and k did not coincide with an intonational boundary in the speech recorded.

[9] For a discussion of what I am calling the cognitive features of the passage in terms of activation, see Chafe 1990: 90–91. Notice the use of "and" which links all clausal intonation units to what precedes (see Chapter 4 on continuation).

the unit preceding the pause. This unit was uttered at a higher pitch, with more volume, and above all, at a slower pace than the previous units (almost in a chanting manner), a phonetic realization of which the pause is an integral part and the main reason why it can be called rhetorical.[10]

Part of the rhetorical articulation at the end of the fragment is also unit l, which has something in common with the type of intonation unit that verbalizes a detail added to the previous unit.[11] Yet in the present context it seems to have a more complex function. Apart from being the verbalization of a detail added to the previous moment's verbalization (a detail which stresses the extraordinary nature of the event), this unit seems to have a rhetorical, or more precisely, a rhythmical function. Being uttered just after the peak of the narrative, it enhances the salience of the peak event (unit k), by modifying it across an intonational boundary (indeed a sentence boundary, marked by the full stop that signals falling intonation). In the two previous units, the discourse had developed into a process with its own pace and articulation; unit j prepares and leads up to unit k, and the l-unit, in counterbalancing the preparatory unit j, provides a rhetorical addition to the peak unit. Its presence seems to be best explained by the fact that its absence would have been undesirable from the point of view of the rhythmical relations between units.[12]

Even in relatively simple and informal cases, then, the transformation of consciousness into speech may result in an object with properties and processes of its own, besides those deriving from the flow of consciousness. For the purposes of the present argument it is opportune to focus on those rhetorical properties that can be discussed under the general heading rhythm. Rhythm is a property of any spoken discourse. Yet its importance and deliberate use depend on the degree to which a narrative is rehearsed and rhetorically presented.[13] No discourse is entirely devoid of rhythm, but in

[10] I have been able to observe these physical features of this discourse, listening to the tape recording of which the cited text is a transcription. Notice also the pause within unit k, a rhetorical feature that does survive transcription.

[11] See Chapter 5 above.

[12] Note that if "totally" had to be placed in a standard English version of the same expression, it would fall exactly where the pause is in the middle of unit k.

[13] For examples of more "professional" informal narratives, featuring both cognitive features (intonation units) and rhetorical features, see Polanyi 1982; Sobol 1992 on modern American storytelling; and especially the translation and transcription of Zuni Indian narrative in Tedlock 1972, who remarks (xix): "What makes written prose most unfit for representing spoken narrative is that it rolls on for whole paragraphs at a time without taking a breath: there is no silence in it." He then goes on to explain his efforts to represent the breaks in Zuni narrative and to create a transcription that does justice to both the cognitive and rhetorical features of the original.

some discourses and discourse types, rhythm is more important than in others, testifying to the varying ratio of cognitive and rhetorical features. In the remainder of this chapter I am concerned with the way in which rhythm as a feature of special speech may come to stylize the cognitively determined features of ordinary speech.

Rhythm and the Remote Consciousness

When we move from informal narratives like the one just presented into more rhetorical territory, an instructive example of the interaction of cognitive and rhetorical (rhythmical) features is the discourse and performance of American folk preachers, described by Bruce Rosenberg as a genuine oral tradition,[14] and known to a larger audience through the oratory of Martin Luther King, Jr., and Jesse Jackson. A folk sermon is typically chanted, at least in its more intense and emotional stages, and presented in short, rhythmical units. The chanting is improvised, but due to the recurrence of each sermon in a preacher's practice as well as to the formal and official stance of the speaker, there is obviously more rehearsal, planned organization, and professional experience than in informal dinner-table conversations. The following passage is cited by Rosenberg as an accurate description of this type of discourse and its performance:[15]

Rev. Ratliff begins his sermon in normal, though stately and carefully measured prose. As he gets into his subject, he gradually raises the intensity of his
delivery (though with well-timed ups and downs). About one third of the
way into his sermon the prose has verged into a very rhythmical delivery,
punctuated into periods (more or less regular) by a sharp utterance which I
suppose might be called a vehement grunt. I haven't timed these periods, but
I would guess that they fall about every three seconds, sometimes less.
Within the rhythmical framework, the rises and falls eventually build to a

[14] Rosenberg 1988, an investigation that started out, in a first edition, as an attempt to exemplify Parry's and Lord's principles of oral composition on the basis of this African-American religious speech genre, but which later came to focus equally on the specific nature and expressivity of this type of discourse (1988: 4–5). On the performed African-American sermon, see also Davis 1985.

[15] Alan Jabbour in Rosenberg 1988: 16–17, from a personal letter to Rosenberg. The description applies to the services of W. T. Ratliff in Durham, North Carolina in 1969, but according to Rosenberg fits over ninety percent of his material.

climax when he lapses into a sort of chant, still with the same punctuation, but with a recognizable tonic [tonal center]. Some of the congregation (who respond *ad libitum* throughout) here lapse into humming along with him.

This description evidently applies to phenomena that are closely related to Chafe's two-to-three-second intonation units. The "periods" described, however, seem to be more pronounced and recognizable than the intonation units of ordinary speech, both intonationally and rhythmically. Moreover, the rhythmically enhanced units apparently play a more important role than just the accommodation of the flow of discourse to the flow of consciousness in the minds of the listeners: delivered at the more emotional stages of a sermon, or when the psychological conditions are right, they actually *invite the audience's active participation* in the flow of discourse. The following transcription of such a performance will serve as a fairly typical example:[16]

    a. John said
    b. I . . . I
    c. I saw four beasts
    d. One with a face
    e. Looked like a calf
    f. Representin' patience
    g. And endurance
    h. 'Nother beast I saw
    i. Had a head like a lion
    j. Representin' boldness
    k. And confidence
    l. 'Nother beast I saw
    m. A face like a man
    n. Representin' wisdom
    o. An' he had knowledge
    p. 'Nother beast I saw
    q. Looked like a bald eagle
    r. Ain't God all right?

This catalogic passage, an instantiation of the four-beast theme from the Apocalypse, exemplifies the interplay of cognitive and rhetorical features

[16] From Rosenberg 1988: 97–98, 222. The speaker is Rubin Lacy from Bakersfield, California. I have followed Rosenberg's presentation, starting each line with a capital, and without Chafe's prosodic punctuation.

when a folk preacher successfully draws on the resources of his tradition. Each unit represents a separate idea on which the performer focuses, and their sequence represents the flow of these ideas through time, as well as their interrelationships, both in the mind of the performer and in the minds of the audience. There is appositional or adding syntax in the *representin'*-units f, j, and n, but also in the lines preceding, which verbalize an added piece of detail as an independent clause.[17] But sharp demarcations between the units and distinct phonetic contour are not as such reflexes of cognitive constraints: a positive, rhetorical factor is at work, operating upon the basic units of speech in their preferred length and in their typical syntactic inter-relationships. This factor consists of the performer's presentation strategy to turn *intonation* as the main physical property of his speech units into *rhythm*,[18] a strategy that not only affects the internal constituency of the units and their relative timing, but also their length.

But rhythm is not an inherent, automatic property of this sermon, or of the speech genre as a whole. The delivery of rhythmical speech units is a matter of performance, and no two performances are identical. Rosenberg actually cites a different, much less rhythmical version of the same theme (with more cognitive features and hesitation phenomena, we may add), which was delivered under much less favorable performance conditions.[19] Apparently the amount of rhythm—in our terms, the ratio of cognitive and rhetorical features—varies from performance to performance, according to audience response and the performer's inspiration at the moment. Without a fixed text serving as norm for future performances, the rhythm of the African-American sermon remains a matter of performer-audience inter-action, and hence dependent on the chemistry of the moment.

It is important to emphasize at this point that rhythm in the sermon preachers' discourse is not a rhetorical manipulation of any preexisting ordinary discourse. As we saw, no discourse is entirely devoid of rhythm or rhetoric, and the African-American sermon differs not in substance but in degree from more casual discourses. The tradition on which the preachers draw, with its roots in biblical rhetoric and African-American Baptist cul-ture, departs from ordinary speech in the rhythmical regularity of speech units at a sermon's more intense moments, but it is not for that reason

[17] Notice the Indo-Europeanists' conception of apposition as a reduced independent clause (Ammann 1922; Schwyzer 1947). See Chapter 3.

[18] On the coincidence of intonation units with rhythmic units in an oral tradition, see also Rubin 1995: 86.

[19] Rosenberg 1988: 98; see also 1988: 90–91 on performer-audience interaction and metrical regularity.

wholly different from speech. The preachers' chanted lines have a poetic quality precisely because they are delivered in the interactive context of a performance. In such a context, the boundaries between cognition and rhetoric, speech and poetry, may become irrelevant to the point at which we may speak of poetry in speech. It takes text, and a textual conception, to separate what is indissolubly connected in a performance, and to isolate poetry as something removed from speech.[20]

Rhythm as a feature of a performance is in a number of ways a complicating factor in an analysis that considers special speech, just as any speech, to be the actualization of the speaker's consciousness. Rhythmical discourse does not merely reflect the speaker's flow of consciousness, but at the same time in a way directs the flow, which has properties and dynamics of its own that are highly conducive to memorization and recall. Rhythm, in fact, increases the impact of speech as an event. The speech may derive from the speaker's cognitive processes, but it is at the same time an independent process in which the speaker himself can participate, given the appropriate conditions, both private or psychological and public, relating to the dynamics of the performance.[21]

It is this potentially ambiguous relation between rhythm, consciousness, and speech that accounts in part for the fact that many performers in traditions of special speech around the world experience their discourse as deriving from a consciousness other than their own, their role in the performance as being that of an interpreter or mediator, and their behavior as being divinely inspired. Rhythm, in other words, contributes to what might be called a dislocation of consciousness: the speech produced is not the present speaker's responsibility but something with which a remote authority is credited, an authority located beyond everyday experience and the source of immutable knowledge and truth.[22]

Rosenberg's preachers consistently claim that their power to produce

[20] On poetry "in" ordinary language, see also Sapir 1921: 221–31; Friedrich 1986: 24–27. On the traditional opposition between ordinary and poetic language, see Fish 1980: 97–111. These authors, however, do not speak of performance.

[21] Cf. Turner 1992: 93–94: "Somehow the rhythm of the words is remembered even when the words themselves are lost to us; but the rhythm helps us to recover the mental state in which we first heard or read the poem, and then the gates of memory are opened and the words come to us at once."

[22] Cf., e.g., Kuipers 1993 on the epistemology of ritual performance; Chafe 1993 on the formulaic and prosodic differences between ordinary speech and the special speech evoking a remote source of authority. The neurophysiological aspects of performance, ritual, and rhythm are explored in d'Aquili and Laughlin 1979. In classical studies, see the work of Détienne (1967) and Vernant (1959) on truth and memory.

rhythmical chant derives from God,[23] and in the Homeric context, it is impossible not to think of the Muses. While other epic traditions stage their performers as telling what they heard, in the Greek context the singer plays the role of an eyewitness.[24] This is possible because the performer is a *theîos aoidós* 'godlike singer' and hence the favorite of the Muses, the ultimate eyewitnesses, who were present on the battlefield of Troy where the epic events were enacted.[25] It is their remote, divine consciousness that the epic poet makes present in the context of the performance. Consider in this connection the words of the Ithakan bard Phemios in the *Odyssey*:

αὐτοδίδακτος δ᾽ εἰμί, θεὸς δέ μοι ἐν φρεσὶν οἴμας
παντοίας ἐνέφυσεν·

(Od. 22.347–48)

I am self-taught and for me in my mind a god made song-paths
of all kinds grow.

These words are often compared with the often cited claim of a Kirghiz bard recorded by the Russian folklorist Vasilii Radlov: "I can sing any song whatever; for God has planted the gift of song in my heart. He gives me the word on my tongue, without my having to seek it. I have learnt none of my songs. All springs from my inner self."[26] The apparent opposition between self and god in these passages has been taken as reflecting a distinction between form (the formulas that are the poet's own contribution to the poem) and content (the god's contribution).[27] But the terms "form" and

---

[23] E.g., Rosenberg 1988: 28–29, 36–37.

[24] On this opposition as the crucial difference between the Homeric and the South-Slavic tradition studied by Parry and Lord see Finkelberg 1990. On the Muses in general, see Ford 1992: 31–34, 52–53, 61, 72–76. On the eyewitness stance see Bakker 1993b; 1996a. See also Chapters 4 and 5.

[25] Cf. *Il.* 2.485.

[26] Translated in Chadwick and Chadwick 1932–40: 182; quoted by Finnegan 1977: 193, who is followed by Thalmann 1984: 224 and Dougherty 1991. Cf. Finkelberg 1990: 303. The phrase "springs from my inner self" could serve as a fairly accurate rendition of the Greek αὐτοδίδακτος. Against the more usual interpretation of this word, "self-taught," Fernández-Galiano objects (in Russo et al. 1992: 279–80) that "there would be little sense in Phemius boasting of being self-taught to Odysseus, a man who himself owes none of his skills to his teachers." Ford (1992: 32) takes the phrase as implying independence from other poets and their work. It seems best to understand αὐτοδίδακτος as "spontaneous," referring to the production of poetry and song in the poet's consciousness. See also Thalmann 1984: 127.

[27] E.g., Lanata 1963: 13–14. Murray, who stresses the intellectual, nonecstatic character of the conception of poetic inspiration in Homer, comes to speak about the divine contribution in terms of knowledge and information (1981: 90–92), although she does object (97) to the form-content interpretation of *Od.* 22.347. On knowledge and the Muses, see Chapter 7 below.

"content" are alien to the self-presentation of these singers.[28] And with the collapse of the form-content distinction, the notion that the poet's self and the divine are opposing factors in the poetic process loses much of its attraction.[29] Rather, what is at stake, among other things, is a moment in the process of verbalization, the transformation of the stream of private consciousness into a stream of public and rhythmical speech. The usual account of speech as deriving from consciousness is insufficient here, for the singer's consciousness not only produces the speech but is also propelled forward by the rhythmical movement of the language. What springs from the self is thus both larger and stronger than the self. The power of such a speech can then be said to originate from a source that is neither opposed to the speaker's consciousness, nor identical to it. And this explains the speaker's claim that a song which is planted by a god springs from the singer's own self.

We could return here to the discussion of rhythm as a rhetorical presentation strategy and move from Phemios and his self-presentation as bard to the practice of Homeric rhythm. To do more justice, however, to the complexity of the latter, and above all its rhythmical periodicity, we have to turn briefly to the rhythm of ancient rhetorical prose. According to Aristotle, as we have seen, the periodicity of this genre of discourse consists in its having number and in its allowing the listener to "anticipate" (*pronoeîn*). At the end of the chapter, we will be comparing these two types of period to each other.

From Cicero to Homer

Rhythm, in a more prosaic vein than contact with the divine, belongs to the many involvement strategies at the disposal of speakers, both casual and formal, that are discussed by sociolinguists.[30] But the discourse analyst of the late twentieth century is by no means the only one to discuss these matters. Students of classical rhetoric will recognize in the sociolinguists' involvement strategies the figures of style from ancient rhetorical theory, the stylistic embellishment of Greek and Latin rhetoric and poetry. But

[28] See also Thalmann 1984: 126–27; Ford 1992: 32–33.

[29] See also Dodds 1951: 10; Maehler 1963: 23.

[30] See in particular Tannen's discussion of conversational artistry, which ends with an analysis (1989: 173–95) of the chanted lines of Jesse Jackson's address to the Democratic Convention of 1988.

while these figures and tropes have been treated as art, and the speeches in which they occur as *Kunstprosa* that is removed from the naturalness and artlessness of ordinary speech,[31] the very fact that ordinary speech abounds in figures suggests that the art of Greek and Latin rhetoric is effective precisely because it draws on the common strategies of everyday speech.[32]

In fact, the ancient theorists of the art of public speaking themselves had a conception of rhetorical style that, though in many ways a forerunner of the modern conception of *Kunstprosa*, was still quite different from it. Being much closer to what may be called discourse analysis than some of their modern students, these writers consider the art of formal public speaking as drawing on, not separated from, the everyday and the ordinary. Style is for them a matter, not only of aesthetics—the static form of a discourse as text—but also of pragmatics: their central concern is a more dynamic conception of discourse as behavior, based on deliberate presentation strategies and a skillful manipulation of the properties of ordinary speech that are essential for understanding and rhetorical success.

One of the most important of these properties is the segmentation of speech into short units, whose cognitive necessity and rhetorical potential we have already seen. Basic speech units are the core of what is "nature" in rhetorical discourse and at the same time are the foundation and starting point of what is "art" in that speech genre. Consider what the Roman orator and rhetorical theorist Cicero has to say on this issue, in a discussion

---

[31] Cf. Denniston 1952: 57, in connection with the artistic nature of the figure of speech referred to in ancient rhetoric and stylistics as hyperbaton, the marked use of a given word outside the syntactic environment to which it properly or logically belongs, and a subject usually treated under the general heading of word order: "The Greeks stylized everything; and it is the most difficult thing in the world to point to any Greek which may be regarded as 'natural,'" the implication being that hyperbaton makes a speech *un*natural and the equation of "artistic" with the latter. See also Norden 1909: 65–66 on rhythm as the cause of "unnatural" word order. Dover's strategy, in his discussion of the word order problem in Greek syntax (1960), is to turn to inscriptions for basic and natural language; this attempt to escape the influence of *Kunstprosa* has to be understood in the same way. In the search for ordinary or natural language, the real problem might well be the difficulty of determining what ordinary language actually is (cf. Fish 1980: 97–111), rather than the shortage of data on nonliterary language.

[32] In the example cited above, for example ("and the next minute, . . . [0.9] they just . . fell over. . . Totally."), the realization of "totally" as a separate unit is reminiscent of hyperbaton as a figure of speech (the "normal" word order being "the next minute they totally fell over"). The discussion of hyperbaton exclusively in terms of word order is typical of the stylistic study of a textual skeleton, not of the discourse itself. Could it be that some cases of deviant, hyperbatic word order in ancient texts are less-than-optimal recordings of passages in which syntactic separation is a consequence of intonational separation in the actual performance, recitation, or delivery of the text? See also the discussion of chiasmus and ring composition in Chapter 5 above.

of style that is remarkable throughout in its insistence on sound, rhythm, and other performance-related matters:

> clausulas enim atque interpuncta verborum animae interclusio atque angustiae spiritus attulerunt: id inventum ita est suave, ut, si cui sit infinitus spiritus datus, tamen eum perpetuare verba nolimus; id enim auribus nostris gratum est, quod hominum lateribus non tolerabile solum, sed etiam facile esse posset. Longissima est igitur complexio verborum, quae volvi uno spiritu potest. (*De orat.* 3.181)

> It was failure or shortness of breath that originated periodic structure and pauses between words; but once invented, this [segmentation] proved so attractive that even if there were a person endowed with unlimited powers of breath, we would still not want this person to deliver an uninterrupted flow of words. For our ears are adapted to what is not merely endurable but also easy for the lungs. The longest stretch of words, therefore, is that which can be completed in one single breath.

For Cicero there are pulmonary constraints on the flow of discourse, a physical necessity resulting in observable and expected breaks in the flow of speech in the performance and yielding a segmentation into relatively short units.[33] Today we would not argue that breathing is solely responsible for breaks in a discourse and would more likely consider it as synchronized with the segmentation resulting from cognitive constraints.[34] For Cicero and from his point of view, however, there is another happy synchrony. Being one of the things in nature that bring beauty and dignity by their very usefulness and necessity,[35] the primary units of discourse are the source of rhythm, which more than anything else characterizes rhetorically en-

---

[33] Κῶλα or *membra* in ancient terminology. Aristotle (*Rh.* 1409ᵇ13–16) is the first to define κῶλον 'limb' as a constitutive part ("clause") of a "period" (περίοδος). See also Dem. *De eloc.* 2–3. Quintilian (*Inst. or.* 9.123) defines the *membrum* (a Latin translation of Greek κῶλον) as a unit that is rhythmically complete but semantically meaningless when detached from the "body" of the period. One level below the *membrum*, Quintilian distinguishes the *incisum* 'incision' (Greek κόμμα), aptly called *articula* 'joint' by Cicero (e.g., *De orat.* 3.186), which he defines as a unit that is both semantically and rhythmically incomplete.

[34] See Chafe (1994: 57), who cites Goldman Eisler 1968 for the relation between speech pauses and breathing.

[35] Cic. *De orat.* 3.178–80. Cicero's examples apply to the makeup of the universe, the organic unity of the human body and the structure of artifacts (columns of temples, for example, which are necessary for the solidity of a structure but add dignity to it as well).

hanced discourse as the skillful manipulation of what is natural to speech. It is the rhythmical aspect of speech units, both in their length and internal constituency and in the movement from one unit to the other, that turns constraint into a positive source of involvement by capturing and directing the attention of an audience. Again, it is instructive to cite Cicero on this point:

> et, si numerosum est in omnibus sonis atque vocibus, quod habet quasdam impressiones et quod metiri possumus intervallis aequalibus, recte genus hoc numerorum, dummodo ne continuum sit, in orationis laude ponetur. Nam si rudis et impolita putanda est illa sine intervallis loquacitas perennis et profluens, quid est aliud causae cur repudietur, nisi quod hominum auribus vocem natura modulatur ipsa? quod fieri, nisi inest numerus in voce, non potest. Numerus autem in continuatione nullus est; distinctio et aequalium et saepe variorum intervallorum percussio numerum conficit, quem in cadentibus guttis, quod intervallis distinguuntur, notare possumus, in amni praecipitante non possumus. (De orat. 3.185–86)

But if this element of rhythm is in all sounds and voices, characterized by certain beats and measurable by its regular intervals, then its presence in discourse, provided it does not occur without interruption, will be a thing worthy of praise. For if a continuous flow of words has to be considered rough and unpolished, is there a better reason to reject it than the fact that nature herself modulates the voice for the ears of humankind?—a thing that would be impossible unless the voice inherently contains an element of rhythm. But in an uninterrupted flow there is no rhythm. It is segmentation and a beat characterized by equal but often varied intervals that creates rhythm. Rhythm is what we notice in falling drops of water, because they are separated by intervals, not in a fast flowing river.

Cicero goes on to point out that the rhythmical movement of the *membra* 'limbs', the short units of discourse, needs considerable management if it is to be felicitous in all regards. Apart from the fact that the rhythmical manipulation of units is an important factor in the creation of certain moods in discourse and in the adaptation of the flow of discourse to the various oratorical genres and styles, there are two major considerations in the rhythmical articulation of discourse. First, the rhythmical movement of rhetorical discourse should not be too close to poetic meter in the internal rhythmical structure of the units, nor in the rhythmical relationships between the units. This stylistic constraint on rhetorical discourse remained valid throughout the history of ancient literary and rhetorical criticism.[36] Second, the rhythmical articulation of rhetorical discourse has to support the syntactic articulation in order to attain the desired periodic structure, in which not only rhythm is brought to completion, but also syntax and thought. The units near the end of a period, for example, have to be longer than the preceding ones in order to avoid truncation and to secure a pleasing ending.[37]

The two considerations work together in establishing rhetoric, not as an artful or even artificial variant of what is for us prose, but as a particular genre of special speech. In its specific deviation from ordinary speech, this genre distinguishes itself most clearly from other, more traditional speech and performance genres, such as the Homeric one. In carrying out the natural rhetorical strategy of adding rhythmical articulation to intonation as a physical property of speech units, the ancient rhetor is faced with the existence of the easily identifiable rhythms of the established poetic genres. Avoidance of these may have been a matter of taste and stylistics from the fourth century B.C.E., when rhetoric had established itself as a discipline with intellectual dynamics of its own.[38] But the earliest stages of the development of ancient rhetoric have to be situated in the fifth century B.C.E., a time less concerned with rhetorical or poetic theory than with actual performance. And in this climate, awareness of the rhythmical possibilities of one's speech may have been more a matter of the awareness of the existence of rival performance genres than the intertextual differentiation of one literary style from the other.

The fifth-century rhetors and sophists Thrasymachus and Gorgias come to mind in this connection. The former is traditionally credited with the invention of rhythmical *Kunstprosa*,[39] and the latter with the introduction

---

[36] Ibid. 175, 182, 184. Cf. also Arist. *Rh.* 1408ᵇ30–31: ῥυθμὸν δεῖ ἔχειν τὸν λόγον, μέτρον δὲ μή· ποίημα γὰρ ἔσται 'A speech should have rhythm, not meter; otherwise it will become a poem'; Isocr. fr. 12: ὅλως δὲ ὁ λόγος μὴ λόγος ἔστω, ξηρὸν γάρ· μηδὲ ἔμμετρος, καταφανὲς γάρ· ἀλλὰ μεμείχθω παντὶ ῥυθμῷ 'A speech should not be "speech" in its entirety, for that would be arid; but it should not be wholly metrical either, for that would be too obvious. A speech should display an even distribution of all sorts of rhythms'. Aristotle recommends the paean (rhythmic patterns of three short syllables and one long syllable) to begin and end periods (*Rh.* 1409ᵃ2–21). See also Siebenborn 1987: 233.

[37] Cic. *De orat.* 3.186. Cf. Arist. *Rh.* 1409ᵇ8–10.

[38] Cf. Cole, who actually limits rhetoric as a concept (1991: 1–30) to this institutional sense and who claims that rhetoric in this sense did not exist before the fourth century (arguing partly on the basis of the absence of the term ῥητορική in fifth century texts).

[39] See Cic., *Orat.* 175; Norden 1909: 41; Kennedy 1963: 68; Eisenhut 1974: 14.

of figures of speech related to the length and configuration of speech units.[40] These two orators are the first in a tradition that defined, analyzed, and designed rhetorical discourse with an ear to poetry. But instead of introducing poetic, metrical elements into prose, as has often been assumed from antiquity onwards,[41] they seem to have been more concerned with the development of a performance genre sufficiently close to poetry (i.e., special speech in performance) to be rhetorically effective (i.e., have a similar emotional or psychological effect), yet sufficiently different from the way in which poetry deviates from ordinary speech to rank as a separate genre.[42] Consider, for example, the following excerpt from Gorgias's epideictic speech *In Defense of Helen*, a demonstration of the power of *logos* that is based on the mythical "case" of Helen, whose abduction by Paris caused the Trojan war:

ἐγὼ δὲ βούλομαι λογισμόν τινα τῷ λόγῳ δοὺς τὴν μὲν κακῶς ἀκούουσαν
παῦσαι τῆς αἰτίας, τοὺς δὲ μεμφομένους ψευδομένους ἐπιδείξας καὶ δείξας
τἀληθὲς παῦσαι τῆς ἀμαθίας. (*Hel.* 2)

What I want is to provide an argumentation in my speech so as to keep her
who is held in bad esteem from accusation, and to demonstrate the lies of
those who blame her, and furthermore to give a demonstration of the truth
and to keep [them] from ignorance.

Presented in the usual way, this passage is an example of early Greek prose, characterized by an antithetic contrast expressed by the particle pair *mén . . . dé*. But this method of written presentation obscures the fact that the passage in performance must have contained silence and hence exhibited the fragmented quality we discussed in the previous chapters. It

---

[40] Examples are antithesis: marked syntactic juxtaposition; isocolon: sameness of two or more cola; homoioteleuton: similarity in sound between the endings of various cola. See Norden 1909: 50–53; Kennedy 1963: 64.

[41] See Cic., *De orat.* 3.173–74.

[42] Cf. the remark of Gorgias τὴν ποίησιν ἅπασαν νομίζω καὶ ὀνομάζω λόγον ἔχοντα μέτρον 'All of poetry I consider to be and refer to as discourse with meter', *Hel.* 9, a statement followed by a description of what cannot but be the psychology of the performance. Gorgias, then, seems to have been concerned with introducing prosaic features into poetry rather than with introducing rhythm and other poetic features into prose. To discuss Gorgianic discourse in terms of prose art, I submit, is to reduce his program to mere stylistic prescriptions pertaining to the properties of his speech as text, whereas he himself seems to have been more interested in his discourse as a way in which an orator can use, for his own ends and in his private interest, the effects of special speech in performance.

consists of short units that match the ideal cognitively determined length of the intonation units of ordinary speech, but which in their rhythmic profile resemble the rhythms of poetry. Following Norden,[43] I now present the passage as a sequence of intonationally and rhythmically marked lines rather than as continuous prose:

a.	ἐγὼ δὲ βούλομαι	But as for me, I want,
b.	λογισμόν τινα τῷ λόγῳ δούς	providing argumentation in my speech,
c.	τὴν μὲν κακῶς ἀκούουσαν	her who is held in bad esteem
d.	παῦσαι τῆς αἰτίας,	to keep [her] from accusation,
e.	τοὺς δὲ μεμφομένους	and as for them who blame her,
f.	ψευδομένους ἐπιδείξας	having demonstrated their lies,
g.	καὶ δείξας τἀληθὲς	and given a demonstration of the truth
h.	παῦσαι τῆς ἀμαθίας.	to keep [them] from ignorance.

For ancient critics, poetry is a type of discourse conforming to a regular metrical sequence, and by that definition this passage from Gorgias is prose. But because, like poetry, Gorgias's *In Defense of Helen* presents rhythmically enhanced speech units in performance, it is certainly *not* prose. Some of the units of the passage, in fact, are almost identical to the recognizable rhythmical units of the various poetic genres. Units a and c, for example, strongly resemble iambic rhythm ($\cup - \cup - \cup -$ and $- - \cup - \cup - - -$), and units e–f are dactylic in feeling ($- \cup - \cup \cup -$ and $- \cup \cup - \cup \cup - -$) and almost hexametrical in their relation to each other. The passage, in short, is speech rhythmically enhanced in such a way as to resemble poetry. It has been partly designed as an imitation of the way in which poetry, as special speech, distinguishes itself from ordinary speech.

Besides rhythmic articulation, we must also consider the syntactic arrangement of the various units. We saw in the previous chapter that the progression of speech units in Homeric discourse is often a matter of framing: units frequently provide context for speech to come. In and by themselves, however, Homeric speech units tend to be syntactically and semantically autonomous: they agree with each other grammatically, without there being government of one by another.[44] In Gorgias's discourse, on the other hand, and in rhetorical prose generally, the framing is a matter of

---

[43] Norden 1909: 64, followed by a rhythmical analysis of other parts of Gorgias's speech.
[44] See Meillet and Vendryes 1968: 598; Meillet 1937: 358–59.

syntactic government of one unit, or set of units, by another. Instead of the continuation or addition I discussed in Chapters 4 and 5, the most characteristic relation between two units is complementation; units tend to be syntactically incomplete or completing, and the way in which one unit anticipates another is thus a matter of syntactic construction.

The particles *mén* and *dé* in units c and e, for example, rather than marking the role of independent clauses in the flow of discourse, as in Homer,[45] signal an antithesis between two ideas within the framework of an overarching construction, in accordance with the use of *mén . . . dé* that is usually singled out as central in Greek grammar. This syntactic intricacy, in which looking forward on the path of speech is "syntacticized" to a considerably higher degree than in Homer (note the parallelism between units d and h), is the hallmark of the periodic style of classical rhetoric, of which Gorgias's passage is an early example. In its mature form, the art of rhetorically manipulating the attention flow of the listener reached the point where the units (Latin *membra*, Greek *kôla*) of discourse are either protases or apodoses in the widest possible sense, in that they either create syntactic expectations or give "what is due" in fulfilling them. It is to this syntactic periodicity and anticipation that the rhythmical articulation of speech units in their rhetorical form is ultimately subservient, in both the theory and the practice of rhetorical discourse from the fourth century B.C.E. onwards.

To consider Homeric discourse unperiodic, in contrast to the periodic syntax of a Gorgias, is problematic and unsatisfactory, as we have seen in the previous chapters. Homeric discourse looks ahead in its progression no less than does rhetorical discourse. Still, we may not want to consider this looking ahead as anticipation in the periodic sense: in spite of all the framing and orientation, there is no period to be completed, and no overarching syntactic construction with respect to which the ordering of speech units is arranged. Instead, there is an entirely different way in which speech units in Homer are anticipating each other in the periodic sense: the dimension of meter. Units in Homer are defined not with respect to the completion of a syntactic whole, but with respect to the completion of a metrical whole. In other words, if we take the rhetorical periodic sentence as one highly complex end point in the marking and manipulation of speech segments, then it appears that Homeric discourse with its metrical

---

[45] See Chapter 4.

period, is another equally complex end point, the perfection of an entirely different genre of special speech.

From Rhythm to Meter

Retracing our steps away from periodicity and anticipation for a moment, let us go back to a type of discourse like that of the American folk preachers discussed above, where, under the right performance conditions, a ratio of cognitive and rhetorical features may obtain that differs from ordinary discourse: the speech rhythm becomes more regular, to the point at which we may speak of meter. Typologically, such a discourse could be seen as a point on a scale ranging from maximum cognition to maximum rhetoric; this scale can also be considered diachronically, as a gradual development from unmarked, ordinary speech to marked, special speech;[46] at a given point on this scale we might envisage the differentiation of two deviations from ordinary speech, the one leading to the *syntactic* periodicity just discussed, and the other to periodicity in the form of a *metrical* period to be discussed now.

Regularized rhythm is a rhetorical strategy to emphasize, as I have argued, the boundedness of intonation units, in order to accommodate the discourse to the listeners' consciousness and to stimulate the participation of the audience in the flow of discourse. Yet at some point rhythm ceases to be simply a property of intonation units and becomes subservient to something else. This happens when the rhythmical movement of the units becomes so regular as to turn into a period, consisting of indefinitely repeated verses or rotations. This is the point at which the *rhythm* emergent in discourse becomes *meter.*[47] Thus meter is not something superimposed on language, a form that exists independently of it; meter emerges from language as part of the process by which special speech emerges from speech. A useful formulation of this understanding of meter is provided by Nagy:

---

[46] Though it would be misleading to characterize the speech genre of the folk sermon as being on its way toward more rhythmical regularity. On the marking of special speech as a diachronic process, see Nagy 1990a: 29–40.

[47] This usage contrasts with those accounts that use the term "meter" for the abstract (ideal) profile of a given verse type, and "rhythm" for the concrete realizations of this type (e.g., Van Raalte 1986: 6; Sicking 1993: 43). I depart from such usage (though without questioning the validity of the observations articulated by it), in the same way that I prefer not to speak of realizations of a "formula" or a "sentence."

"At first, the reasoning goes, traditional phraseology simply contains built-in rhythms. Later, the factor of tradition leads to the preference of phrases with some rhythms over phrases with other rhythms. Still later, the preferred rhythms have their own dynamics and become regulators of any incoming phraseology."[48]

The simplest case of meter, and minimally different from mere rhythmically streamlined intonation units, is the coincidence of the metrical period with the basic segments of speech and performance. This type of meter, which of all the metrical systems is closest to speech and in which rhythmical properties belong just as much to the discourse units (formulas) as to the meter, is exemplified in oral traditions all over the world. In the context of the older Indo-European languages, *Rig-Veda* verse may serve as an example, and in later times we find a variety of medieval traditions and verse types. Other examples, some of which are modern, include the Finnish *Kalevala*, as well as the verse of the South Slavic tradition investigated in the 1930s by Parry and Lord.[49] All these cases may be characterized, for the purposes of the present discussion, in terms of adding, both in the usual sense of adding style, applying to the absence of syntactic anticipation, and in the sense that each new speech unit added to the previous one is as such a new instance of the metrical period.

Homeric discourse and metrics is much more complex than this, and also an important step further removed from ordinary speech in its rhetorical sophistication. The Homeric metrical period, the dactylic hexameter, is much longer than speech units usually are, and this turns the movement from unit to unit into something much more complex, metrically and rhetorically, than the mere recurrence of an identical period. Instead of coinciding with the metrical period, speech units in Homeric discourse are in their rhythmical profile *subservient* to it, as part of an ongoing rhythmical flow, and this creates *anticipation* and *periodicity*, not in the syntactic sense of *rhetorical period* but in the equally rhetorical sense of *metrical period*.

It has often been pointed out that the dactylic hexameter is a long verse, with one, two, even three caesuras, which accordingly displays an internal structure that accommodates two, three—according to some even four—

[48] Nagy 1974: 145; see also Nagy 1990a: 37. Useful formulations are also to be found in Devine and Stephens 1993: 399–400; 1994: 101. See also Allen 1973: 14.

[49] On *Rig-Veda* see Kurylowicz 1970; Dunkel 1985: 119–20; Nagy 1990b: 31. For Old English see Cable 1974; 1991; Foley 1990: 110–20. For *Kalevala* see Schellbach-Kopra 1991: 135–36. On Serbo-Croatian see Lord 1960: 54–55; Foley 1990: 85–106. General remarks in Turner 1992: 61–105.

cola. Much discussion has been devoted to the exact status of these caesuras and cola: are they metrical or syntactic?[50] It may not in the end make much difference whether we speak of metrical units or of syntactic units seen in terms of meter. The same rhythmical properties will be assigned to the verse as to its manifestation in language. As long as we consider meter the perspective and starting point, it may not even make much difference whether we see the hexameter as a *unit* of discourse in itself, or as a *mode* of discourse, a rhythmic principle regulating the flow of discourse. What is of interest here is the specific nature of this flow of discourse, treated as a progression of cognitively determined speech units. It is this cognitive flow, I submit, on which we must base our discussion of the rhetoric of the Homeric hexameter.

Instead of speaking of discourse in terms of meter, then, we are dealing with meter in terms of discourse, as part of our discussion of the emergence of poetry out of speech. In terms of cognition, the hexameter cannot be an original discourse unit: it is simply too long to be grasped in its entirety by the poet's and listener's consciousness. Instead, I propose, the hexameter is a matter of rhetoric, of the deliberate manipulation of speech units for the purposes of special speech in performance. The Greek epic tradition, at an early date, must have developed a verse (in the literal sense of "period": something that returns to its beginning) that deliberately exceeded the span of human consciousness, creating a complex universe of discourse that is suitable for the reenactment of complex epic stories and the words of their characters.[51] The exact metrical details of this process will probably remain forever in the dark, but the origin of the hexameter from smaller units is a very plausible scenario, if not an inevitable one from a cognitive point of view. Instead of a coalescence of two shorter verses, however, we would have to think of an increasingly elaborate rhythmical interdependence of the basic units of speech.[52]

---

[50] Some approaches treat cola as linguistic phenomena, with caesuras resulting from colon boundaries. See Fränkel 1968: 100–156, for a four-colon theory. See also Porter 1951; Barnes 1986. Other accounts stress the structural, metrical properties of the verse. See for example Beekes 1972; Van Raalte 1986: 28–103; Sicking 1993: 70–71; Bakker 1988: 165–71. This approach may lead, whether or not explicitly, to a stance against historical and genetic accounts of the hexameter. See for example Hoekstra's critique (1981: 33–53) of the genetic accounts proposed by Nagy 1974 and West 1973.

[51] On the dactylic hexameter being longer than syntactic units (seen as formulas rather than as speech units) see Parry 1971: 191–239; Russo 1966; Ingalls 1972.

[52] The origin of the hexameter is often thought of as the coalescence of a hemiepes $-\cup\cup-\cup\cup$ $-$ (X) and a paroemiac X $-\cup\cup-\cup\cup--$, reflected in the middle caesura (West 1973; 1982: 35;

The space opened up by the long metrical period allows the poets to move in various ways from one period to the other, thus producing the complex colometry that was taken up by subsequent hexameter poets. The least complex situation is exemplified by a passage that served in Chapter 3 as an example of Homeric adding style: the metrical period is realized as two intonation units that have now become metrical units, conforming to the two halves of the verse divided by the middle caesura, which occurs either immediately after the third long position (the so-called penthemimeral caesura) or, when the third foot is a dactyl, after the first short syllable of that foot (the feminine or trochaic caesura):[53]

a.	‖ Πρῶτος δ᾽ Ἀντίλοχος	And first Antilokhos,
b.	| Τρώων ἕλεν ἄνδρα κορυστὴν	of the Trojans he took a helmeted man,
c.	‖ ἐσθλὸν ἐνὶ προμάχοισι,	valiant among the foremost fighters,
d.	| Θαλυσιάδην Ἐχέπωλον·	Thalusias's son Ekhepolos.
e.	‖ τόν ῥ᾽ ἔβαλε πρῶτος	He first struck him,
f.	| κόρυθος φάλον ἱπποδασείης,	on the crest of his horse-haired helmet,
g.	‖ ἐν δὲ μετώπῳ πῆξε,	and he planted [it] in his forehead,
h.	| πέρησε δ᾽ ἄρ᾽ ὀστέον εἴσω	and it pierced right through the bone,
i.	‖ αἰχμὴ χαλκείη·	the bronze spearpoint,
j.	| τὸν δὲ σκότος ὄσσε κάλυψεν,	and darkness covered his eyes,
k.	‖ ἤριπε δ᾽ ὡς ὅτε πύργος,	and he fell as when a tower [does],
l.	| ἐνὶ κρατερῇ ὑσμίνῃ.	in the tough battle.

(*Il.* 4.457–62)

In this fragment, the movement from the verbalization of one focus of consciousness to another in the adding style is subjected to a metrical cohesion between pairs of units that shows Homeric discourse at its rhetorically least marked and least complex: each unit that begins the metrical period (units a, c, e, g, i, and k) is followed by a unit completing it (units b, d, f, h, j, and l), and each pair is separated by what in terms of hexameter

---

Haslam 1976: 202). Berg (1978), followed by Tichy (1981), argues for another coalescence with the Aeolic meter of the pherecrateus × × – ◡ ◡ – – as second member, yielding what in hexameter metrics is called the hephthemimeral caesura as the genetically important joint. See also Gentili (1977; 1988: 15) who argues for an original looser association of the cola that were to produce the hexameter. The most elaborate discussion is Nagy's (most recently 1990a: 459–64), who proposes a common ancestor for the hexameter, the Aeolic pherecrateus, and the dactylic cola of "dactylo-epitrite" meters.

[53] In this representation, ‖ signifies the beginning of a metrical period, and \| the primary division of the period, the middle caesura of the verse.

metrics is the middle caesura. This pattern of rhythmical segmentation often yields one of two paired rhythmical units (minimal strophes or distichs), depending on where the middle caesura falls:

$$-\cup\cup-\cup\cup-|\cup\cup-\cup\cup-\cup\cup--$$
$$-\cup\cup-\cup\cup-\cup|\cup-\cup\cup-\cup\cup--$$

In the example above, units c–d, units g–h, and units k–l are of the second type, and the others are of the first type. In either case, the second unit of the line complements the first. So between the two units (cola), there is a mutual expectancy that is not unlike that between a protasis and an apodosis in a rhetorical period: the one fulfills what the other promises. In the next chapter we will see that in certain central cases this expectancy is no less a matter of the meaning of the two units.

The two-colon period just described is the default case of rhythmical articulation in Homeric discourse. It displays controlled variation not only in that each complementing unit has a different rhythmical profile from its opening unit, but also in the way in which entire periodic distichs (the two units of a verse taken together) relate to each other. When any two adjacent verses are considered together, the result we observe is a more or less tightly organized interplay of four rhythmical profiles. Whatever role the middle caesura has played in the origin of the hexameter, its rhetorical role is beyond question: in either of its two possible realizations, it is the primary resting point in the movement from the beginning to the end of the metrical period.

But Homeric discourse frequently moves beyond this level of rhythmical and rhetorical complexity. Other subdivisions of the time span of the metrical period are possible, yielding cognitive breaks after either the trithemimeres (i.e., a break in the middle of the second foot) or the hephthemimeres (i.e., a break in the middle of the fourth foot), or at both places:

$$-\cup\cup-|\cup\cup-\cup\cup-|\cup\cup-\cup\cup--$$

In the last case, the characteristic result is what Kirk has called a rising threefolder, a division of the time of the metrical period into three units of increasing length:[54]

---

[54] See Kirk 1985: 20–21. Minton notes (1975: 33–34) that this type of division is more frequent in Hesiod than in Homer. In many cases (as perhaps in the example given) the first break is less marked or even very weak, so that a case could be made for a bipartite organization with a single break at the hephthemimeres.

‖ τὸν δ' εὗρον	− − −	and him they found,
φρένα τερπόμενον	∪∪−∪∪−	delighting his mind,
φόρμιγγι λιγείῃ ‖	− −∪∪− −	with the clear-sounding lyre.
		(*Il.* 9.186)

The rising threefolder constitutes, as Kirk notes, a "substantial minority of Homeric verses,"[55] and we could see it as a rhetorical strategy to alleviate the monotony of an indiscriminately prolonged series of periodic distichs. The rhetorical function of the tripartite hexametrical period would be a factor whether or not the participating cola have played a role in the origin of the hexameter. We also find tripartite sequences with other, less regular rhythmic profiles, e.g.:

a.	‖ εἰ δ' ἄγε,	−∪∪	well then,
b.	τοὺς ἂν ἐγὼ ‖ ἐπιόψομαι,	−∪∪−∪∪−∪∪	whomever I will choose,
c.	οἱ δὲ πιθέσθων. ‖	−∪∪− −	let them obey.
			(*Il.* 9.167)

The central unit is longer than in the previous example, beginning earlier, right after the first dactylic foot, and running up to the bucolic diaeresis. In spite of the tripartite structure the middle caesura, falling after *egò* in unit b, is not absent and could be seen as slight break, rhetorical rather than cognitive, in the middle of unit b. The default rhythm of the hexameter, in other words, is not disrupted.[56] The following example contains a tripartite hexameter that can be seen as a disruption of the basic rhythm of the period:

a.	‖ τὸν βάλε δεξιὸν ὦμον·	him he hit in the right shoulder,
b.	‖ ὁ δ' ὕπτιος ἐν κονίῃσι	and he, on his back in the dust,
c.	‖ κάππεσεν οἰμώξας,	he fell with a cry,
d.	‖ ἕταροι δέ μιν ἀμφὶ φόβηθεν	and his comrades around him they scattered,
e.	‖ Παίονες·	the Paionians,
f.	ἐν γὰρ Πάτροκλος	for in [them] Patroklos,
g.	φόβον ἦκεν ἅπασιν	fear he sent into all of them,
h.	‖ ἡγεμόνα κτείνας,	having killed their leader,
i.	‖ ὃς ἀριστεύεσκε μάχεσθαι. ‖	who was the best of them in the fighting.
		(*Il.* 16.289–92)

---

55 Kirk 1985: 20.

56 Cf. also *Il.* 24.1: λῦτο δ' ἀγών, | λαοὶ δὲ | θοὰς ἐπὶ νῆας ἕκαστοι ‖ ἐσκίδναντ' ἰέναι 'and the games ended, | and [as for] the people, | to the swift ships each | they went dispersing', where a slight break may perhaps be discerned after λαοὶ δὲ, uttered as a separate unit before its clause.

After two distichs (units a–b and c–d), the next verse is a tripartite period (units e–g) like the one in the previous example. But this time there is no rhythmic anticipation, as in the case of the distich or the rising threefolder. The middle unit f, with its five heavy syllables, seems out of place rhythmically, and would have been more appropriate as the first unit of a period.[57] This metrical disturbance results from the insertion of unit e, a unit that is added to what precedes in the sense discussed earlier.[58]

The cognitive boundary between unit e and the preceding unit d is much less strong than that between unit e and the following unit f, and we might for that reason say that unit e is *enjambing*. Enjambement, commonly seen as the mismatch between a metrical unit (the hexameter verse) and a linguistic unit (the sentence), has long occupied an important place in the discussion of Homeric meter and style.[59] In the perspective developed here, where sentence recedes in favor of speech unit as a cognitive entity and verse in favor of metrical period as a rhetorical one, the notion of enjambement might have to be modified accordingly. As we have seen in Chapters 4 and 5, the two major operations in Homeric syntax, continuation and framing, require a space that almost always exceeds the metrical period. To the extent that sentence is a phenomenon from a different medium, therefore, I suggest that we refrain from using the term "enjambement" whenever the progression of speech units is in accordance with the metrical period.[60] This happens, for example, in the transitions from unit b to c and from unit g to h in the passage just cited, where we see a clause uttered within a frame and an adding participial phrase.[61] In these cases the cognitive boundary between two speech units coincides with the rhetorical boundary between two periods.[62]

But there are varying degrees to which the movement from one focus of

[57] Names like Patroklos (consisting of three long syllables) are much more at home either at the beginning of the line or before the middle caesura (see O'Neill 1942).

[58] See Chapter 5. The present case is an example of disambiguation.

[59] Since Parry's 1929 article (1971: 251–65) enjambement has played an important role in discussions of oral composition. See, e.g., Lord 1960: 54; Kirk 1966; Edwards 1966; Bakker 1990b; Higbie 1990 (the fullest account); Clark 1994.

[60] Cf. the earlier treatment of this topic in Bakker 1990b.

[61] On the reasons for not viewing κάππεσεν (unit c) as the "verb" of a sentence of which ὁ is the "subject," see Chapter 5.

[62] This is what Parry (1971: 253) called unperiodic enjambement, the type of enjambement that is in accordance with the adding style (see also Chapter 3 above). Notice, however, that Parry would not consider the first enjambement, between units b and c, unperiodic; he would assign it, instead, to the more severe category of necessary enjambement (in which two necessary parts of a sentence are separated by the end of the line—on this point, see the previous note). For the various typologies of enjambement see Parry 1971: 253; Kirk 1976: 148; Higbie 1990: 29.

consciousness to the other does not coincide with the cyclic rhythmical movement of the period. Sometimes the boundary between two periods is only blurred, as it is between units d and e, and the disturbance that results is absorbed by unit f and contained within the metrical period. But sometimes the cognitive units are at variance, not with the default rhythm *within* the period, but with the movement *across* two or more periods. For example, a unit may start at the bucolic diaeresis and move beyond the time that is left in the period (i.e., the clausula $- \cup \cup - -$) into the next period. The remarkable thing about such necessary or violent enjambement, with a strong mutual cohesion of the linguistic material on either side of the rhetorical boundary,[63] is not that it occurs, but that it *occurs in clusters*, series of rhythmical mismatches creating tension that is sustained across two or more periods. To bring out the dynamic character of these rhetorically charged moments, we might speak of *antimetry* to characterize the secondary rhythm that is temporarily set up against the movement of the hexametric period.[64] The second assembly of the Trojans provides an example:

a. ‖ ἐς δ' ἀγορὴν ἀγέροντο,	and they gathered for the assembly
b. ǀ πάρος δόρποιο μέδεσθαι.	before thinking of food,
c. ‖ ὀρθῶν δ' ἐσταότων	and with everybody standing
d. ǀ ἀγορὴ γένετ᾽,	the assembly, it was held,
e. οὐδέ τις ἔτλη ‖ ἕζεσθαι ·	and no one dared sit down,
f. πάντας ǀ γὰρ ἔχε τρόμος,	for fear, it held them all,
g. οὕνεκ᾽ Ἀχιλλεὺς ‖ ἐξεφάνη,	since Achilles, he had appeared
h. δηρὸν δὲ ǀ μάχης ἐπέπαυτ᾽ ἀλεγεινῆς. ‖	and long he had stopped from the dire fighting.

$$(Il.\ 18.245-48)$$

The description begins with a distich (units a–b) and a further unit (c) that divides the time of the metrical period in the usual manner. The fourth unit (d), containing old information that is not cognitively salient (*agorè génet'* 'the assembly it was held'), serves as a bridge to unit e, where the antimetry begins; the unit runs into the next period, producing a limping, unhexametrical rhythm.[65] Unit f then carries the sequence of ideas to the

---

[63] Some cases of adjective and noun separated by the end of the verse are *Il.* 1.78; 8.75, 128; 17.360, 371; 13.191; 24.122. Cf. also Edwards 1966: 125–33; Higbie 1990: 55–56, 115–16.

[64] Edwards (1966: 136–37; 1991: 42–44) tends to stress the emphasis received by the word following the verse boundary in such cases.

[65] The rhythm is unhexametrical because by Meyer's First Law phrases of the form $- \cup \cup - -$ or $- \cup \cup - \cup$ almost never begin the verse, no doubt to avoid the very sequence with which it ends (Beekes 1972; Van Raalte 1986: 93; but cf. Kirk 1966: 97).

point at which the next antimetrical movement starts (unit g), at the bucolic diaeresis, exactly the same time in the metrical period as the previous
one. Units e and g do not, of course, pretend to be "false starts," hexameters
beginning too early and thereby weakening the basic metrical cadence: no
attempt has been made to conceal the beginning of the metrical cycle, as
appears from the hiatus in unit e between *étlē* 'dared' and *hézesthai* 'sit
down', and the virtual single-short rhythm due to the shortening of the
long final vowel of *étlē* in line end. Indeed, the antimetrical effect of unit e
and g derives precisely, not from their weakening the metrical cycle but
from their acknowledging it; the units move against the basic rhythm, thus
creating a tension that cannot but be rhetorically effective. This tension, we
observe, is connected with an increase in semantic salience. Unit f, bridging the time between the two antimetrical units e and g, is as to its content
also less prominent than the two surrounding units causing the metrical
turbulence. This attraction of metrical (rhetorical) and semantic salience is
even clearer in the next example:

a. αἰδοίης ἑκυρῆς ὀπὸς ἔκλυον,   of my honored mother-in-law I heard the
                                  voice,
b. ἐν δ᾽ ἐμοὶ αὐτῇ ‖ στήθεσι   and within me the heart, it is pounding in my
   πάλλεται ἦτορ   breast,
c. ἀνὰ στόμα,   up to my mouth,
d. νέρθε δὲ γοῦνα ‖ πήγνυται·   and my legs below, they cannot move,
e. ἐγγὺς δή τι κακὸν   yea, something terrible is close
f. Πριάμοιο τέκεσσιν.   to Priam's children,
g. αἲ γὰρ ἀπ᾽ οὔατος εἴη ἐμεῦ ἔπος·   may the word it be far from my ear:
h. ἀλλὰ μάλ᾽ αἰνῶς ‖ δείδω   but terribly I fear. . . .

(*Il.* 22.451–55)

Andromakhe's verbalization of her anxiety constitutes a highly functional
case of antimetry: in three installments (units b, d, and h) she expresses her
feelings, and each time her discourse breaks through the metrical structure,
producing the halting, unhexametric rhythm of antimetry.[66] One might

---

[66] One might argue that unit b consists, after all, of two cognitive units separated by the end of
the verse, but in that case the cohesion between them would be so strong that the effect produced
would be in practice the same as described here. The same applies to units e and g in the previous
example: one might want to argue that οὕνεκ᾽ Ἀχιλλεύς (unit g) is a unit on its own that frames
ἐξεφάνη in the way described in Chapter 5. But that would not affect the analysis proposed here:
repeated antimetrical effects would still occur, since the cohesion between ἕζεσθαι and ἐξεφάνη
and the units preceding would be much stronger than between these verbal forms and the units
following (f and h).

want to consider such cases[67] as a suppression of meter that is uncharacteristic of oral composition and not likely to occur in the practice of improvisation.[68] Yet from the point of view of performance and audience attention—that is, rhetoric—one cannot help finding them very effective. They may even be indispensable, if not to underscore emotional or chaotic scenes by means of meter, then at least to avoid a metrically too correct and therefore potentially dull sequence of units.

Metrical versus Syntactic Periods

By way of apodosis to this chapter, we may add to this discussion of the emergence of meter from discourse that the unperiodic nature of Homeric syntax is by no means less complex than the periodic and hypotactic discourse of later periods. Rather, Homeric discourse is an equally complex result of the marking of ordinary speech into special speech, though of a completely different kind. As noted above, the essence of special speech lies in the connection between the discourse of the special occasion and ordinary discourse as the source on which it draws for its rhetorical effect. As such the concept of special discourse is useful in bringing out a common denominator of Homeric discourse and classical rhetorical prose, a similarity that gets lost in the more usual opposition between a formulaic *Kunstsprache* and the periodic *Kunstprosa* of later times.

Yet the concept is no less useful in bringing out the differences. Classical rhetoric, in increasing the importance of syntactic anticipation in speech and turning it into hypotaxis, can be said to have deviated from ordinary speech in an important step toward what we would call prose. By contrast, Homeric discourse has retained the characteristic flow of speech, but subjected it to the constraints of the hexametric period. It is this rhythmical period, the primary characteristic of the discourse of the performance, that turns Homeric speech into the stylization of ordinary speech. The flow of speech in the performance may be driven by the consciousness of the Homeric performer, but this consciousness, in its turn, is driven by the rhythmical flow of the hexametric period. Insofar as the audience cannot help participating, this process can rightly be called rhetorical.

---

[67] Cf. also *Il.* 6.407–11; 8.125–29; 10.149–54; 12.184–85; 13.687–92; 16.60–62, 107–10, 335–40, 367–68, 395–96, 552–53; 19.92–96; *Od.* 2.167–68.

[68] See Kirk 1976: 168–69 on *Il.* 16.306–50.

CHAPTER 7

Epithets and Epic Epiphany

The Mythic Idea . . . finds expression in the . . . belief . . . that the name of a person is an integral part of his being. For this belief rests on the ulterior assumption that personality consists not only in the visible corporeal self but also in some wider preterpunctual essence of which the name is a peculiarly appropriate symbol inasmuch as it indeed represents the individual even when his body is absent or defunct.
—Theodore H. Gaster, "Myth and Story"

The primary units of ordinary speech can be stylized, as we have seen in the previous chapter, into metrical units, in a process that involves selecting the most common and regular rhythmic profiles of the language. This process, however, is not limited to meter and the other physical properties of speech; it also involves, and crucially so, the meaning of speech units. Phrases referring to ideas that are of thematic importance for the special speech act of the performance are more likely than other phrases to contribute to the rhythmical or metrical properties of the discourse that prompts them.

The idea of recurrence of speech units in connection with meter inevitably leads us to the notion of the formula in Homeric and other oral diction. As we saw in the first two chapters, the formula has commonly been seen as the criterial property of oral style, and the singers' dependence on it as the key to the problem of oral composition. The conception of formulas as stylized intonation units does not dilute Parry's and Lord's claims for the formula's function in the oral tradition. It makes them more specific, in fact, by placing them within the general framework of human cognition, its possibilities and limitations: the primary bits of special speech can have their specific mnemonic function in the recomposition of the epic story because of their cognitive foundation in the primary bits of ordinary speech.

In the present chapter, we will look at the noun-epithet formula, thematically one of the most important phrase types in Homeric diction. We will not be concerned in the first place with the systematic way in which these expressions interact with each other in that diction (see Chapter 1), nor with the question whether they are meant to be significant at times, in spite of their being formulas. What interests me here is not so much the phrases themselves, with their semantic and metrical characteristics, as the reason why they are used. The principal question will be: Where do noun-epithet formulas occur? Is there a typical context that motivates their occurrence and perhaps even requires their existence? My argument in this and the next chapters will reverse the procedure usually followed: instead of asking when noun-epithet phrases and other formulas become meaningful owing to the originality of the poet who uses them, I will try to determine when they become formulaic owing to the recurrence that results from their importance.

In line with the general method presented in this study, then, I do not begin with a given poetic or stylistic feature like the formula, taken by itself in isolation from speech and language. Instead, I start from ordinary language and see how one of its features is stylized to play a role in the semantics of Homeric special speech. In this chapter speech is considered a behavior that responds to the requirements of a context, as those are acknowledged by speakers and listeners together. In the next chapter I show how this behavior can become routinized to yield formulas within the metrical environment created by Homeric discourse.

Making, Using, and Doing

Formulas are stylized speech units, but speech units in ordinary language may also be formulaic, a connection first made by Paul Kiparsky, who has drawn attention to the similarities between Homeric formulas and the "bound expressions" of ordinary language, the idioms that are characterized, among other things, by their "frozen syntax."[1] The formularity of ordinary language, however, is not limited to a few isolated idioms; it also involves real syntax, the very grammar of a language. Consider what the linguist Dwight Bolinger has to say on this issue: "At present we have no way of telling the extent to which a sentence like *I went home* is a result of invention, and the extent to which it is a result of repetition, countless

[1] Kiparsky 1976: 73–83.

speakers before us having already said it and transmitted to us in toto. Is grammar something where speakers 'produce' (i.e., originate) constructions, or where they 'reach for' them, from a pre-established inventory?"[2] I have suggested already that speech has to be seen as a process, rather than as a product,[3] and against the background of Bolinger's question I now propose that speakers are much less often than is sometimes assumed the authors or makers of the things they say. The idea that language is primarily creation belongs to the literate conception of discourse, and is of relatively limited importance when it comes to the study of the oral conception of language.[4] In many frequently recurring speech situations, success depends on *not* being the originator of one's words, and on the listener acknowledging this.[5] Useful as Bolinger's formulation is, however, it has the unsatisfactory effect of turning speech from originality into traditionality, its notional opposite and a concept no less literate in its conception.

I believe there is some advantage in realizing that we tend to conceive of linguistic expressions as things; Bolinger, for example, characterizes grammatical constructions as items to be "reached for." But such a reification rests, whether explicitly or not, on the conception of linguistic expressions (words, phrases, sentences) as textual items. In writing, it is possible to write an expression, any expression, twice, so that the second writing is turned into a quote, and as such a repetition of the first one. Even the very idea of the "use of a linguistic expression" treats the use as somehow external to the expression "itself" and so already in a sense repetitious.[6] The idea of linguistic constructions as prefabricated rather than newly made, then, turns speakers from makers into *users*, who reach for tools to make something out of what others have made before.

Moving away from linguistic expressions as things and seeing them more as events, cognitive as well as acoustic, we may accordingly change our view of speakers and their typical activity. Being neither makers nor users, they are more like actors, *doers* who engage in recognizable behavior. Saying something that has been said before entails less the repetition of some utterance than a judgment on the part of the speaker that a given context is similar to a previous one, calling for the same behavior. This behavior is

---

[2] Bolinger 1961: 381, cited by Tannen 1989: 37. Tannen's entire discussion of "repetition in conversation" (1989: 36–97) is very instructive.

[3] See Chapter 3.

[4] On the notion of conception in orality and literacy, see Chapter 1.

[5] Bakker 1993a: 6–10.

[6] See Derrida 1978: 247–48, on a similar notion of writing as repetition.

neither wholly original nor wholly traditional, and in fact this distinction may well collapse into a concept belonging to a different kind of aesthetic. What the repeated words, by themselves, actually mean (in a traditional or in a novel way) is less important than that the speaker considers them suitable behavior for a given context. The meaning is also less important than that the listener is able to recognize and acknowledge the similarity between the present context and a previous one. Repeated phrases, even whole speech acts or discourses, may become like rituals, enacted by speakers who assume that the actual words spoken will acquire a "plus-value" in the speech context at hand: the listener not only recognizes their actual, literal meaning, but beyond that also the very reason why they are used. This account of the ritual aspects of ordinary speech behavior provides us, I believe, with a basis from which to approach the stylized recurrence of phrases in the context of the epic performance.

The Meaning of Noun-Epithet Formulas

It may not be too misleading to state that the opposition between traditionality and originality has dominated the debate about the meaning and function of noun-epithet formulas in Homeric formulaic diction.[7] Parry set the stage for traditionality by arguing that noun-epithet formulas fill a metrically salient part of the line in a systematic, prefabricated way. The meaning of the epithet in this account amounts to an ascription of a property to a god or hero that may or may not fit a given context. The lexical value of the epithet is ultimately irrelevant, since the attribution is subservient to the metrical circumstances.[8] Ever since Parry's startling argument attempts have been made, in various ways and with varying degrees of antagonism with respect to the original insight, to modify his approach to the formula. Noun-epithet formulas, it was held, do not merely serve a metrical function, if their function is metrical at all; they may also be appropriate to their referent, to their context, or to both.[9]

---

[7] For a recent reevaluation of traditionality and originality, see Peradotto 1990: 100 n. 2.

[8] To be sure, Parry made the important distinction (e.g., 1971: 145) between fixed and generic epithets, the former pertaining exclusively to one hero, the latter not. Parry insisted that although the meaning of the fixed epithet is different from that of the generic epithet (in telling something significant about a given character), the reason for its use may still be ease of versification in a given context.

[9] E.g., Whallon 1969: 1–32; Parry 1973: 161–67; Austin 1975: 11–80, esp. 69–73; Tsagarakis 1982: 34–39; Vivante 1982; Beck 1986; Cosset 1990; Lowenstam 1993: 13–57; Machacek 1994.

The discussion has thus been one of metrical form vs. meaning in context. Yet whether one conceives of the Homeric noun-epithet formula as meaningless in spite of its having a given lexical meaning, or as meaningful in spite of its being a formula, the central assumption remains that what is at stake is the literal meaning of a formula, its lexical value, and whether the formula is semantically insensitive or appropriate to a context. In trying to come to terms with the strange and ubiquitous formulaic repetitions, we convert those formulas, and the context in which they occur, into what is the essence of our literary conception of language: words on paper, occurring within the context of other words on paper.

In his recent account of traditional verbal art, trying to bridge the gap between the "mechanism" of oral-formulaic theory in its original form and the "aesthetics" of literary appreciation, John Miles Foley has suggested that the use of an epithet is for epic performers and their audiences a moment at which something is invoked that exceeds the importance of the literal meaning of the epithet in a particular context. Foley calls this semantic phenomenon, which is typical of oral traditions, "traditional referentiality," and he introduces it as a key concept in a new aesthetics of traditional verbal art:[10]

> Traditional referentiality . . . entails the invoking of a context that is enormously larger and more echoic than the text or work itself, that brings the lifeblood of generations of poems and performances to the individual performance or text. Each element in the phraseology or narrative thematics stands not simply for that singular instance but for the plurality and multiformity that are beyond the reach of textualization. From the perspective of traditional context, these elements are foci for meaning, still points in the exchange of meaning between an always impinging tradition and the momentary and nominal fossilization of a text or version.

This traditional referentiality, Foley points out, is a matter of metonymic relationships between the epic phrases in their particular contexts and their traditional referents. Epithets can be seen, in Foley's formulation, as "metonymic pathways to the poetic conjuring of personalities";[11] they stand as individual instances, not in a one-to-one but in a *pars pro toto* relation to the traditional theme or idea which they represent. The noun-epithet formulas

[10] Foley 1991: 7.
[11] Ibid., 23; see also Foley 1992: 281.

polútlas díos Odusseús 'much-suffering godlike Odysseus' or *glaukôpis Athênê* 'owl-eyed Athene', for example, are not just metrically convenient references to Odysseus or Athene at a particular moment; nor are they the ascription of a property to these epic figures that may or may not suit a given context. Rather, uttering the phrase is a summoning to the present of the Odysseus or the Athene of all moments, the Odysseus or Athene that is provided by the tradition.[12]

Elaborating slightly on Foley's formulations, we might say that the epithet is much more than the ascription of a property by an attributive adjective. Rather, the epithet *is* the quintessential property, a criterial attribute not expressed by, but turned into language. Instead of ascribing a property to an absent referent, noun-epithet formulas make this absent referent present,[13] conjuring it, in its most characteristic form, to the here and now of the performance, as an essential part of the universe of discourse shared between the performer and his audience. As recurrent instantiations of the mythical reality of the past, the noun-epithet formulas are not secondary, as repeated phrases, to any original or first use of the expression. Indeed, if there is any first use, it is the god or hero herself or himself, as the normative original of all the recurrences of a noun-epithet phrase. In other words, what comes back again and again is not so much the phrase as the god or hero with whom it is associated.

Foley's account of traditional referentiality charges noun-epithet formulas with an immanent meaning that transcends the literal meaning of the phrases as textual items and is fully accessible only to those who are within the tradition: the poets and their audiences. But immanent, extratextual meaning may be less a matter of the meaning of the traditional phrases themselves than of certain contexts in which they are used. Nor is the principle of traditional referentiality confined to traditional oral epic. Language in general, in fact, is a matter of inherent meaning. By this I mean

---

[12] The extratextual significance of epithets gains an extra dimension in the case of πολύτλας δῖος Ὀδυσσεύς 'much-suffering godlike Odysseus', a formula associated with the theme of Odysseus's νόστος 'homecoming', which freely occurs in the *Iliad* (8.97; 9.676; 10.248; 23.729, 778) where, from a strictly chronological point of view, events are recounted that occur before Odysseus has had the chance to become "much-suffering." As Nagy puts it (1990b: 23): "Odysseus is πολύτλας 'much-suffering' throughout the *Iliad* because he is already a figure in an epic tradition about adventures that he will have after Troy. My saying 'after' here applies only to the narrative sequence: the *Iliad* is recording the fact that Odysseus already has an *Odyssey* tradition about him—which is certainly not the final *Odyssey*, the fixed text that has come down to us."

[13] On the notion of the presence of past events in the present of the epic performance, see Bakker 1993b: 15–25; Ford 1992: 54–55.

simply that words and phrases inevitably come with conventional associations, if only because the speaker is not the first one to use them.[14] And insight into these associations is inevitably not just a matter of the expressions themselves, but of the contexts in which they are used.

As anyone who has learned foreign languages—not in the classroom but in the actual arena of linguistic performance—can testify, knowing the literal meaning of a given expression is relatively easy; much more demanding is to know when to utter the expression, or to recognize the specific meaning of the moments at which it is used. The real meaning of any given expression includes the significance of its contexts in a given culture, not as textual junctures, but as recurrent events, whose social or thematic importance is recognized by the speech community in question, be it a private and idiosyncratic community of two, a subculture, or the entire language community. Immanent meaning, in short, is a matter of language as behavior, of the rituals belonging to a speech culture. Among the most characteristic rituals of the speech community of the Homeric tradition is the noun-epithet formula, and in light of what precedes we can now define the study of these elements as follows: the question we have to ask is not whether the noun-epithet formula, or rather, its literal meaning, is appropriate when it occurs in a given context; the important question, rather, is what motivates the ritual of which they are the prime articulation when they occur.

Epiphanies and Their Stagings

I suggest, then, that we view noun-epithet formulas as minirituals, performed in the context of the Homeric performance. Insofar as the naming of, say, Odysseus as *polútlas díos Odusseús* 'much-suffering godlike Odysseus' is not so much the use of a given formulaic expression as an action performed, I will speak of an *epiphany* of the hero in question. Usually the term "epiphany" is used for the appearance of a divinity in a human context, a moment that may be represented as such in the performance.[15] In the use to be made here of the term, on the other hand, the appearance is

---

[14] In his accounts of the dialogism of meaning in language, Bakhtin explicitly includes previous uses of a given word, their purposes and contexts, in the dialogue (1986: 93). These previous uses cling to any given word and give it a semantic aura much larger than its strict lexical force.

[15] See Pucci 1987: 110–23, 244.

not represented in but effected by the performance; the epic figure, god or hero, makes his or her appearance out of the timeless world of the myth into the time frame of the performance, a moment that is closer to ritual and cult than to our sense of poetry.[16] When do these epiphanies occur? In the most Homeric of the Homeric speech rituals, noun-epithet formulas are very often preceded by phrases of the following type:

τὸν δ᾽ ἀπαμειβόμενος προσέφη	and him in answer he addressed
τοῖσι δ᾽ ἀνιστάμενος μετέφη	and rising he spoke among them
τὸν δ᾽ ἠμείβετ᾽ ἔπειτα	and him s/he answered then
τὸν δ᾽ αὖτε προσέειπε	and him in his turn s/he addressed
τὸν δ᾽ ὡς οὖν ἐνόησε	and him when s/he saw
τὸν δὲ ἰδὼν ἐνόησε/ἐλέησε	and seeing him he thought/pitied
τὼ δὲ πεσόντ᾽ ἐλέησε	and them as they fell he pitied

Of a different structure, but comparable in function, is:

εἰ μὴ ἄρ᾽ ὀξὺ νόησε	if s/he had not seen sharply

In terms of the discussion of Homeric syntax offered in Chapters 4 and 5, these phrases, except for the last one, are moments of *continuation* with respect to the preceding discourse (notice the particle *dé*); with respect to the subsequent discourse they have a *framing* function, and the unit added, the noun-epithet formula, is the first unit uttered within the frame.[17] Continuation and framing together yield the *relational* function of these units: they serve as link between a character named by the noun-epithet phrase that follows and a character who is already on the scene. The pronoun in an oblique case (*tòn* 'him', *toîsi* 'to them', etc.), with which all the units begin, designates the character(s) already on the scene (and active in the mind of the performer and his audience), setting up the antagonist for the protagonist of the discourse to come, the character who makes his epiphany with the noun-epithet formula.

The pronoun is in syntactic terms the object of the verb, but its primary function is not limited to its specific clause. In having a relational function,

---

[16] See Bakker 1995: 110. Ford (1992: 34, 55) uses "epiphanic" and related terms like "magical" to evoke the "vividness" of Homeric poetry. See also Bakker 1997a, on what is near and what is far in the Homeric performance; Kahane 1997, on "stitching together the past and the present."

[17] See Chapter 5, also on the noun-epithet phrase not being the subject of the preceding clause.

the pronoun integrates the unit into the ongoing flow of discourse, relating the new character to one(s) already on the scene.[18] Similarly, over and above its being the predicate of its clause, the verb serves a relational function in specifying how the new character is linked to the character already on the scene. That relation is typically one of speaking or of perception. In the case of speaking, the formula along with the noun-epithet formula that follows is an introduction to direct speech; the character named by the noun-epithet formula is usually already on the scene. In the case of perception, on the other hand, the epiphany takes place in ongoing narrative, and the hero or god named by the noun-epithet formula tends to make an entirely new appearance.

Phrases of the type just described are almost always followed by a noun-epithet formula, as we shall see in more detail in Chapter 8. Now if the noun-epithet phrase is not just a unit added to the preceding one or uttered within a frame, but an epiphany of the god or hero, we may want to assign a special value to the preceding phrase as well. In what follows I will speak of *staging formulas*.[19] A staging formula is the phrase that sets the scene for the heroic or divine epiphany, staging the hero or god in the proper way. If the noun-epithet formula is a small and recurrent speech ritual, then the staging formula provides the appropriate setting for that event. Phrases functioning as staging formula thus transcend the act of perception or the answer that they report.

In terms of the preceding chapter, an epiphany and its staging together form one complete metrical period: the staging formula starts at the beginning of the metrical period and runs to one of the metrical resting-points, either the trochaic caesura or the hephthemimeres.[20] The staging is then complemented by a noun-epithet formula of the appropriate length. The noun-epithet formula almost always follows when a staging formula is uttered. Metrical completion, then, goes hand in hand with a strong semantic bond between staging and epiphany, to the point that the epiphany

---

[18] Note that there is an important difference when the pronoun is in the nominative (ὁ δὲ 'and he'): in those cases the pronoun and the noun-epithet formula (if there is one) designate the same person, and this has important consequences for the status of the noun-epithet formula, on which see the next chapter.

[19] See Bakker 1995: 109–11.

[20] Cf. Parry's list (1971: 11–13) of what he calls "predicate hemistichs." Some of these, however, are not staging formulas in my sense (notably when they begin with a pronoun in the nominative case, such as αὐτὰρ ὁ μερμήριξε 'and he pondered', for which see Chapter 8). Parry's "predicate" implies that the noun-epithet formula is a subject; the problems of this seemingly obvious idea have been discussed in Chapter 5.

and its staging glue together the two cola of which the metrical period consists. We may say, then, that a staging formula creates a standard environment for the noun-epithet formula: once a stage has been set up, it will be occupied by a god or hero. Notice, however, that the converse is not true: a noun-epithet formula may be uttered when something other than a staging unit precedes, an observation that will be further explored in the next chapter. Yet to say that there exists a strong, grammatical bond between staging formulas and noun-epithet phrases does not in itself do more than take the occurrence of the staging formula for granted; it does not explain when and where it is used. In other words, we have to be concerned with what motivates the creation of the proper environment for a noun-epithet formula. What the formulas literally mean is clear enough and trivial; what interests us is the significance of the speech event which they constitute.

Epic Discourse As Secondary Action

Usually the relation between the epic song and the heroic past is seen in terms of glorification and commemoration. But from the point of view of heroes as depicted in Homer the epic song is no less a matter of *justification* of heroic deeds. Homeric heroes are frequently presented as being aware of songs that will be sung about them in the future, and this is an end to which they direct their behavior. Consider for example what Hektor says at the moment at which he is about to be killed by Achilles:[21]

νῦν αὖτέ με <u>μοῖρα</u> κιχάνει.
μὴ μὰν ἀσπουδί γε καὶ <u>ἀκλειῶς</u> ἀπολοίμην,
ἀλλὰ μέγα ῥέξας τι καὶ <u>ἐσσομένοισι</u> πυθέσθαι.

(Il. 22.303–5)

But now my <u>fate</u> is upon me.
Let me at least not perish <u>ingloriously</u> without a struggle,
but do some big thing first, that <u>men to come</u> shall know of it.

Hektor does what he does with an eye on the future. He knows that he is in the middle of epic action, and so he is conscious of the medium that

---

[21] See also *Il.* 3.352–54; 6.357–58; 7.87–91.

carries him. He is determined to show courage in order to make possible a song in the future. One could almost reverse the relation of causality that is normal and uncontroversial to us when we talk about historical discourse, in which the event in the past is what prompts the historian's discourse of the present. In the historical conception of Homeric epic, the discourse of the present, conversely, is what may be said to prompt the heroic deed of the past. Heroic deeds like Hektor's valiant resistance, in fact, belong to the present no less than they do to the past, insofar as they are reexperienced in each new performance. Nothing in the epic is independent of the medium in which it is reenacted, and the idea of the past as something "before" song seems alien to the implicit poetics of the Homeric tradition.[22]

I would suggest, then, that for the Homeric poet and his audience the past is not simply a historical reality that is the subject of a song. There is an *interdependence* between the deed of the past and the song of the present. Each exists because of the other. If we call the epic events, as they transpire on the battlefields of Troy and as they are seen by the Muses, the *primary action*, then the performance in the future would be the *secondary action*. The secondary action of song completes the primary action of epic, and neither one is meaningful without the other. To describe the epic action as primary action in its relation to the secondary speech action of the future, the performance of the *Iliad*, brings out a distinction between two kinds of event occurring in epic narrative. Some things that happen in the epic tale may be moving or frightening to the audience, but they are not essential for the story. Had they not happened, the *Iliad* would still be the *Iliad*. One might even consider the possibility that they sprang from the minds of poets, in their desire to depict the epic world in as vivid a manner as possible, and that the audience acknowledged this.[23]

Some other events occurring in the epic, however, are truly primary action. Frequently, heroes or gods decisively contribute to the epic action, in such a way as to cause the action of the performance. At such moments the character is the author of the epic tale: the story as the performer and his audience know it would have been different, or would not have existed at all, if the god or hero had not performed the act in question. These junctures are shifts at which the very fate of epic characters, or the right course

---

[22] See Bakker 1997a for the temporal consequences involved here (the "now" being the future of the "then").

[23] Cf. Pratt 1993: 37–42 on "commemorative fiction."

of the epic action, is at stake.[24] Those moments may or may not be moving or frightening, but their thematic importance for the epic tradition is beyond doubt. It is at these moments, I propose, that epic characters get staged, and ritually named by the epithet that is the principal bearer of their *kleos*. The noun-epithet formula is not used here solely because it is metrically useful; nor is the epithet as such meant to be appropriate in its context. What is appropriate is the appearance of the epic figure himself, who as an agent then is directly responsible for the experience of the performance now, in performing a deed that bridges the gulf between the past and the present.

The most obvious type of action that significantly contributes to the course of events as rebehaved and reexperienced in the performance is the very action of which the performance consists: speech. The epiphany of a hero or god in the epic performance is most direct and forceful when the hero is represented as doing what the performer does himself, when indeed the performer becomes the epic character, in uttering the authoritative speech of the latter. The typical speech act of heroes, in fact, as has been recently suggested, is itself a performance, designated by the term *mûthos*.[25] It is when they speak that epic characters are most present, by way of strategies of mimetic impersonation that also occur freely in conversational narrative.[26]

Mimetic impersonation takes up about forty-five percent of the text of the *Iliad* as we have it. Various strategies to introduce the mimesis of an epic character's speech are deployed in Homer,[27] but the most conspicuous way to realize this shift is the naming of the speaker with a full noun-epithet formula preceded by a staging. This combination transcends the lexical meaning of its words and marks the speech introduced as primary action that carries the story line at the moment of its production. Speech intro-

---

[24] In this connection it is interesting to pay attention to the word for "fate" that Hektor uses in the example just quoted. The μοῖρα 'portion' of an epic hero such as Hektor is not so much his destiny as preordained by the gods, as the fate allotted to him by the process of the epic tradition. For fate and tradition see Nagy 1979: 134–35, 265–68; Schein 1984: 62–64. See also Bakker 1997a on the interrelationships of fate, tradition, and temporal reference in Homer.

[25] See Martin 1989: 12–37, 231–39. See also Nagy 1996: 61, who argues that for the performer the gods and heroes actually spoke in the dactylic hexameters of the epic performance.

[26] See Tannen 1989: 98–133.

[27] The various strategies and their formulaic articulation are presented and discussed in Edwards 1970. See also Riggsby 1992, a formulaic analysis along the lines of Visser 1987, 1988, and Bakker and Fabbricotti 1991.

duced in this way is always formal, often competitive, and uttered in response (friendly or unfriendly) to a peer. Such speech, I contend, should be distinguished from speech that does not create the action of the performance but is created by it, speech that is part of epic action, as a hero's comment in a less formal situation. In the first book of the *Iliad*, for example, the speeches representing the quarrel between Achilles and Agamemnon are consistently introduced by staged epiphanies, whereas the verbal action of the two protagonists in the wake of the quarrel is introduced differently.

The quarrel itself, with its antiphonal speeches, is quintessential Iliadic action, of the same importance as the speech act of poetry itself, to be carried out by the two heroes in their full epic identity: swift-footed godlike Achilles and Agamemnon lord of men. Without the quarrel the wrath of Achilles would not have occurred, and without the wrath of Achilles the *Iliad* loses its reason for being. The immediate practical consequence of the quarrel in the story, on the other hand, the transferral of Briseïs that Agamemnon had announced, is merely the consequence of the pivotal speech events reenacted earlier. Accordingly, the direct speech accompanying the transferral is of a different order, more informal, and therefore not coded as epic. Thus it is an unstaged and epithetless Agamemnon who sends his heralds out to take Briseïs away from Achilles, and it is an equally epithetless Achilles who addresses the heralds, saying that what is happening is not their fault.[28] But it is a fully staged Achilles marked with all his epic trappings who afterwards addresses his mother to give her, as a real performer, *his* version of the quarrel:

> τὴν δὲ βαρὺ στενάχων προσέφη   and her he addressed sighing deeply,
> πόδας ὠκὺς Ἀχιλλεύς·   swift-footed Achilles
>
> (*Il.* 1.364)

The speech following this staging is of course just as fundamental as the discourse of the earlier quarrel, since Achilles' words send Thetis to Zeus to ask him to give the victory to the Trojans and to punish Agamemnon and the Greeks, thus setting the action of Achilles' wrath in motion.

Typical examples of staged founding speech include conversations between gods in which the course of events is decided on, such as the meeting of Athene and Apollo in *Il.* 7.23–42, the foundation for the action around

---

[28] *Il.* 1.318–25, 330–44.

the duel between Hektor and Aias that is to follow.[29] Unstaged speech, by contrast, is not only speech that results from or is part of founding action. It may also be speech that, if implemented, would result in action that deflects or even obviates the events of which the epics as we have them are the reenactment. Such speech is anti-action and tends for that reason not to be staged and heroically marked. Thus during Hektor's visit to the city in the sixth book of the *Iliad*,[30] all proposals made to him that, if followed, would keep him from his heroic fated course are unstaged.[31] But all the answers are made by huge Hektor of the flickering helmet,[32] in speech that is formally staged for representing Hektor in his quintessential identity as the hero who cannot escape his epic fate and death. His performances within the walls of Troy effectively counteract the proposals that might deflect him from this track. Similar is the case of Odysseus's great speech to Achilles as a member of the embassy. The speech is unstaged, not marked as the stuff that epic is made of. Indeed, if Achilles had accepted Agamemnon's proposals as voiced by Odysseus, the *Iliad* would not exist.[33] By his very rejection Achilles produces founding action, and his performance is preceded, accordingly, by a staging and a noun-epithet formula (*Il.* 9.307).[34]

[29] Even more fundamental is Zeus's speech in *Il.* 8.5–27, his formal ban on divine participation in the battle. This speech is unstaged in the grammatical sense used here, but is more fully introduced (*Il.* 8.2–4) supragrammatically. See also *Il.* 11.186–94, Zeus's announcement of the glory of Hektor as part of the Διὸς βουλή, the plan of Zeus mentioned in the proem and instigated by Achilles via Thetis in the words just quoted.

[30] Note that the visit as a whole is caused by staged action on the part of Helenos at *Il.* 6.75–76, a combination of a speech introduction and an *if not* situation (on which see below).

[31] Hekabe is unstaged at *Il.* 6.253 and asks Hektor to "stay" (258). Helen is unstaged at 343 and asks him to "come in and sit down" (354). Most important, Andromakhe is unstaged at 406 and says (431): ἀλλ' ἄγε νῦν ἐλέαιρε καὶ αὐτοῦ μίμν' ἐπὶ πύργῳ 'but come, have mercy now and stay here at the tower'.

[32] *Il.* 6.263, 359, 440.

[33] *Il.* 9.224. One line earlier, however, Odysseus is presented in a significant way (νόησε δὲ δῖος Ὀδυσσεύς 'and he took notice, godlike Odysseus', not a staging in the sense used here) at the moment when Aias nods at Phoinix to start the speechmaking. The offer of Agamemnon endangers Achilles' status in epic, and as Nagy (1992b: 324) suggests (arguing from the semantics of the verb νόησε, on which see below), Odysseus may well have this very purpose in mind. Thus we may say that the speech as such is anti-action, but that Odysseus's attempt at undermining Achilles' stature is true epic action.

[34] Notice also Agamemnon's unheroic, indeed anti-Iliadic, and therefore unstaged words ("let's go home") introduced at *Il.* 9.16, and his equally anti-Iliadic speech at *Il.* 2.110–41: the extraordinary focusing on the scepter, the profound symbol of Agamemnon's kingship, has, in light of the speech that Agamemnon produces, leaning on the scepter, the effect of an ironic anti-staging. The speech by Phoinix is staged (9.432), in contrast with Odysseus's. But this speech will have some effect, since it makes Achilles soften his intentions.

Staging and Heroic Names

Direct speech in epic, then, may be marked as the primordial action of which epic narrative is the reenactment.[35] In such cases the staging of the speaking god or hero and his or her subsequent epiphany by a noun-epithet formula is the appropriate grammatical encoding. The peculiar relation between the original speech act and its representation in the performance may be further specified: what is staged is not only the god or hero but also the name. The quintessential identity of the epic figure is matched by the appearance of a quintessential name, a significant moment in the rhythmical flow of speech, to which the previous discourse leads up. We may assume that the thematic importance of these epiphanic noun-epithet phrases has reinforced the impact of their rhythmical profile on the process by which regular metrical sequences emerge from discourse.[36] In light of the discussion of the previous chapter, this pattern of reasoning might imply that the very origin of the Homeric hexameter lies in the importance, and hence the recurrence, of the thematic bond between a noun-epithet formula and the preceding staging formula.[37] This would give the unusual existence of a verse spanning the time needed for two or more speech units a poetic or semantic motivation, and the epic heroes, especially Achilles and Odysseus, would become the creators of the hexametric discourse which enacts their *kleos.*[38]

By contrast, there are heroes for whom no noun-epithet formulas at the end of the verse exist, or no clearly established set of such formulas. In the perspective presented here this observation has more than a merely metrical importance. These heroes cannot be staged in the heroic way, nor do they have epiphanies or contribute to hexameter metrics in the way Achilles, Odysseus, Hektor, Athene, and other central characters do.[39] The Trojan

---

[35] But it should be emphasized that unstaged speech is by no means unimportant, poetically or otherwise; one need only think of Antilokhos's words to Achilles (*Il.* 18.18–21, the message of the death of Patroklos) to see that unstaged speech can have an enormous dramatic impact.

[36] See also Chapters 6 and 8, as well as Nagy 1990b: 29 (on the relation between formula/theme and meter).

[37] Cf. O'Nolan's remarks (1969: 14–17) on the possible role of noun-epithet formulas in the development of the dactylic hexameter, two of which are cited in Chapter 8 below.

[38] Kahane observes (1994: 116–17) that the names of Achilles and Odysseus (as well as those of Apollo and Athene) are almost always verse-final, characterizing this position as "a typical heroic feature" (119).

[39] This reasoning leads us into territory that has recently been explored by Kahane (1994: 135–41), in a study on the semantic significance of metrical positioning. On the basis of the

speakers Antenor and Poludamas, for example, who at different occasions try to dissuade Hektor and Paris from taking the course of action that has produced the *Iliad*,[40] have names that cannot be accommodated in noun-epithet formulas at the end of the verse and thus lack heroic staging possibilities. We may add that the negative and indignant answers of Paris and Hektor, being fatal for the Trojans but essential for the epic, are fully staged.[41]

Other, more prominent warriors have less than fully epic names as well. Aineias has an ambiguous status in Trojan society, as emphasized by the *Iliad* itself.[42] There is much to lose and nothing to win for him in the world of the *Iliad*, and his general role is apparently to share, rather than create, the action that gives him less *kleos* than he deserves. The case of Sarpedon, furthermore, whose name does not yield noun-epithet formulas, is remarkable for the insistence on godlike honor among his people, that is, epichoric hero cult after his death:[43] something desirable but less so than the *kleos* conferred by poetry in which he cannot make a staged epiphany. Neither Aineias nor Sarpedon are quite at home in the epic world of the *Iliad*, and neither of them really fits in the metrical world that constitutes its secondary action.

One might object that the different metrical behavior of Sarpedon and others is merely the consequence of the form of their names as handed down by tradition (three long syllables), and that epic discourse has to adapt itself to these intractable, atomic bits of naming. Yet it is unlikely that epic names are raw material, distinct from epic discourse; rather, the name of a hero is indissolubly connected with the discourse that enacts his *kleos*. This means that less than full heroic status on the level of meter cannot but be

---

metrical behavior of the names of Telemakhos and Patroklos, especially their absence from the final, heroic position in the verse (where Achilles and Odysseus are very much at home) Kahane argues that Telemakhos is a subordinate character, a "non-Odysseus" (137); on Patroklos see below.

[40] Antenor in *Il.* 7.347 ("let's give Helen back to Menelaos"). Poludamas in *Il.* 12.210 ("let's refrain from the battle around the ships"); *Il.* 18.249 ("let's adapt to the changed circumstances and go into the city"). Antenor's speech and Poludamas's second speech are characterized by the participle πεπνυμένος, a word of uncertain meaning, which "is seldom used of great heroes . . . but is a regular description of youthful or subordinate characters" (Hainsworth on *Od.* 8.388, in Heubeck et al. 1988: 373; cf. Kahane 1994; 137).

[41] *Il.* 7.354–55; 12.230; 18.284.

[42] *Il.* 13.459–61; 20.178–83. See Nagy 1979: 265–75, on extra-Iliadic poetic traditions for Aineias.

[43] *Il.* 16.453–57. See Nagy 1990b: 122–42. On Sarpedon in general, see Janko 1992: 370–73.

related to less than heroic stature in the epic events themselves: whoever proposes what is from the point of view of the *Iliad* non-action cannot be expected to be the bearer of a stageable noun-epithet formula. And whoever has no such epic status cannot be expected to determine the epic course of events.

There is one exception that proves the rule: Patroklos. This character behaves very flexibly in Homeric hexametric discourse (partly due to the heteroclitic nature of his name), but his name is never staged, even though a verse-final noun-epithet formula would not have been impossible.[44] The less than epic stature of Patroklos seems to account for this: Patroklos is the character whose actions are preordained and determined by forces stronger than himself.[45] Yet at various points Patroklos cannot help doing what constitutes the *Iliad*, in the most direct way. In spite of himself, Patroklos makes some crucial founding speeches whose ambiguous status is reflected in the unusual way in which they are staged. Once trapped in the chain of events of which our *Iliad* is the poetic representation, Patroklos makes what is one of the most crucial speeches of the *Iliad* from the point of view of epic action: his plea to Achilles to send him instead into the battle, wearing Achilles's armor. The speech is staged in an unusual way. Instead of the normal epiphany of the character, Patroklos is directly addressed by the performer:[46]

τὸν δὲ βαρὺ στενάχων προσέφης,   and him deeply sighing you addressed
Πατρόκλεες ἱππεῦ ·   Patroklos horseman

(*Il.* 16.20)

The metrical explanation that is usually adduced for the apostrophe is correct in spite of itself:[47] there is no alternative for the vocative expression.

[44] The noun-epithet formula Πάτροκλος ἀμύμων 'blameless Patroklos' has been suggested (e.g., Parry 1972: 10). The epithet ἀμύμων (on whose enigmatic meaning see Parry 1973; Lowenstam 1993: 49–52) is actually applied to Patroklos (*Il.* 17.379), adding significance to the absence of a noun-epithet phrase formed by it.

[45] Kahane characterizes Patroklos (1994: 139–41) as a silent hero who is denied "the privilege of speech," and who is "as close as the epic will ever approach to describing an anti-hero." In Bakker 1997a Patroklos is characterized as the ultimate νήπιος, not in the sense of "fool," but as the character who "is conditioned by the inherent limits of human knowledge." In other words, he is a character who cannot look beyond the proto-action in which he finds himself, a fact that is reflected in the secondary action that is poetry.

[46] See also *Il.* 16.744, 843. For more on apostrophe of characters in Homer, see Kahane 1994: 107–13, 153–55 with more literature; Bakker 1993b: 22–23; on the apostrophe of Patroklos at *Il.* 16.787, see Bakker 1997a.

[47] On the metrical explanation, see Matthews 1980.

But rather than an incidental gap in the formulaic system leading to a suppletive paradigm, this absence seems poetically motivated. Patroklos is not a normal hero, and the direct address does not *effect* an epiphany, it *presupposes* one: Patroklos is already present in the performance for the performer to address him. Patroklos, the Iliadic character who is most out of touch with the first action of the *Iliad*, enjoys a special status in its secondary action: he is a listener in the performance like ourselves.[48]

Plotting the *Iliad*

Fundamental proto-action that consists in speech may be staged, as I argued, but the god or hero in question need not be new to the stage. In fact, the very nature of the context in which the speech is presented (formal, competitive, with antagonistic peers as audience and interlocutors) often requires that the epic speaker be already on the scene.[49] This is different in the case of staged action other than speech. Here the epiphany tends to be a sudden first appearance, the creation of presence out of absence, of activity out of inactivity.

As we have seen, many staging formulas in ongoing narrative display the same internal structure as speech introductions: they consist of a pronoun in an oblique case (e.g., *tòn dè* 'and him', *toùs dè* 'and them') followed by a verb which denotes perception as well as the mental activity resulting from it, most often the verb *enóēse*:

τὼ δὲ πεσόντ᾽ ἐλέησε	and them as they fell he pitied
τὸν δ᾽ ὡς οὖν ἐνόησε	and him when s/he saw
τὸν δὲ ἰδὼν ἐνόησε/ἐλέησε	and seeing him he thought/pitied

These stagings are clauses that, surely enough, report an act of perception or commiseration, but it is important to repeat that literal meaning is less important than function in context, which is the staging of an epiphany. Staging is the function to which the relational function of the pronoun and

---

[48] See Frontisi-Ducroux 1986: 23–25 on the interchangeability of Patroklos as audience of Achilles (e.g., *Il.* 9.184–91) with the audience of the *Iliad*. See also Nagy 1990a: 202; 1996: 72.

[49] Notice, however, that speech action may be a first appearance in an assembly scene. In such cases the epiphanic naming of the hero takes up the entire line, as is possible for some characters. See, e.g., *Il.* 1.102: τοῖσι δ᾽ ἀνέστη ‖ ἥρως Ἀτρεΐδης εὐρὺ κρείων Ἀγαμέμνων 'and to them he rose, ‖ hero Atreus's son, wide-ruling Agamemnon'. Cf. *Il.* 1.69 (Kalkhas); 2.77 (Nestor); 7.355 (Paris), 366 (Priamos); *Od.* 2.225 (Mentor).

the verb is subservient:[50] these elements provide a link between the epiphany of the new character and the previous action, or better, the protagonist(s) of that previous action. With the pronoun as starting point,[51] the staging moves via the verb to the epiphany proper, the noun-epithet formula.

Perhaps the most significant occurrence of a staging that features the verb *enóēse* is Achilles' sudden appearance in Book 11, at the moment when he, being absent from the fighting, takes an interest in the wounded Makhaon, who is transported by Nestor from the battle:

‖ Νέστορα δ' ἐκ πολέμοιο φέρον	and Nestor they bore away from the battle,
ǀ Νηλήϊαι ἵπποι	the horses of Neleus,
‖ ἰδρῶσαι,	sweating,
ἦγον δὲ Μαχάονα,	and they carried Makhaon,
ποιμένα λαῶν.	shepherd of the people,
‖ τὸν δὲ ἰδὼν ἐνόησε	and seeing him he took notice,
ǀ ποδάρκης δῖος Ἀχιλλεύς·	swift-footed godlike Achilles.

(Il. 11.597–99)

Achilles' sudden and unexpected appearance has momentous consequences: the *Iliad* would not exist if Achilles had not taken notice. The immediate consequence of Achilles' act of perception is a second epiphany, this time of Patroklos, who is summoned out of his tent by Achilles:[52]

ǀ ὁ δὲ κλισίηθεν ἀκούσας	and he hearing from his tent,
‖ ἔκμολεν ἶσος Ἄρηϊ,	he came out, similar to Ares,
ǀκακοῦ δ' ἄρα οἱ πέλεν ἀρχή.	and it was the beginning of evil for him.
‖ τὸν πρότερος προσέειπε	him (=Achilles) he first addressed,
ǀ Μενοιτίου ἄλκιμος υἱός·	the valiant son of Menoitios:
‖ τίπτέ με κικλήσκεις, Ἀχιλεῦ;	why do you call me, Achilles?
τί δέ σε χρεὼ ἐμεῖο;	what need of me [comes to] you?

(Il. 11.603–6)

Patroklos cannot make a normal heroic appearance with his own name, and so an ersatz noun-epithet phrase has to be used, presenting him as "the

---

[50] Cf. De Jong, who discusses (1987: 102–7) what she calls "perception passages" (including the stagings analyzed here) as "embedded focalization," expressing the point of view of a character. She does, however, recognize (106–7) what I call the staging and relational potential of perception.

[51] See Chapter 5 above.

[52] See also *Il.* 11.837, another significant speech by Patroklos, on which see Bakker 1997a.

valiant son of Menoitios." His staging is unusual in that it is not so much the poet who stages him as Achilles himself: in listening to Achilles Patroklos creates the *Iliad*, because Achilles sends him to identify the person in Nestor's chariot, and as a result, Patroklos heeds the advice of Nestor and eventually enters the battle as a substitute for Achilles.

In this connection we note that the verb used to stage Achilles, *enóēse* 'took notice', may have an epic meaning that goes beyond mere seeing.[53] Or more precisely, this meaning derives from the contexts in which it is used, and crucially, from the audience's familiarity with those contexts. Within the context of a staging formula, the cognitive act *noêsai*, as performed in the mythic past, seems to be related to what the poet does in the present: having mental activity that reconstitutes the epic tradition, even if the mental contribution to the course of epic events is made unwittingly.[54] Achilles is here the author of the epic action.[55]

The course of events leading up to this important double epiphany has been carefully charted and grammatically encoded in a network of epiphanies that helps the audience find a way through these crucial moments, which serve as the groundwork for much of the action of the *Iliad*.[56] It is staged action in which Paris, appearing in full epic form (*Aléksandros, Helénēs pósis ēükómoio* 'Alexandros, husband of Helen with the fair hair') wounds Makhaon; and it is Nestor with all his epic trappings (*Gerḗnios hippóta Néstōr* 'Gerenian horseman Nestor') who takes up the task of transporting the wounded Makhaon out of the battle, in order to be noticed by Achilles.[57]

There is a second significant wounding in this part of the narrative, equally connected with the consequences of Achilles' epiphany. When

---

[53] I would therefore not call the staging formula τὸν δὲ ἰδὼν ἐνόησε "prolix" or merely resulting "from the interplay of formulas" τὸν δὲ ἰδὼν and ἐνόησε in this position in the line (Hainsworth 1993: 287). The two verbs of perception are not synonymous.

[54] Suggestive venues here are offered by Frame, who insists (1988: 28–30) on the etymological connection of νοέω and νόστος (root *nes- 'return to light and life', i.e., the fulfillment of epic *kleos*). Ruijgh (1967: 371–72) proposes "save" as the original meaning for the root *nes- (corresponding to Gothic *nasjan* 'save'), citing Latin *servo* 'conserve', 'observe').

[55] Cf. the words of Zeus, the author of all authors, at *Il.* 15.64–65: ὁ δ' ἀνστήσει ὃν ἑταῖρον ‖ Πάτροκλον 'and he (=Achilles) will set up his companion, ‖ Patroklos', using terminology (ἀνστήσει 'will set up') that is not too far removed from the term "staging" used here.

[56] On the structural and thematic properties of this part of the *Iliad*, see also Schadewaldt 1966: 74–79.

[57] *Il.* 11.505, 516. Nestor is set in motion by a speech of Idomeneus, a hero with a choriamb-shaped (– ∪ ∪ –) and therefore unstageable name. The verse introducing this speech (*Il.* 11.510: αὐτίκα δ' Ἰδομενεὺς προσεφώνεε Νέστορα δῖον 'and immediately Idomeneus addressed him, godlike Nestor', a case of type 9 in Edwards 1970: 15) has rather the effect of staging the addressee.

Patroklos encounters the wounded Eurupulos, he is detained and kept from making his fatal appearance in the battle until Book 16. This wounding thus has considerable importance for the narrative structure of the repeated action that is our *Iliad*, and it comes as no surprise that the appearance of Eurupulos is staged; equally staged is the act of wounding him, performed again by Paris. The staging formula used in both cases is *tòn d' hōs oûn enóēse* 'and him when he saw', a regularly occurring phrase with the verb *enóēse(n)* in the same metrical position. The first time, this phrase links Eurupulos to the beleaguered Aias:

‖ τὸν δ᾽ ὡς οὖν ἐνόησ᾽	and him when he saw,
	Εὐαίμονος ἀγλαὸς υἱὸς	radiant son of Euaimon
‖ Εὐρύπυλος	Eurupulos
πυκινοῖσι βιαζόμενον βελέεσσι,	overwhelmed by the density of the spears

(*Il.* 11.575–76)

Like Patroklos, Eurupulos is not a stageable hero, but the tradition has provided him too with a periphrastic phrase of the same rhythmical structure as a noun-epithet formula, to be used whenever staging is motivated. The second time (11.581) the *enóēse(n)* formula stages Paris as "godlike Alexandros" (*Aléksandros theoeidḕs*). His wounding of Eurupulos is an act with far-reaching consequences for the action of the *Iliad*. The appearance of Patroklos, then, and the path to be taken by him in the course of the narrative, leading him from Achilles via Nestor and Eurupulos back to Achilles and to his death, appears to be carefully plotted by a series of stagings and epiphanies.

Nor is Paris's wounding of Eurupulos an isolated phenomenon; it is part of a series of woundings by the Trojan archer,[58] each of which is staged.[59] And this series in its turn is part of the wounding and retreat of the major Greek heroes, which itself sets the scene for Patroklos's fated heroic appearance.[60] Agamemnon's wounding somewhat earlier, for example, is performed by Koön, an otherwise insignificant figure who contributes in his

[58] See Hainsworth 1993: 267.

[59] Apart from the wounding of Eurupulos just mentioned, there is the wounding of Makhaon (*Il.* 11.505–6, see above) and of Diomedes (*Il.* 11.369), in each of which Paris features as Ἑλένης πόσις ἠϋκόμοιο 'husband of Helen with the fair hair'.

[60] One knows that the wounding of the Greek chiefs (except for the Aiantes, who remain active throughout the battle of the ships) plays an important role in Nestor's advice to Patroklos, as well as in the subsequent plea of the latter to Achilles to send him into the battle in his stead; see *Il.* 11.659–62 (=16.24–27).

own small way to the action of the *Iliad*, paying for it with his life. He is staged for his one-time heroic performance by the *tòn d' hōs oûn enóēse* formula, which sets him up vis-à-vis his opponent:

τὸν δ' ὡς οὖν ἐνόησε	and him when he saw
Κόων, ἀριδείκετος ἀνδρῶν,	Koön (nom.), glorious among men
πρεσβυγενὴς 'Αντηνορίδης,	the firstborn son of Antenor

(Il. 11.248–49)

Typologically, this staging is the moment at which the hero whose *aristeia* or finest hour is underway meets the warrior who wounds him and puts him temporarily out of action.[61] The structural importance of this formulaic event is sufficient motivation for the staging of Koön, who by seeing Agamemnon is marked as one of the authors (albeit a very minor one) of the Iliadic story.[62] Other instances of the *tòn d' hōs oûn enóēse* formula consist of cognitive activity on the part of the gods, in moments that lift the narrative from the human to the divine plane, where founding speech action is to take place.[63]

By contrast, acts of perception that do not involve a staging and an epiphany do not so much involve a new appearance of a hero as a switch to a hero that was mentioned earlier in the narrative, an operation discussed in Chapter 5. The character most often involved in this kind of moment is Hektor, who is almost continuously on stage and hence is a participant to whom the narrator must often return:

"Εκτωρ δ' ὡς ἐνόησ'	and Hektor when he saw
'Αγαμέμνονα νόσφι κιόντα,	Agamemnon as he was withdrawing,
Τρωσί τε καὶ Λυκίοισιν	to the Trojans and the Lukians
ἐκέκλετο μακρὸν ἀΰσας·	he shouted with a great voice

(Il. 11.284–85)

---

[61] See Krischer 1971: 23–24, 31, for this "formal convention" of Greek epic.

[62] Identical are the circumstances under which Pandaros is staged as the wounder of Diomedes during the *aristeia* of the latter; as in the case of Eurupulos and Patroklos, an epiphany with a periphrastic formula is used (*Il.* 5.95: τὸν δ' ὡς οὖν ἐνόησε Λυκάονος ἀγλαὸς υἱός 'and him when he saw, radiant son of Lukaon'). See also the wounding of Hektor in Book 14, where Aias is formally staged as the wounder, even though he is already on the scene (*Il.* 14.409: τὸν μὲν ἔπειτ' ἀπιόντα μέγας Τελαμώνιος Αἴας 'and him when he left, huge Aias son of Telamon [hit him]').

[63] *Il.* 5.711; 7.17. In the former case the epiphany is followed by speech action (on the part of Hera) that literally spells out its founding nature: "If we do not intervene now, Menelaos will not go home after having sacked Troy."

This is a topic switch, not an epiphany, and Hektor's subsequent speech ("the best man of the Greeks withdraws; now Zeus is going to grant me the victory") is not so much epic proto-action as the consequence of Zeus's message to Hektor.[64] In some other cases there is a new appearance, but the character has a name that makes him unstageable.[65]

Reversal Passages

Finally, we discuss a category of epiphanies that make explicit what has so far remained implicit: the story of the *Iliad* would not be the same, or would not exist at all, if a character had not in some cases done what he or she did. I am referring to what has been called the "if not situation" or "reversal passage."[66] The reversal passage is the articulation of a moment at which a hero or god crucially intervenes at the very last moment when an important epic figure is in mortal danger, or when the course of events threatens to stray off course. The intervening hero is thus not merely the savior of a life, but more importantly, the agent who is responsible for the epic tradition at this point. Such a crucial appearance on the epic stage cannot be better reenacted than with a staged epiphany. One of the more typical examples is the end of the encounter between Achilles and Aineias:[67]

a. ἔνθα κεν Αἰνείας μὲν   and then, Aineias,
b. ἐπεσσύμενον βάλε πέτρῳ   he would have hit him in his onrush with a
                                                  stone,

---

[64] *Il.* 11.187–94 (cf. 202–9), Zeus's message transmitted by Iris to Hektor: "When Agamemnon is wounded I will give you the victory, till dusk sets in." Other cases, all involving Hektor: *Il.* 5.590; 11.343; 15.422; 16.818; 20.419; 22.136. On topic switches see Chapter 5.

[65] See above. Typical instances are Sarpedon's and Aineias's appearance in the battle by way of perception (e.g., *Il.* 16.419–20: Σαρπηδὼν δ᾽ ὡς οὖν ἴδ᾽ ἀμιτροχίτωνας ἑταίρους ‖ χέρσ᾽ ὕπο Πατρόκλοιο Μενοιτιάδαο δαμέντας 'and Sarpedon when he saw his comrades with the unbelted tunic ‖ die under the hands of Patroklos son of Menoitios'; *Il.* 5.166: τὸν δ᾽ ἴδεν Αἰνείας ἀλαπάζοντα στίχας ἀνδρῶν 'and him Aineias saw, creating havoc among the ranks of men'). Is it coincidence that in these cases not ἐνόησε 'took notice' but the more neutral ἴδε 'saw' has been used?

[66] Cf. Fenik 1968: 175; De Jong 1987: 68–81; Lang 1989; Morrison 1992: 61; Nesselrath 1992: 1–27. See also Chapter 4 above on the use of καί in this type of passage.

[67] Notice the evidential particle ἄρ(α) in the protasis (unit g), stressing the factual nature of the statement, but at the same time marking it as a conclusion drawn from visual evidence (see Bakker 1993b: 15–23; 1997a).

c. ἢ κόρυθ᾽ ἠὲ σάκος,   on his helmet or on his shield,

d. τό οἱ ἤρκεσε λυγρὸν ὄλεθρον,   which would have kept bitter death from him,

e. τὸν δέ κε Πηλεΐδης   and him Peleus's son,

f. σχεδὸν ἄορι θυμὸν ἀπηύρα,   he would have taken his life from nearby with
                            the sword,

g. εἰ μὴ ἄρ᾽ ὀξὺ νόησε   if he had not seen sharply,

h. <u>Ποσειδάων ἐνοσίχθων·</u>   <u>Poseidon earth-shaker.</u>

(Il. 20.288–91)

In linguistic terms, this passage reverses the familiar order of the counterfactual condition. The protasis, reshaped here to function as a staging formula (unit g), does not precede but follows its apodosis (units a–f), and it is not affirmative but negative. The construction, with its vivid verbal component *oksù nóēse* 'he saw sharply', thus produces what might be called a hyperfactual statement:[68] Poseidon intervenes to prevent the course of events from becoming what can from the point of view of the epic tradition only be anti-action, the black hole of what could have happened but did not. The death of Aineias at the hands of Achilles would have been in conflict with known and accepted poetic traditions; in Homeric parlance, it would have been "beyond fate" (*hupèr moîran*).[69] It is at the moments when this nonpast, the reversal and denial of epic *kleos*, is most visible that epic tradition can most clearly reassert its own reality and celebrate the *kleos* of the figure to whom this is due. The presence of this figure, coded by a noun-epithet formula, gains extra relief in contrast with the action that he or she has just prevented.[70]

[68] See also the useful formulation of Lang 1989: 6: "An affirmative protasis contemplates a possibility which was not realized, while a negative protasis reports what happened to prevent an unexpected result." See also De Jong 1987: 68–69.

[69] *Il.* 20.336, in Poseidon's own words to Aineias; cf. *Il.* 20.302–5. At *Il.* 2.155 and *Od.* 5.436–37, a beyond fate phrase is actually used in the reversal passage.

[70] It seems preferable, therefore, to take fate in Homer as what happened in the world of myth (whether or not the event is covered by the *Iliad*), rather than as some causality inherent in the epic events. Thus the "fatality" of an epic event is due to the certainty of its performance in the present (see Bakker 1997a). It also seems preferable to see the poetics of reversal passages as reinforcing the tradition of what happened, rather than challenging it. The challenge of a consciously composing individual poet (Morrison 1992; 1993) would lead us again into the anachronistic territory of the opposition between traditionality and originality. And finally it seems preferable to see tradition as an *intention* on the part of poets and performers rather than as an inherent property of any discourse or text (see Bakker 1995: 105; 1997a; Bauman 1992: 128). This conception of tradition and traditionality could even include individual attempts by performers to reinforce the tradition, e.g., by including a reversal passage. Such attempts would count as original by our standards, though not by the performers' own.

Poseidon's epiphany is staged by the most characteristic staging formula *ei mè ár' oksù nóēse* 'if s/he had not seen sharply', which features the same important verb *(e)nóēse* that we saw earlier; the formula is followed by a noun-epithet formula in all of its occurrences.[71] The noun-epithet formula thus occurs in a grammatical context which in its turn is motivated by the preceding counterfactual apodosis. That discourse segment, marked by the Aeolic irrealis particle *ke(n)*, is no less a staging device for the epiphany of the savior than the *if not* staging formula proper. Noun-epithet formulas, accordingly, tend to be used even when the more explicit staging formula *ei mè ár' oksù nóēse* is absent.[72]

The epithet tends *not* to occur, on the other hand, in those cases where the occurrence of the event prevented in the nick of time would *not* have significantly or unacceptably changed the course of events. In the battle over Patroklos's body, for example, Hektor and Automedon would have attacked each other with swords, if the two Aiantes had not intervened:[73] the event prevented is not a non-event, and its prevention not an act that is essential for the course of events of the *Iliad* to take place.[74] The action of the Aiantes, therefore, is not a staged epiphany.

Plotting in the *Odyssey*

The reader may have noticed that thus far examples from the *Odyssey* have been conspicuously absent. There is a good reason: staged epiphany

---

[71] *Il.* 3.374; 5.311–12, 680; 8.91, 132; 20.291. Cf. also *Od.* 23.242; Hes. *Theog.* 838 (a juncture at which the fate of no less than the whole world is at stake). Πατὴρ ἀνδρῶν τε θεῶν τε 'father of men and gods' at *Il.* 8.91 is not strictly speaking a noun-epithet formula, but it has similar cultic and epiphanic potential.

[72] E.g., *Il.* 5.389; 6.73–76 (the merger of a reversal passage and a speech introduction); 7.106–7; 8.218; 11.505; 12.292; 16.700; 17.71; 18.166; 21.212 (reversal passage and speech introduction), 545. Not all the noun-epithet formulas in these cases, however, are heroically located at the end of the line (e.g., 16.700; 21.545) and not all interventions are equally crucial, but the use of epithets under less epiphanic and crucial circumstances is inherent in their being, or becoming, grammatical. See Chapter 8.

[73] *Il.* 17.530–31. Cf. 23.491, 733; 24.713.

[74] See De Jong's (1987: 75–77) and Morrison's (1993: 65) category of "less dramatic situations." Lang (1989: 9) makes a useful distinction between a type A ("something *contrary to fact* would have happened, had not someone acted to prevent it"); a type B ("something *destined to happen later but contrary to present fact* would have happened now, had not someone acted to prevent it"); and a type C ("some action or passion would have *continued*, had not someone put a stop to it")—emphases added. Noun-epithet formulas tend to occur in type A, the pure reversal passages.

occurs much less often here than in the *Iliad*, except for the introduction to speech.[75] This is not the appropriate moment to go into the issue in great detail, but we may briefly try out some reasons. The narrative of the *Odyssey* is much less suited to the kinds of staging I have discussed: their relational nature makes them more at home in Iliadic battle description, where progress on the path of speech is a matter of the appearance and reappearance of warriors. A natural method of continuation is to take off from one character as a means to activate another, and so to effect the juxtaposition of heroic opponents that is the proper function of the staging formula. The *Odyssey*, by contrast, is not so much description as narrative in the modern sense of the term, involving a more limited number of epic agents, and it accordingly has less need for staged interaction between agents.[76]

But the reason might also be a deeper one. In the poetics of the *Iliad*, as I have argued, the epic tale is secondary action, rebehaved behavior, the re-creation of the key events in the mythical past. And from the standpoint of the Iliadic heroes, as they engage in their proto-action, the poetic representation of what they do (and so the continuation of their *kleos*) is the work of future generations: it is the songs of the future that make their present action meaningful. The *Odyssey*, by contrast, presents its very action *as already in the future*: only Odysseus can listen to poetry that celebrates his own *kleos*. The *Odyssey* does not report action that will result in *kleos*; its very action is *kleos*, the working and power of words. And those words are not necessarily conceived of as unfailing signs pointing to the mythical past, but as behavior that is fascinating or treacherous in its own way.[77] The *Odyssey*, then, seems too conscious of its own medium to be interested in seeing itself as the reenactment of mythical proto-action, and in ritually staging the prime agents of that action.

The difference between the poetics of the two traditions seems to be reflected in one staging formula that, even though it does occur in the

---

[75] See Lang 1989: 22–23, on the distribution of reversal passages in the Homeric poems; of the eleven occurrences in the *Odyssey*, four occur in Iliadic contexts (narratives about Menelaos, Aias, and the Trojan War). The use of the τὸν δ' ὡς οὖν ἐνόησε formula in the *Odyssey* is discussed in the next chapter.

[76] On description vs. narrative, see Chapter 4.

[77] See Segal 1994: 89, in an essay bearing directly on the issues presented here: "The great deeds of the past . . . are now especially designated as a part of heroic song qua song. Their 'objective' existence as unquestioned events that the audience accepts when it is under the 'spell' of the poet's magic . . . yields momentarily to an awareness of the form that makes possible that spell."

Iliad,[78] seems primarily an Odyssean ploy. Again the verb *enóēse* is the prime feature:

> ἔνθ' αὖτ' ἄλλ' ἐνόησε   and then she saw/planned something else

This staging is *transitional* rather than *relational*: it effects an episode boundary in the tale, rather than an interaction between two protagonists. The character staged in this way, who in the *Odyssey* is always female and usually Athene,[79] does not, as a participant in the epic proto-action, engage in interaction with some other participant. Rather, she manipulates the action as an *external agent*, playing a divine trick in order to steer the course of events in a desired direction. For instance, Athene drugs characters into sleep and appears before a character in the shape of someone else, thus making an epiphany *represented within the epic tale*, rather than one that is *effected by the performance*.

Only once does her action seem to come close to an intervention such as we saw in the reversal passages discussed above:[80] when Nausikaa and her maids are at the point of leaving the beach, Athene intervenes:

> ἔνθ' αὖτ' ἄλλ' ἐνόησε   then she thought of something different
> θεὰ γλαυκῶπις Ἀθήνη,   goddess owl-eyed Athene

(*Od.* 6.112)

Athene wakes up Odysseus in order for him to meet the girl and thus contributes further to his return (*nóstos*). The important difference from the reversal passages discussed above, however, is that Athene's intervention takes place in a situation that she has created herself, having put the idea of going to the beach in Nausikaa's mind.[81] She does not react to circumstances as Iliadic gods in reversal passages, she creates them. Athene, in short, is a manipulator, not a participant. She appears in the course of

---

[78] Two times at close quarters (*Il.* 23.140, 193), Achilles being the hero staged on both occasions.

[79] For Athene (θεὰ γλαυκῶπις Ἀθήνη 'owl-eyed goddess Athene'), see *Od.* 2.382, 393; 4.795; 6.112; 18.187; 23.344; Helen (Ἐλένη Διὸς ἐκγεγαυῖα 'Helen born from Zeus'), 4.219; Penelope (περίφρων Πηνελόπεια 'very thoughtful Penelope'), 16.409. Twice the same idea is used while no staging occurs: 5.382 (Athene); 6.251 (Nausikaa).

[80] In one other case the *if not* staging formula actually occurs, with ἄλλ(ο) replacing ὀξύ (*Od.* 23.242): εἰ μὴ ἄρ' ἄλλ' ἐνόησε θεὰ γλαυκῶπις Ἀθήνη 'if she had not seen/planned something else, goddess owl-eyed Athene').

[81] *Od.* 6.21–40.

events, not in the context of the performance. And so her epiphany is a narrative device rather than a celebratory moment.

The occurrence of noun-epithet formulas and staging formulas that are not epiphanic in the sense used in this chapter, however, is not always a matter of the differences between the poetics of the *Iliad* and the *Odyssey*. In either poem, noun-epithet formulas frequently occur outside the contexts reenacting the moments at which the survival of the epic tradition is at stake. This does not invalidate the interpretations offered in the preceding pages; rather, it says something about the grammaticality of thematically important phrases. To appreciate fully the mechanism involved here, we consider in the next chapter a similar phenomenon in the use of ordinary language. After this discussion we will be better equipped to deal with the use of epithets in the Homeric grammar of poetry.

CHAPTER 8

The Grammar of Poetry

Don't tell your friends about your indigestion:
"How are you!" is a greeting, not a question.
—Arthur Guiterman, *A Poet's Proverbs*

In the previous chapter we saw that noun-epithet formulas, uttered within the specific context of their staging formula, constitute an important speech ritual, with a meaning that exceeds the propositional content of a phrase "x saw/answered y." The speech ritual is a matter of special speech in that it pertains specifically to the performance as the reenactment of the heroic events from the past. Important aspects of noun-epithet formulas, however, are left unaccounted for in this discussion. These can be summed up by the observation that the noun-epithet formula is not only uttered within a context; it also constitutes a context, a metrical one that is defined with respect to the metrical period and its recurrence in the Homeric performance. In the present chapter I offer a metrical discussion of the noun-epithet formula, which complements the semantic and thematic one of the previous chapter.

The relation between phrases and meter takes us back to Chapter 6. There I argued that meter as a rhetorical strategy may emphasize or otherwise manipulate the typical segmentation of the spoken medium. The rhythmical, prosodic features of intonation units may become regularized to the point that they become metrical. So meter emerges from discourse, as I argued, but at some point it becomes so rigid as to constitute a structure in itself, regulating the flow of speech. The shift from meter as nascent and emergent to meter as a structure in its own right implies a parallel shift in perspective on the Homeric epithet. In the previous chapter, where staged epiphany was at the center of the discussion, the focus was not even on the epithet as such and its meaning, but on the noun-epithet formula as a whole, of which the epithet is an integral part. In the present chapter we will be viewing epithets as separate elements that can be added to a name or omitted. This different conception and use of epithets is occasioned, I argue, by the development of meter from regularized speech rhythm to poetic, structuring principle.

As in the previous chapters I start from the intonation unit of speech. Viewing noun-epithet formulas as stylized intonation units, we note that metrical expansion may apply both to the internal structure of units as they are defined with respect to the metrical period and to the way in which they relate to each other. Conditioned by the contexts of meter, an epithet may expand a noun or name, and the combination of the epithet with the name as one unit may expand the idea expressed by another unit—a phenomenon I discussed in Chapter 5 as "addition" and "framing." Within the context of meter I shall speak of expanding phraseology as material that is *peripheral* with respect to a given *nucleus*. On the level of the single intonation unit or formula a nucleus can be equated with the "essential idea" of Parry's definition of the formula;[1] but it may also be the framing unit that serves as starting point for the unit(s) to follow, this time defined not only as cognitive but also as metrical moments.

Peripheral elements constitute the formulaic element in Homeric metrical diction, in the strong sense of the formulaic system proposed by Parry and Lord.[2] We only have to look at the epithets for, say, Odysseus to see that they are all of a different length, and so economical in Parry's sense. But the metrically conditioned deployment of peripheries is merely the area where the stylization of speech comes to be defined in terms of meter rather than vice versa, without its constituting Homeric discourse as such. Formulaic peripheries are the tip of an iceberg, and as such they are not merely inevitable stopgaps or traditional formulas that serve the purpose of versification. Peripheral elements are the most extreme, grammatical case of the expansion phenomena I discussed in Chapter 5. Just as a framing unit may be uttered not for its own sake but to accommodate the description that is to follow, so it is the periphery, not the nucleus, that constitutes the really essential idea—it verbalizes the detail that is the concern of epic

---

[1] Parry 1971: 13, 272. See also Chapter 1 above, as well as the discussion of Parry's definition in Bakker 1988: 152–64.

[2] See Chapter 1 above, as well as Bakker 1995.

discourse. To put this aesthetic of expansion in perspective, let us now turn for the last time to the phenomenon of recurrence in ordinary speech.

Routinization and Deroutinization

The presence of formulas in a language or idiom is obviously a factor conducive to repetition in the discourses conducted in that language. In line with the argument of Chapter 7, however, in which I suggested that linguistic expressions be viewed as behaviors rather than as things, we may also reverse the statement: formulas are not only a source for repetition, but also a consequence of certain recurrent contexts in which a given expression is required. The result of such recurrence may be routinization: within one's total behavior a given way of expression may prove so useful as a method of coping with a recurrent speech situation that it becomes standardized, serving as the model for future expressions to be uttered under the same circumstances. The routinization may even increase to the point at which the expression comes to be used in situations that are merely similar, not identical, to the original context. In such cases the original meaning of the phrase may come to be bleached, by the loss of one or more features proper to the original context.[3]

We saw in Chapter 6 that what is involuntary has a natural counterpart in deliberate enhancement: the segmentation of speech that is due to cognitive constraints was shown to be stylized by rhythm. In the same way the routine or idiomatic utterance of given expressions in ordinary speech is balanced by an opposite phenomenon: the tendency to use routinized, idiomatic phrases for new purposes. In terms that have been used in the study of grammar, one might speak of a process of *deroutinization* as a counterpart of *routinization*.[4] This tendency to deroutinize certain ways of expression may be called innovation, not in the sense that original and

---

[3] This is what I have discussed elsewhere (Bakker 1988: 14–18, 239–65, 273–74) as the use of a linguistic item outside its "prototypical" use in the original context. The principle of prototypicality derives from the study of how people create and experience categories (Rosch 1973; 1978) and has been applied to the study of linguistic categories such as noun or verb (e.g., Hopper and Thompson 1984; Givón 1984–91: 12–23) as well as of the lexicon (e.g., Geeraerts 1988). The idea of routinization, furthermore, can be applied not just to the utterance of phrases but also to the system of the language itself, grammar being the process by which certain phrases become grammatical by constant recurrence. On this process of grammaticalization, see Heine et al. 1991; Hopper and Traugott 1993; cf. Bakker 1995: 106–8.

[4] See Hopper and Traugott 1993: 65.

unique expressions are produced for which no model exists yet, but that new things are done with old means. In this sense, the deroutinization of expressions and constructions in order not to have to make new phrases is a matter of simplicity or "economy," a term to which Parry's technical usage lends a special significance.

As far as recurrence in speech is concerned, then, we may distinguish three categories or stages: (1) a formative stage, in which a given expression comes to serve a function in certain contexts; (2) a routinization stage, in which the expression, now an idiom, is uttered under circumstances that are in part different from those for which it was originally devised; and (3) a deroutinization stage, in which the expression comes to serve a new function. These three categories will serve as a general framework for a discussion of noun-epithet formulas, to which we now turn.

The Grammar of Poetry

It is clear that meter will have a large role to play when we try to study the recurrence of Homeric expressions along the lines just sketched. The question is exactly what role. The influence of meter was formulated by Parry, as we saw in Chapter 1, in terms of formulaic systematicity, extension, and economy. Following this lead, Lord described the influence of meter as a grammar of poetry: "In studying the patterns and systems of oral narrative verse we are in reality observing the 'grammar' of the poetry, a grammar superimposed, as it were, on the grammar of the language concerned. Or, to alter the image, we find a special grammar within the grammar of the language, necessitated by the versification."[5]

It is true enough that the verse necessitates certain patterns and regularities, but it is equally true, as I argued above,[6] that meter is not an external constraint, independent of discourse. In fact, meter is conditioned by certain phrases just as much as it is itself a conditioning factor, and we might see its relation to the stylized speech units of epic discourse as reciprocally defining: phrases confer their rhythmical and prosodic properties on meter, after which they become metrical, part of the system that is meter and occurring within the contexts created by that system. Noun-epithet formulas are a particularly clear example of this phenomenon, as is

[5] Lord 1960: 35–36.
[6] See Chapters 6 and 7.

pointed out by Kevin O'Nolan in an article on this feature of heroic narrative:[7]

> Much of the examination of formulas in Homer seems to assume a fixed dactylic hexameter into which the poet-composer must fit his various formulas like so many building bricks. The fact seems to be that epithet formulas are a feature of heroic storytelling, not simply of epic hexameter. It must be obvious that these formulas of their nature have a slow organic growth and to assume that this slow growth took place in the context of an established hexameter verse is unreasonable. . . . The hexameter cannot have sprung fully fledged into existence but is likely to have developed . . . from a prototype which had a fixed tail-end and a free fore-part. One might imagine a sort of creeping paralysis of versification starting at the line end. The preponderance of epithet nouns at that point suggests that that feature of heroic storytelling helped to develop and mould the hexameter.

The exact reconstruction of the origin of the hexameter cannot be our concern here. What is of interest is that the hexameter, as the rhetorical strategy discussed in Chapter 6, was not always there, and that the thematically important noun-epithet phrases have, diachronically, contributed more than other phrases to the emergence of meter. Achilles, Odysseus, and the other major figures of epic have helped, via their names, to shape the epic verse, a medium that came to constitute the universe within which their *kleos* is reenacted.

Thus whereas all phraseology is subject to meter such as we observe it in our Homeric text, some phrases are more metrical in essence than others. The importance of this statement lies in the double nature of the word "metrical," referring both to what contributes most to meter and to what behaves most systematically and economically within the metrical grammar of poetry. The central concern of the present argument is that it is the same phrases to which both senses of "metrical" apply. This observation may lead us back to the three stages mentioned in the previous section, which we may now reformulate in terms of meter: (1) a given phrase may serve an important and recurrent function in the discourse of special speech, so that (2) its rhythm becomes so regularized as to become meter,

---

[7] O'Nolan 1969: 14, 17. Cf. Nagy 1974: 140–49; 1992b: 18–35, esp. 29–32; on the great antiquity of noun-epithet formulas (going back to Mycenaean or even proto-Mycenaean times), see most recently Ruijgh 1995: 75–91.

after which (3) it may come to serve new functions within the very metrical contexts that it has thus created. Applied to the specific case of noun-epithet formulas, this tripartite scheme yields the following picture:

1. *Formative Stage.* In effecting an epiphany that marks founding action crucial for the reality of the performance (see Chapter 7), the noun-epithet formula, along with its staging formula, serves a commonly needed discourse function.

2. *Routinization Stage.* The use of the noun-epithet formula is triggered by the preceding staging formula, which is no longer motivated by the momentous circumstances of the previous stage; in other words, the noun-epithet formula along with its staging formula has become an idiom, and the bond between the two has become fixed.

3. *Metrical Stage.* The noun-epithet formula occurs in isolation from a staging formula; the noun-epithet formula comes to be reanalyzed as a metrical phrase, so that it can serve a function in the expansion aesthetic of Homeric discourse, while its original meaning is still visible; on account of this original meaning the formula can function, according to the rules of the grammar of poetry, as a periphery with respect to a nucleus, or the epithet as periphery with respect to the noun.

Before we continue with the discussion and illustration of these three possibilities, it is worth emphasizing that although the idea of stage implies the notion of consecutive development, the relationship between a noun-epithet formula of the first stage and one of the third stage is not simply a diachronic one in the sense that the one precedes the other in time: noun-epithet formulas continue to be used in formative, epiphanic contexts, even after the metrical stage has been reached. As in ordinary speech, old and young in Homeric diction exist side by side, and two uses of a given expression between which a diachronic relation can be established are often, synchronically, simply different senses or uses of the expression. The decision, then, not to treat contexts in which staged epiphanies occur as older than the other contexts does not so much bespeak a Unitarian stance with regard to the Homeric Question as an insight drawn from the study of speech.[8]

---

[8] On synchrony and diachrony in the study of linguistic items see the discussion of the particle περ in Bakker 1988: 73–75, 120, 146 n. 38–39; 1993d: 15. The synchronic productivity of what must belong to a diachronically older stage is particularly pertinent in Homer, of course, because

The development from stage to stage does not simply involve an increase in the role of meter. Meaning is also crucially involved, in that the metrical behavior of the noun-epithet formulas as optional third-stage peripheries would be impossible without their essential original meaning in the first stage. Illustration of this principle will be my prime concern at the end of this chapter. The first of these stages has already been discussed in the previous chapter. So I continue now with the second one.

Beyond Staging: Routinization

It is easy to observe that noun-epithet formulas and their staging formulas, apart from the specific contexts in which they effect a staged epiphany as described in the previous chapter, are examples of idiomatic rigidity.[9] First we note that after a staging formula (e.g., *tòn d' apameibómenos proséphē* 'and him answering he addressed'), the occurrence of a noun-epithet phrase is so routinized, indeed obligatory, as to be virtually a matter of a grammatical rule.[10] It follows that instead of competing with other kinds of expression within the context created by a staging formula, the noun-epithet formulas compete with each other, and this substitutability within a limited set of phrases is connected with their rhythmical and prosodic equivalence: they contract paradigmatic, systematic relationships with each other on the basis of their rhythmical profiles. This circumstance, we note, is nothing other than Parry's principle of extension and economy of formulaic systems, and we are now in a position to see that this regularity is not only a *source* but also a *consequence* of epic verse-making.[11]

---

of the coexistence of different dialects, representing different stages in the development of epic diction; see Ruijgh 1995: 59–91.

[9] See Kiparsky's account of Homeric formulas in general (1976: 73–84) in terms of the "bound phrases" of ordinary language. See also Chapter 7 above.

[10] Strictly speaking the frequent πατὴρ ἀνδρῶν τε θεῶν τε 'father of men and gods' is not a noun-epithet formula, but for the purposes of Chapter 7 it can count as one. In some cases, we see a noun followed by an independent clause (*Od.* 15.434), a relative clause (*Od.* 15.430), or a participial phrase (*Il.* 1.413; *Od.* 24.280). At *Il.* 13.768 (ἀγχοῦ δ' ἱστάμενος προσέφη αἰσχροῖς ἐπέεσσι 'and standing close in he addressed him with insulting words'), κορυθαίολος Ἕκτωρ 'Hektor with the flickering helmet' has apparently been judged less pertinent than the speech description; see also Edwards 1970: 10–12. Cf. also *Il.* 3.396, where a modified perception formula is followed, not by a character staged, but by the object perceived: καί ῥ' ὡς οὖν ἐνόησε | θεᾶς περικαλλέα δειρὴν 'and when she saw | of the goddess the very beautiful neck').

[11] For more detail on this point, see Bakker 1995; for extension and economy, see also Chapter 1 above.

Furthermore, staging formulas of any length and type always *precede* noun-epithet phrases, an ordering that is obviously in the nature of the very concept of staging.[12] This frozen syntax reveals the special role of noun-epithet phrases in the semantics and metrics of the epic tradition. The fixed linear ordering of the noun-epithet phrases and their stagings reflects the rigid behavior of these phrases as ritual namings in Homeric discourse: only rarely do they precede their verb,[13] and their participation in the dynamics of word order in the Homeric Greek clause is quite limited.[14] For example, noun-epithet phrases do not combine with the ubiquitous connective particle *dé*. Noun-epithet formulas are typically framed, not framing speech units as we observed in Chapter 5. The routinized coalescence of the noun-epithet formula with the staging formula, finally, may well have produced the dactylic hexameter itself, the particularly strong bond between the staging and the epiphany being the semantic motivation for the coalescence (see also Chapter 7).

In the formative use discussed in the previous chapter, the staging formula provides a context for the noun-epithet formula, and is in its turn motivated by the importance for the performance of the moment of the epiphany. Moreover, a staging formula presents a character who is new to the stage. The exception is the introduction of speech, which can be marked as epiphanic even when the speaking character is already on the stage.[15] But in general, if an epiphany is to be felicitous, the character must really appear. Thus at the sight of Patroklos about to kill Sarpedon, Zeus makes his sudden appearance in a staging plus noun-epithet formula that lifts the action from the battlefield to the divine plane, where the important conversation between Zeus and Hera concerning the fate and death of Sarpedon is to take place:

[12] Parry observes (1971: 55) that noun-epithet phrases used at the beginning of the verse (a type not discussed here) are always the subject of a verb in the preceding line. See, e.g., Ζεὺς ὑψιβρεμέτης 'high-thundering Zeus', διογενὴς 'Οδυσσεύς 'Zeus-born Odysseus', "Εκτωρ Πριαμίδης 'Hektor son of Priam'. See also Edwards 1966: 121–22.

[13] The cases that I have found all involve (with the exception of *Il.* 1.506) noun-epithet formulas beginning at the hephthemimeral caesura (such as πολύμητις 'Οδυσσεύς 'many-minded Odysseus') preceded by the particle ἀτάρ 'but': *Il.* 5.29; 10.488; 11.153, 732, 744; 17.580; 23.110; *Od.* 21.404; Hes. *Scut.* 455, 470; *h. Dem.* 302. These cases, however, are not so much exceptions to the rule of the order of staging and epiphany as instances of the use of epithets discussed below.

[14] See also Edwards 1966: 121. To a limited extent noun-epithet formulas combine with the particle ἀτάρ; see further below.

[15] An important category of the introduction of speech by a character who appears on the stage is the verse-final τοῖσι δ' ἀνέστη 'and to them he rose' group of staging formulas followed by a line-long epiphany. See Chapter 7.

τοὺς δὲ ἰδὼν ἐλέησε	and seeing them he took pity,
Κρόνου πάϊς ἀγκυλομήτεω,	the son of Kronos with the crooked wits,
Ἥρην δὲ προσέειπε	and he addressed Hera,
κασιγνήτην ἄλοχόν τε·	his sister and wife

(Il. 16.431–32)

The staging formula, here reporting an act of commiseration, lives up to its relational potential: it stages an important new character vis-à-vis what is already on the scene, and it thus effects a shift of scene that is crucial for the reality of the epic tradition: Zeus lets himself be persuaded not to allow the anti-fact of the fated Sarpedon staying alive.[16] The prevention of anti-action is also what takes place when Zeus awakes from Hera's charms, at the beginning of Book 15 of the *Iliad*. During Zeus's mental absence, the Greeks have gained the upper hand with the help of Poseidon, and the plan of Zeus and hence the course of the *Iliad* has nearly been reversed. The same staging formula is used to make Zeus see Hektor, but this time the circumstances under which it is used are quite different:

a.	Ἕκτορα δ' ἐν πεδίῳ ἴδε κείμενον,	and he saw Hektor lying in the plain,
b.	ἀμφὶ δ' ἑταῖροι ‖ ἥαθ',	and around him his comrades they sat,
c.	ὁ δ' ἀργαλέῳ ἔχετ' ἄσθματι	and he was taken by painful breathing,
d.	κῆρ ἀπινύσσων,	unconscious in his heart,
e.	αἷμ' ἐμέων,	vomiting blood,
f.	ἐπεὶ οὔ μιν ἀφαυρότατος βάλ' Ἀχαιῶν.	since not the weakest of the Achaeans had hit him,
g.	τὸν δὲ ἰδὼν ἐλέησε	and seeing him he took pity,
h.	πατὴρ ἀνδρῶν τε θεῶν τε,	the father of men and gods,
i.	δεινὰ δ' ὑπόδρα ἰδὼν	and looking darkly terribly,
j.	Ἥρην πρὸς μῦθον ἔειπεν·	Hera he addressed.

(Il. 15.9–13)

At the moment of his staging in unit g, Zeus is already on the scene, and the act of perception linking him to Hektor and reported in the staging formula *tòn dè idṑn eléēse* 'and seeing him he took pity' is already underway, as appears from unit a. Hence there is no epiphany or shift of scene, as there was in the previous case. The staging formula simply says that Zeus took

---

[16] Cf. *Il.* 8.350, where Hera is staged under similar circumstances. On the notion of anti-action, see Chapter 7.

pity, without much relational implication.[17] What these differences suggest is that the staging formula, with the fixed grammatical combination of the noun-epithet phrase in its wake, has been used under circumstances that differ from the situation in which it stages an epiphany.[18] In other words, the staging formula motivates the use of the noun-epithet phrase, as a routinized idiomatic reflex, but seems itself not as strongly motivated as in more prototypical situations, where the formulas have the special features I have discussed.

Thus the noun-epithet phrase occurs in what may be called a grammatical context and as part of an idiomatic expression. Yet this is not to say that it is diminished in poetic and semantic force; on the contrary, the idiomatic combination of staging and noun-epithet phrase in the excerpt from Book 15 derives its significance precisely from the crucial nature of the speech action that is to follow, in which Zeus undoes Hera's scheming and firmly reestablishes the plot of the *Iliad*.[19] In other words, the basic meaning of the noun-epithet formula persists in the idiomatic combination and motivates its use in a slightly different context.[20]

The case of the parallel staging formula *tòn dè idṑn óikt(e)ire* 'and seeing him he felt compassion' is similar and may even provide evidence of a further step in the process. This commiseration formula is often considered to be synonymous with *tòn dè idṑn eléēse*,[21] yet it seems to denote a more intimate relation than the latter expression: a feeling of compassion for a friend whom one sees in distress, as opposed to the emotions of Zeus, who notices that a mortal is about to die.[22] As such, the formula seems to be

---

[17] Cf. also the case of τὸν δὲ ἰδὼν ῥίγησε 'and seeing him he shuddered', which is twice used for Diomedes reacting to Hektor menacingly approaching; once (*Il.* 5.596) Diomedes is new to the stage, and once (*Il.* 11.345) he is not.

[18] In Bakker 1988: 186–95, I have discussed this "semantic integration" of the formula.

[19] In *Il.* 15.54–78, Zeus actually poses as the author of the plot, summarizing the course of action and predicting the deaths of Sarpedon, Patroklos, and Hektor: words that blur the distinction between god and poet.

[20] See Hopper and Traugott 1993: 90, for a discussion of this phenomenon in grammatical terms: the persistence of the original lexical meaning of an item after it has become incorporated within another word as a bound morpheme.

[21] E.g., Janko 1992: 315, on *Il.* 16.5. Cf. also τὼ δὲ πεσόντ' ἐλέησε 'and when they had fallen he took pity', a staging formula that activates a character at the sight of a fallen warrior (*Il.* 5.561, 610; 17.346, 352; apparently two examples of clustering).

[22] The verb ἐλέω (and the corresponding noun ἔλεος) connotes a sense of shame, reverence, and feeling for proportion (note the frequent combination with αἰδώς and its cognates, e.g., *Il.* 21.74; 22.59, 82, 123–24, 419; 24.44, 207, 503) and seems therefore more apt for the expression of

more appropriate for two characters who are already on the stage than for the activation of one character vis-à-vis another. In any case, the formula is used to convey compassionate feelings in the intimate tête-à-têtes between Patroklos and Eurupulos and between Achilles and Patroklos, as well as Achilles's sympathy for Antilokhos during the funeral games for Patroklos:

| τὸν δὲ ἰδὼν ᾤκτειρε | and seeing him he felt compassion, |
| Μενοιτίου ἄλκιμος υἱός. | the valiant son of Menoitios. |

(Il. 11.814)

| τὸν δὲ ἰδὼν ᾤκτ(ε)ιρε | and seeing him he felt compassion, |
| ποδάρκης δῖος ’Αχιλλεύς. | swift-footed godlike Achilles. |

(Il. 16.5; 23.534)

In these passages neither Patroklos nor Achilles is "staged," as the term is defined in Chapter 7; no shifts of scene are effected and no epiphanies take place. And if the interpretation of ōikt(e)írō just presented is right, then these effects are not likely to occur, since this verb would presuppose an already established relation on the scene. This would imply that on account of the meaning of its verb, the phrase tòn dè idṑn ṓikt(e)ire is not a staging formula at all, but an expression based on one, created on the analogy of tòn dè idṑn eléēse. In other words, even though tòn dè idṑn ṓikt(e)ire displays the formal characteristics of a staging formula (relational pronoun, idiomatic and fixed bond with a noun-epithet formula), it is an analogical extension of a staging formula, a phenomenon testifying to the routinization in the use of idiomatic, grammatical forms: once the use of a given form becomes so routinized as to become grammatical, it can generate new forms by analogy. Yet again, as in the case discussed earlier, the original meaning of the noun-epithet formula, for all its grammaticality, does not bleach but rather persists in the new environment: Patroklos's words addressed in compassion to Eurupulos and Achilles' address to Patroklos are among the more important speech acts in the Iliad.[23]

Our final example involves the phrase tòn d' hōs oûn enóēse, which we studied in the previous chapter. This formula frequently paves the way, as we saw, for a structurally important appearance on the scene. Yet this

---

formal relationships involving mutual responsibilities. Accordingly it is ἐλέω, and not οἰκτείρω, that is used in the imperative ("pity me and show respect"), at least in Homer. On αἰδώς see Redfield 1994: 115–18; on αἰδώς and pity, see Cairns 1993: 49, 92–93.

[23] On Patroklos's speech (Il. 11.816–21) see Bakker 1997a.

staging device can also be used differently, in passages where staging and epiphany do not seem to be the appropriate concepts anymore. In Book 21 of the *Iliad*, as Achilles is wreaking havoc on the Trojans near the river Skamandros, he meets with Lukaon, a son of Priam whom he had previously captured and sold into slavery, but who now has returned to the battle:

τὸν δ' ὡς οὖν ἐνόησε	and when he saw him,
ποδάρκης δῖος Ἀχιλλεὺς	swift-footed godlike Achilles,
γυμνόν,	naked,
ἄτερ κόρυθός τε καὶ ἀσπίδος,	without helmet or shield,
οὐδ' ἔχεν ἔγχος,	and he did not have his spear,
ἀλλὰ τὰ μέν ῥ'	but all that,
ἀπὸ πάντα χαμαὶ βάλε·	he had thrown it to the ground,
τεῖρε γὰρ ἰδρὼς	for sweating wore him out,
φεύγοντ' ἐκ ποταμοῦ,	as he escaped from the river,
κάματος δ' ὑπὸ γούνατ' ἐδάμνα·	and exhaustion overmastered his limbs beneath,
ὀχθήσας δ' ἄρα εἶπε	and vexed he (=Achilles) spoke
πρὸς ὃν μεγαλήτορα θυμόν·	to his own great-hearted spirit.

(*Il.* 21.49–53)

This is not an epiphany. Achilles is already on the scene, and the staging formula does not effect a shift of scene.[24] The normal perception formula, which now begins to mean simply what its words literally mean, seems to have been used in a situation other than the one for which it was originally meant. Yet this is not merely a deviant, suboptimal use of the formula, or an undesirable but inevitable consequence of oral composition. This is how language works.

Reanalysis

There are very few staging formulas without a noun-epithet phrase, but there are many noun-epithet phrases without a staging formula. To account for this asymmetrical relationship, which testifies to the metrical potential of the noun-epithet phrase in the grammar of poetry, we turn to an important concept in the study of language change: reanalysis. It fre-

---

[24] The two instances of the formula in the *Odyssey* (15.59: Telemakhos seeing Menelaos; 24.232: Odysseus seeing Laertes) are similar, in that the perceiver is already on the stage.

quently happens that an extant form comes to be used for a new purpose, after which it can be reanalyzed in terms of the new function. A straight-forward example is the development in spoken English of clauses with a *verbum sentiendi* (verbs expressing thought or attitude, such as *I think* or *I guess*) into epistemic parenthetical phrases:[25]

    a. *I think that* we're definitely moving towards being more technological.
    b. *I think* exercise is really beneficial, to anybody.
    c. It's just your point of view you know what you like to do in your spare time *I think*.

In example a, *I think* is a main clause governing a subclause introduced by the complementizer *that*; the complementizer is absent in example b, a phenomenon that syntacticians call *that*-deletion. It appears preferable, however, to analyze the case as intermediate between examples a and c; in the latter the phrase acts as an epistemic parenthetical, a phrase "function-ing roughly as an epistemic adverb such as *maybe* with respect to the clause it is associated with."[26] In other words, what is a syntactically necessary main clause in example a is reanalyzed as a syntactically optional epistemic adverb in example c, and the complement clause of example a is turned into a main clause modified by the adverb.[27]

In the case of noun-epithet formulas we are not concerned with main clauses, complement clauses, and epistemic adverbs, of course, but the general principle is similar: a necessary phrase comes to be optional, as a consequence of a shift from one function to another. The new function is owing to the recognition of meter as a grammatical factor. In the previous chapter we saw that the original context for a noun-epithet phrase is the staging formula that provides the proper environment for an epiphany. But what is staged, as we saw in Chapter 7, is not only the epic character but also his or her name: the staging formula provides an environment that not only is epiphanic but also has the potential of being reanalyzed as metrical, owing to the rhythmical profile of the noun-epithet formula. In other

---

[25] See Thompson and Mulac 1991: 313.

[26] Ibid.

[27] See also Hopper and Traugott 1993: 58–59, on the history of the negative marker *pas* in French, which started out as an independent lexical item (meaning "step") that could strengthen negation in the case of verbs of movement. In this restricted context the word *pas* was reanalyzed as a negation marker, after which its use could be extended to verbs expressing an idea other than movement.

words, the noun-epithet phrases may change their function from staging an entity to occupying a certain metrical space, and this shift means that they can occupy the same metrical space outside the context provided by the staging formula. Once this step has been made, the way is clear for a more general function in the grammatical system of the epic verse.

Noun-epithet formulas freely occur outside the context of speech introductions and other staging formulas. They occupy the same metrical slot, but are not tied anymore to the phrase that occupies the first half of the verse. Instead of competing with each other, they now compete with any other phrase that has the same metrical profile.[28] To take a simple example, the speech unit *mermḗrikse d' épeita* 'and then he/she pondered', which begins the metrical period, can be complemented, both semantically and metrically, by a number of expressions that elaborate on the act of deliberation, verbalized either as an adding unit or as a new step marked by the particle *dé*:[29]

|| μερμήριξε δ' ἔπειτα   and then he pondered,
| κατὰ φρένα καὶ κατὰ θυμὸν || in his mind and in his spirit

(*Il.* 5.671; *Od.* 4.117; 24.235)

|| μερμήριξε δ' ἔπειτα,   and then he pondered
| δόκησε δέ οἱ κατὰ θυμὸν || and he decided in his spirit

(*Od.* 20.93)

Yet the second half-line could have been a noun-epithet formula which has not been used for some reason, and sometimes the noun-epithet formula actually occurs:[30]

---

[28] Contrast this with Parry's remark (1971: 14): "This fidelity to the formula is even more evident in the case of πολύτλας δῖος Ὀδυσσεύς 'much-suffering godlike Odysseus', which the poet uses five times in the *Iliad* and thirty-three times in the *Odyssey*, without ever thinking of using other words to express the same idea, without ever so much as considering the possibility of utilizing the portion of the line taken up by the epithetic words for the expression of some original idea." It may be true that in all thirty-eight cases an alternative was never considered, but that does not mean that there are no places where the formula could have been used but has not been used. See also Bakker 1995: 113–18.

[29] Cf. *Il.* 8.169: τρὶς μὲν μερμήριξε κατὰ φρένα καὶ κατὰ θυμόν 'thrice he pondered in his mind and in his spirit'. For a discussion of dative or prepositional expressions with words for mental faculties (φρήν, θυμός, κῆρ, κραδίη, etc.) in the context of formulas and versification, see Jahn 1987.

[30] In *Il.* 5.671 the use of πολύτλας δῖος Ὀδυσσεύς may have been prevented by an overabundance of the name of Odysseus in the immediate context, and in *Od.* 24.235 the decisive factor no doubt was the occurrence of the formula three lines earlier.

| μερμήριξε δ' ἔπειτα | and then she pondered |
| βοῶπις πότνια Ἥρη ‖ | cow-eyed mistress Hera |

(Il. 14.159)

In such contexts the noun-epithet formula is optional in the sense that it is not tied up with the preceding phrase. It has been used as a phrase that fits metrically, chosen from a range of phrases with the same metrical profile. But this certainly does not mean that it is dictated by the meter. In fact, the use of *boôpis pótnia Hḗrē* 'cow-eyed lady Hera' in the example may well be necessary in the sense that any phrase can be necessary if it is the only way to say what must be said in a given context. The reason why the phrase is used is less to fill out the line with a convenient way of saying "Hera" than to serve as an introduction to the seduction scene between Hera and Zeus that follows: the pair of units quoted is balanced by a parallel pair in the next line, resulting in a rhetorical juxtaposition of Hera to Zeus, each of whom ends the metrical period in the same way:

‖ μερμήριξε δ' ἔπειτα	and then she pondered,
βοῶπις πότνια Ἥρη	cow-eyed mistress Hera,
‖ ὅππως ἐξαπάφοιτο	how she could deceive
Διὸς νόον αἰγιόχοιο ·	the mind of Aigis-bearing Zeus.

(Il. 14.159–60)

Thus it does not follow from the reanalysis of noun-epithet formulas as metrical phrases that meter becomes in and of itself a positive factor in their use. Rather, meter provides the contexts in which the use of certain phrases that lack the required metrical profile is ruled out. Only very rarely does meter constitute the sole reason for the use of a given phrase.

In certain cases the noun-epithet formula cut loose from its staging formula seems optional in the stronger sense of omissible or redundant. It can be excised, it seems, without any real loss of meaning. Yet even here meter is not the exclusive factor, with the formula as a mere stopgap. Rather, what is at stake is the stylization by means of noun-epithet formulas of the redundancy that is natural to speech. Consider for example the following cases, belonging to a type of expression that has already been at the center of attention in Chapter 5:[31]

---

[31] For the formula in the third extract, see also ἡ μὲν ἄρ' ὣς εἰποῦσ' ἀπέβη(,) πόδας ὠκέα Ἶρις 'now she, having spoken thus, went away, swift-footed Iris' (*Il.* 8.425; 11.210; 18.202; 24.188).

| ‖ αὐτὰρ ὁ μερμήριξε | but he, he pondered |
| ‖ πολύτλας δῖος Ὀδυσσεύς | much-suffering godlike Odysseus |

(Od. 5.354)

| ‖ αὐτὰρ ὁ βοῦν ἱέρευσεν | but he, he sacrificed a bull, |
| ‖ ἄναξ ἀνδρῶν Ἀγαμέμνων | ruler of men Agamemnon |

(Il. 2.402)

| ‖ ἡ μὲν ἄρ᾽ ὣς εἰποῦσ᾽ ἀπέβη | now she, having spoken thus, went away |
| ‖ γλαυκῶπις Ἀθήνη | owl-eyed Athene |

(Il. 5.133; Od. 1.319; 6.41)

‖ ὣς φάθ᾽,	thus he spoke,
ὁ δὲ κλισίηνδε κιὼν	and he, moving to the tent
πολύμητις Ὀδυσσεὺς	many-minded Odysseus

(Il. 10.148)

The difference with staging formulas is instructive: we saw that these expressions begin with what I called a relational pronoun in an oblique case, presenting the participant on the scene as a starting point for the appearance of the new character, the bearer of the epithet.[32] What we see here, by contrast, is that the pronoun and the noun–epithet formula refer to one and the same character. The pronoun is in the nominative case, and the noun–epithet formula is added as an optional apposition.[33] Instead of an epiphany, the staging of a new character vis-à-vis a character who is already on the scene, we have here the situation described in Chapter 5: a switch to the other character on the scene, or a return to the character who was mentioned shortly before.[34] The name of this character may or may not be mentioned again, depending on whether the poet thinks that the audience will need the name to identify the character, and also on whether other material is available to fill the same metrical slot. This is not so much the encoding of founding action as the stylization of speech, where such loose additions are quite normal. And the principle regulating the stylization is the metrical grammar of the hexameter.

[32] See Chapters 5 and 7.

[33] Cf. Il. 5.133, quoted in the text, with Od. 15.43, in which the noun–epithet formula has been rejected in favor of a phrase that must have been felt a more useful continuation in context: ἡ μὲν ἄρ᾽ ὣς εἰποῦσ᾽ ἀπέβη πρὸς μακρὸν Ὄλυμπον 'and she, having spoken thus, went off to tall Olympos'.

[34] See Chapter 5. See also Bakker 1995: 111 n. 35.

But the function of noun-epithet formulas in the grammar of poetry extends further than this stylized addition of speech units. Once metrical reanalysis of the noun-epithet phrase has taken place, widening its distribution, a further reanalysis may ensue. If the noun-epithet formula has come to function as an optional, loosely added phrase, the epithet itself can also be reanalyzed as occupying a certain metrical space distinct from the name. This means that it can be left out if the metrical space which it occupies has to be used for other purposes. Consider for example the following pairs of additions to a topic switch (see also Chapter 5):

ὁ δ' ἐπεύξατο δῖος Ἀχιλλεύς	and he, he boasted, godlike Achilles
	(*Il.* 20.388; 22.330)
ὁ δέ οἱ σχεδὸν ἦλθεν' Ἀχιλλεὺς	and he, he came close to him Achilles
	(*Il.* 22.131)
ὁ δ' ἀνείρετο δῖος Ὀδυσσεύς	and he, he asked her, godlike Odysseus
	(*Od.* 7. 21)
ὁ δὲ μερμήριξεν Ὀδυσσεύς	and he, he pondered, Odysseus
	(*Od.* 6.141; 17.235)
ὁ δ' ἄρ' ἔσθορε φαίδιμος Ἕκτωρ	and he, he ran forward, brilliant Hektor
	(*Il.* 12.462)
ὁ δ' ἀπέσσυτο δώματος Ἕκτωρ	and he, he rushed from the house, Hektor
	(*Il.* 6.390)

We have discussed the noun-epithet phrase as an indivisible unity, the epiphany of an epic character. What we see here is a simple name that is either preceded or not preceded by an adjective. In other words, once the noun-epithet phrase has come to be used beyond its original locus, the staged epiphany, it is no longer essentially different from the simple noun, and the epithet may be dropped if need be.

Nuclei and Their Peripheries

The idea of the epithet as an optional phrase takes us into territory already covered by Parry himself, who states in his discussion of the choice of epithets:[35]

---

[35] Parry 1971: 84.

In every noun-epithet formula there are two elements, of which one is fixed and the other variable. The fixed element is the substantive. Apart from its variation in the genitive and dative plural, it has always the same metrical value, and this predetermined value is what the poet must reckon with. The variable element is the epithet. It can be assigned whatever metrical value the poet chooses, and it can begin or end pretty much as he wants. So the poet creates the noun-epithet formula of the desired measure by adding the x syllables of the epithet to the predetermined syllables of the substantive.

This formulation differs from the one used here so far, in that Parry speaks of the *addition* of the epithet as a metrical entity, whereas I have been speaking of its *omission*. This difference is not arbitrary, for it depends on what we take to be the basic unit in the verse: the simple name or the combination of the name and the epithet. It is for the latter possibility that I have opted thus far, arguing for the multiple effects that staging produces, epiphanic and metrical: it is the *combination* of the name with the epithet, together with the staging formula, that produces the verse, and the names to which an epithet can be added at all tend to occupy, if not accompanied by the epithet, the same metrical position as they do in the fixed combination of name plus epithet, that is, in most cases, the end of the metrical period. Epithets, then, so long as we take into account their original epiphanic use, are omitted rather than added.

Parry's conception of epithets as thematically congenial additions to a name does apply, however, if we see the optional addition not as the essence of the epithet—which lies in the epiphany—but as a further stage of reanalysis, in which the epithet as a metrical form does not so much leave space for material that is more appropriate in a given context as occupy space for want of that material. In this way the epithet becomes what I have called elsewhere an element that is peripheral to a nucleus.[36] A peripheral element specifies, in semantic terms, a property of the nucleus that is inherent, indeed so essential as to be self-evident. On account of this very importance, a peripheral element is optional semantically, for what is inherent in something can be expressed or it can be left understood. And this optional status in terms of meaning can be exploited for the sake of metrics and versification: one may lengthen a nucleus with the extra syllables of the periphery, but one could also leave the periphery out, without any signifi-

---

[36] Bakker and Fabbricotti 1991; Bakker 1990a; Bakker and Van den Houten 1992: 3–5. See also Bakker 1988: 186 (still without this particular terminology).

cant loss or disruption of meaning. Thus there is no harm in calling Odysseus *polúmētis* 'many-minded' once one has decided to make this epithet omissible.[37]

In fact, there is considerable gain in doing so. The metrical reanalysis of epithets does not reduce them to what Parry calls "stylistic superfluity" that is added to an "essential idea."[38] The metrical reanalysis goes hand in hand with a semantic one, whereby the addition of the epithet becomes an aesthetic principle in its own right, a matter of ornamental extension. Viewed in this way, the grammar of epithets and other peripheral elements becomes the tip of an iceberg, the grammatical and metrical consequence of a pervasive tendency in Homeric discourse that has been discussed in various ways and from various viewpoints in Part 2 above. After defining speech as process through time in Chapter 3, I argued in Chapter 4 that time, of which there is only a limited quantity, can be an important means in a performer's hands to emphasize the importance of a given idea: what stays longer in focus is more prominent for that reason.[39] In Chapter 5 I elaborated on this point by discussing the way in which a given idea can frame what lies ahead and thus organize the flow of speech. In the present context, finally, we speak of the expansion of nuclear ideas as an operation within the metrical space of the hexameter.[40] Seen in terms of this metrical expansion aesthetic, the peripheral status of epithets with regard to their nouns is but a part of a much wider phenomenon.

The principal domain of operation for the peripheral expansion of nu-

---

[37] Notice that the two central heroes, Achilles and Odysseus, the quintessential performers of founding action, and hence most amenable to staging, are also the ones whose epithets lend themselves best to reanalysis. Thus not only are the simple names (very strongly localized at the heroic end of the verse, see Kahane 1994: 156) analyzable as the omission of their epithets, but the combination of generic epithet and name (δῖος Ὀδυσσεύς 'godlike Odysseus' and δῖος Ἀχιλλεύς 'godlike Achilles') can also be seen as involving the omission of πολύτλας 'much-suffering' and ποδάρκης 'swift-footed', respectively. Moreover, the phrase ὠκὺς Ἀχιλλεύς 'swift Achilles' is not only the prosodic variant of δῖος Ἀχιλλεύς 'godlike Achilles' (Parry 1971: 39), but also, and perhaps more significantly, involves the omission of πόδας 'of foot'. These heroes, then, are more than any other characters, hexametrical heroes.

[38] Parry 1971: 13–14.

[39] See also my discussion of inclusion as articulated by the particle καί in Chapter 4.

[40] In his discussion of "Item Plus," Russo mentions the noun-epithet formula (1994: 378) as "one of several 'tropes of extension,' . . . the epithet bestowing an extension that is always appositional and is explanatory to the extent that it enlarges the idea or image." Russo calls the expansion aesthetic nonformulaic, whereas I would stress that expansion straddles the difference between formulaic and nonformulaic. In other words, nucleus and periphery are where "Item Plus" hits the grammatical, metrical surface.

clei is the intonation unit, reanalyzed as a metrical unit. Two situations are possible. First, a peripheral element may fill out the metrical space unoccupied by the nuclear element, so as to complement the metrical colon. In this case the nucleus coincides with Parry's essential idea, and it is specifically the periphery (e.g., the epithets associated with a given name) to which Parry's notion of economy applies: the various epithets surrounding as peripheral expansions a given name that acts as nuclear idea tend to be unique expressions metrically. Second, the periphery may also be an entire unit with regard to another unit, an operation that mostly serves to complement the hexameter line, but that may also involve two (or more) lines. Peripheral expansion, then, may either occur unit-internally or across a unit boundary. The two kinds of expansion may occur in the same line, with the principle operating on two levels. In the example that we have seen already, for instance,

a. ‖ μερμήριξε δ' ἔπειτα   and then she pondered,
b. | βοῶπις πότνια ῞Ηρη ‖   cow-eyed mistress Hera

(Il. 14.159)

the two ancient cult epithets for Hera, boôpis and pótnia,[41] reanalyzed now as metrical elements, serve to complement the essential idea "Hera" in unit b both metrically and semantically. The relationships between the three elements can be seen as recursive, in that pótnia can be analyzed as a periphery to Hḗrē, whereas boôpis in its turn acts as periphery to pótnia Hḗrē. Represented schematically (with arrows pointing from nuclei to their peripheral extensions):[42]

But the noun–epithet formula in its entirety can be seen as an extension to unit a. That is, it completes the metrical period, and at the same time repeats the idea "Hera" at the important moment when the plan for de-

---

[41] See Ruijgh 1995: 75–77.

[42] Compare the case of ἀκόντισε δουρὶ φαεινῷ 'made a cast with the shining spear', where δουρὶ φαεινῷ 'with the shining spear' functions as periphery to ἀκόντισε 'made a cast' but is itself the combination of a nucleus (δουρὶ) and a periphery (φαεινῷ). See further Bakker and Fabbricotti 1991: 69.

ceiving Zeus first occurs to her.[43] Unit a may also be seen as peripherally
extended. Its two main components are the verb and the connective particle *d(é)*. The latter serves as nuclear idea for the extension by *épeita*, as part
of the peripheral system of the central particle *dé*, a system that also features
the particle *ára* in the lengthened forms *d' ára* and *d' ár' épeita*.[44] The
nucleus-periphery relations in the passage can be represented schematically,
with arrows again pointing from nuclei to their peripheries:

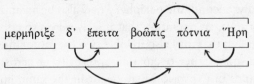

Boiled down to its "essential idea" the passage would thus be "and she
pondered," but that reduction would amount to a perversion of Homeric
style. It is the periphery, not the nucleus, that constitutes the essence of
Homeric discourse.

Other systems of peripheral extension are the dative or prepositional
expressions for "in his heart," (involving the elaborate and much discussed
Homeric vocabulary for mental and emotional organs) as a peripheral
element to a verb of emotion or cognition.[45] Again, the peripheral extension may either fill out the metrical unit of which its nucleus is the core
idea, or serve as an expanding unit itself. Of the latter possibility we have
already seen an example:

a. ‖ μερμήριξε δ' ἔπειτα   and then he pondered,
b. | κατὰ φρένα καὶ κατὰ θυμὸν ‖   in his mind and in his spirit

(Il. 5.671; Od. 4.117; 24.235)

Unit b serves as periphery to unit a and its internal structure (two functional synonyms linked by the extending particle *kaí*) is a characteristic
example of Homeric expansion.[46] The verb *mermērízō* 'ponder' can also be
expanded within the confines of a metrical unit:

---

[43] The noun-epithet phrase does not mark an epiphany, nor does the phrase clarify the
discourse flow, since it is clear who is doing the pondering.

[44] See Visser 1987: 92 (and 148 for a similar treatment of μέν). On ἄρα see Grimm 1962;
Bakker 1993b: 16–23; 1997a. Note that ἔπειτα δέ is different from δ' ἔπειτα; see Chapter 4.

[45] See Jahn 1987: 247–98.

[46] See also O'Nolan 1978. On καί specifically, in connection with Homeric aesthetics and
discourse flow, see Chapter 4 above.

|| ἔνθ' ἔβη εἰς εὐνὴν   then he went to bed,
| πολλὰ φρεσὶ μερμηρίζων. || pondering many things in his mind

(Od. 1.427)

Other examples of peripheral expansion include the use of the particle *kaí* as periphery to the frequent concessive participial phrases of Greek epic (*kaì akhnúmenós per* 'even though he was grieved'),[47] or the systematic deployment of expressions for "with the spear" in battle narrative as peripheral element to a verb of wounding or killing.[48] All these expressions are, like the epithet with regard to its name, natural extensions of the essential idea that is their nucleus.

But it should be pointed out once more that the metrical usefulness of these peripheral elements as they function in the grammar of poetry does not imply by any means that they are fillers with a meaning that is semantically empty or indifferent. The combination of particles *d' ára*, for example, functions as the metrical equivalent of the simple *dé* 'and' without loss of meaning for *ára*: an evidential particle that is used in conclusions drawn from visual evidence and which thus marks the narrative as deriving from a special, privileged source.[49] Likewise, the original epiphanic meaning of the epithet as it is attached to the name of a hero persists in each occurrence of the new use. It is not too much to say, in fact, that this new, reanalyzed use could never have developed without the impetus of the epic epiphany.

The metrical function of epithets as peripheral elements is thus not the *essence* of the use and function of epithets but rather the *consequence* of their original, essential meaning. The connection between meter and grammar that I have stressed in this final chapter is useful in bringing out limitations of metrical utility and formulaic composition that have sometimes been neglected. Like grammar, meter is the result of saying the right thing in certain recurrent contexts. But once it has emerged as a structure in its own right, meter itself comes to constitute contexts. These metrical contexts do not call anymore for "the right thing" to be said; rather, they specify what can *not* be said: phrases that do not fit in the meter, and that hence do not even exist for the performers and their appreciative audiences. Speaking the special speech of the Homeric tradition requires a deeply ingrained knowl-

---

[47] See Bakker 1988: 173–86.
[48] See Bakker and Fabbricotti 1991.
[49] See Bakker 1993b; 1997a.

edge of the phonetic, rhythmic properties that any utterance must have in order to serve as heroic discourse. But this knowledge in itself does not tell the performer what to say: like the grammar of an ordinary language, meter in Homer is a constraint, not a compulsion. The systems of peripheral omission and extension that I briefly reviewed in this chapter are an adaptive response to the metrical constants. Resulting from those phrases that are quintessentially epic, the epithets are among the phrases that best fit the metrical contexts that they helped to create. As such they are always a good thing to say, even though sometimes it is better to say something else.

Speech and Text:
A Conclusion

Speech and special speech: these were the key terms in my attempts to rethink the written criticism and reception of Homeric poetry. Using terms and concepts that present Homeric syntax as a *flow* through time rather than as a *structure* on the two-dimensional space of the written page, and speaking of recurrent behavior rather than of repetition, I have tried to devise a vocabulary that views speech, and Homeric formulaic speech in particular, as a medium in its own right, rather than as a style that is defined with respect to the written styles of later periods.

The conception of orality that was in the forefront in the preceding pages is different from the historical or literary conceptions that view orality as the stage preceding literacy, or as a kind of literature that is different from our own. Adopting the ahistorical stance of the discourse analyst, I have tried to approach Homeric poetry from the point of view of speech, and speaking, the most natural way of using language. Still, the investigation has been a historical one in the philological sense of that term: we have been reconstructing something from the past, not a text or some other physical reality, but a *medium*. This medium of speech has become obliterated by the opposite medium of writing which has carried Homeric poetry through the ages.

The reconstruction of speech is in a sense the deconstruction of text. The presentation of Homeric passages in the form of the speech units that formed the basis of almost all the operations in the preceding chapters may seem cumbersome to some readers. Yet such a reaction merely confirms that categories of textual reception were disabled in the attempt to detextualize the salient features of Homeric style, and redescribe them in terms of the speech of which the text is a transcription. No speech that is transcribed in such a way as to highlight the typical features of the spoken medium makes for easy reading.

Yet something is missing here, something that formed the core of the conception of speech that I presented in the preceding chapters, even that of writing in Chapter 2. To speak of the Homeric text as the transcription of speech is an oversimplification insofar as neither speech nor text are one-time events. I have spoken at some length of recurrence at various junctures in the preceding argument,[1] and we may now return to this concept in our final assessment of the findings of this study.

I argued that recurrence, not as the repetition of identical phrases, but as routinized behavior, is an essential feature of speech, the basic medium of language. In ordinary discourse the regularization and normalization resulting from recurrence is a matter of grammar, or rather, of the process of becoming grammatical.[2] In the special discourse of the Homeric performance, analogously, the result of recurrence is regularization of the prosody of speech in the form of meter. Meter is synchronically a matter of stylization, one of the aspects of poetry in speech; diachronically, however, meter is a matter of becoming metrical, of speech into poetry.

Unlike the grammarian of a living and continuously evolving language, the grammarian of Homeric special speech is in a position to study the final result of regularization, the point after which no change will ever occur. This is, of course, the Homeric text as it is transmitted in the medieval codices. In fact, this text is itself the result of recurrence, of numerous redactions in the course of which the process of normalization and regularization, inherent already in the process by which speech becomes special speech, reached its final stage.

The writing of Homer, as I argued in Chapter 2, was originally a matter of transcription, of the transcoding of one medium (speech) into another (text), in order to facilitate future performances.[3] But there is no reason to suppose that the first transcripts were anything like the text we possess today. In this regard it may be helpful to listen to students of traditions of

---

[1] See Chapters 1, 7, and 8.

[2] In linguistics the term "grammaticalization" is used. See Heine et al. 1991; Hopper and Traugott 1993. See also Chapter 8.

[3] See Nagy's definition (1992a: 42) of transcript: "A transcript is not the equivalent of performance, though it may be an aid to performance." Cf. Nagy 1996: 112. I would add that in a transcript the act of narration is not yet fictionalized: the text is not meant to stand on its own as inscribed discourse.

special speech who are in a position to produce the transcription of speech that they have witnessed themselves: "The measuring out of long runs of lines with equal numbers or syllables, moras, or feet does not occur in audible texts from cultures whose verbal arts are not under the direct influence of literary traditions. In most languages, such fine-grained metrical schemes require an atomization of speech sounds that is precisely the forte of alphabetic and syllabic writing systems."[4]

Such imposition of the categories of the writing system cannot be due to transcription as a one-time event, the creation of an unedited transcript of a performance, to be copied as is into the future. Writing too was a process, not of mere transcription, but of textualization,[5] the gradual transformation of words from elements of sound into elements of orthography. Such a transformation is crucially bound up with the *textual perception* of meter as something regular. Writing, I submit, is responsible in the last resort for meter as we know it, not as the emergence of regular rhythmical patterns from the prosody of speech, but as the principle determining the poetic style of the text.

A case in point is the frequent Homeric phenomenon of *diectasis* 'drawing out' a contracted vowel over three moras, as in *mētióōnto* or *mēkhanáasthai*, where the long vowel *ō* or *ā* has been distended so as to occupy a metrical space that is longer than one *longum*. Such forms are often seen as artificial creations of the epic *Kunstsprache*, inadmissible in the ordinary language and created to avoid the "impossible" single-short rhythm of the "natural" forms *mēkhanâsthai* and *mētiônto* (– ᴗ – – and – ᴗ – ᴗ).[6] I would rather hold that the artificiality is a matter of spelling, and that the *diectasis* is a strategy to make the meter regular in the text, whereas what happens in the reality of the performance is merely the marked pronunciation of a certain word. In other words, a phonetic entity has been converted into an orthographic item, part of a textualization of the epic tradition that cannot

---

[4] Tedlock 1983: 8. Cf. Hymes 1994. See also Chapter 6.

[5] For the difference between transcription and textualization, cf. the German terminological distinction between *Verschriftung* 'textification' and *Verschriftlichung* 'textualization' proposed by Oesterreicher (1993), who usefully points out (271) that pure transcription, without any interference of the transcribing, recording medium, is in principle possible only with the help of modern recording technology. Thus in practice any transcription of speech into writing brings in elements belonging to the latter medium, however superficial or unimportant.

[6] E.g., Chantraine 1948–53: 75–83. Janko rightly stresses (1992: 17) that diectasis forms are signs of innovation in the *Kunstsprache*, in that the bards prefer them over the older, uncontracted forms μηχανάεσθαι and μητιάοντο; yet he also treats the distended words as forms rather than as spellings.

but have contributed to a further, and final, regularization of the dactylic hexameter.[7]

What I propose, then, is that the increasing textualization of the Homeric tradition is an extension of the process of regularizing the prosody of ordinary speech into meter. In other words, the special speech of the Homeric tradition, with its increasingly rigid meter and its need to sustain itself across performances, has an in-built tendency to textualization, to inscribe itself, as a result of an increasingly textual reception. This would seem a paradox at first sight: we have been concerned, as I just suggested, with the reconstruction of the medium of speech, and so with the deconstruction of the text. But if we have now reconstructed a medium that tends to textualize itself, has not our own investigation deconstructed itself, undermining the methodology that it asserts?

The paradox disappears when we realize that the textualization of the Homeric tradition has been only a very partial one. Special speech becomes written, and so poetry, but the aspects of it that undergo textualization are precisely those aspects by which it is marked with respect to ordinary speech: the prosodic regularity of meter. In other respects Homeric discourse has remained remarkably close to speech in its typical segmentation and syntactic progression. These features have caused enough baffled reactions, in ancient and modern times, to justify the attempts made in the preceding chapters to rethink some of our textual terminological apparatus. And if our notion of special speech has inherent affinities with the text that Homer has become, so it has with the speech from which that text originates.

[7] See Gentili 1988: 231.

Bibliography

Allen, W. Sydney. 1973. *Accent and Rhythm: Prosodic Features of Latin and Greek. A Study of Theory and Reconstruction.* Cambridge: Cambridge University Press.

Ammann, H. 1922. *Untersuchungen zur homerischen Wortfolge und Satzstruktur.* Freiburg: J. Holtze.

Arnheim, Rudolph. 1969. *Visual Thinking.* Berkeley: University of California Press.

Auerbach, Erich. 1953. *Mimesis: The Representation of Reality in Western Literature*, trans. Willard Trask. Princeton: Princeton University Press.

Austin, Norman. 1966. "The Function of Digressions in the *Iliad.*" *Greek, Roman, and Byzantine Studies* 7: 295–312. Reprinted in *Essays on the "Iliad." Selected Modern Criticism*, ed. John Wright, 70–84. Bloomington: Indiana University Press, 1978.

——. 1975. *Archery at the Dark of the Moon: Poetic Problems in Homer's "Odyssey."* Berkeley: University of California Press.

Bakhtin, Mikhail M. 1981. *The Dialogic Imagination: Four Essays by M. M. Bakhtin*, trans. Caryl Emerson and Michael Holquist. Austin: University of Texas Press.

——. 1984. *Problems of Dostoevsky's Poetics*, ed. and trans. Caryl Emerson. Minneapolis: University of Minnesota Press.

——. 1986. *Speech Genres and Other Late Essays*, trans. Vern W. McGee. Austin: University of Texas Press.

Bakker, Egbert J. 1988. *Linguistics and Formulas in Homer: Scalarity and the Description of the Particle "Per."* Amsterdam: Benjamins.

——. 1990a. "Homerus als Orale Poëzie: De Recente Ontwikkelingen." *Lampas* 23: 384–405.

——. 1990b. "Homeric Discourse and Enjambement: A Cognitive Approach." *Transactions of the American Philological Association* 120: 1–21.

——. 1991. "Foregrounding and Indirect Discourse: Temporal Subclauses in a Herodotean Short Story." *Journal of Pragmatics* 16: 225–47.

——. 1993a. "Activation and Preservation: The Interdependence of Text and Performance in an Oral Tradition." *Oral Tradition* 8: 5–20.

—. 1993b. "Discourse and Performance: Involvement, Visualization and 'Presence' in Homeric Poetry." *Classical Antiquity* 12: 1–29.

—. 1993c. "Topics, Boundaries, and the Structure of Discourse: An Investigation of the Particle *dé*." *Studies in Language* 17: 275–311.

—. 1993d. "Concession and Identification: The Diachronic Development of the Particle περ." In *Miscellanea Linguistica Graeco-Latina*, ed. L. Isebaert, Collection d'études classiques 7, 1–17. Namur: Société des études classiques.

—. 1995. "Noun-Epithet Formulas, Milman Parry, and the Grammar of Poetry." In *Homeric Questions*, ed. J. P. Crielaard, 97–125. Amsterdam: Gieben.

—. 1997a. "Storytelling in the Future: Truth, Time, and Tense in Homeric Epic." In *Written Voices, Spoken Signs*, ed. Egbert J. Bakker and Ahuvia Kahane. Cambridge: Harvard University Press.

—. 1997b. "The Study of Homeric Discourse." In *A New Companion to Homer*, ed. Ian Morris and Barry Powell. Leiden: Brill.

Bakker, Egbert J., and Florence Fabbricotti. 1991. "Peripheral and Nuclear Semantics in Homeric Diction: The Case of Dative Expressions for 'Spear.'" *Mnemosyne* 44: 63–84.

Bakker, Egbert J., and Nina van den Houten. 1992. "Aspects of Synonymy in Homeric Formulaic Diction: An Investigation of Dative Expressions for 'Spear.'" *Classical Philology* 87: 1–13.

Bakker, Egbert J., and Ahuvia Kahane, eds. 1997. *Written Voices, Spoken Signs: Performance, Tradition, and the Epic Text*. Cambridge: Harvard University Press.

Bannert, Herbert. 1988. *Formen des Wiederholens bei Homer: Beispiele für eine Poetik des Epos*. Wien: Österreichische Akademie der Wissenschaften.

Barnes, Harry R. 1986. "The Colometric Structure of Homeric Hexameter." *Greek, Roman, and Byzantine Studies* 27: 125–50.

Bartlett, F. 1932. *Remembering: A Study in Experimental and Social Psychology*. Cambridge: Cambridge University Press.

Bassett, Samuel E. 1938. *The Poetry of Homer*. Sather Classical Lectures 15. Berkeley: University of California Press.

Bauman, Richard. 1992. "Contextualization, Tradition, and the Dialogue of Genres: Icelandic Legends of the *Kraftaskáld*." In *Rethinking Context: Language as an Interactive Phenomenon*, ed. Alessandro Duranti and Charles Goodwin, Studies in the Social and Cultural Foundations of Language 11, 125–45. Cambridge: Cambridge University Press.

Bäuml, Franz H. 1980. "Varieties and Consequences of Medieval Literacy and Illiteracy." *Speculum* 55: 237–65.

—. 1984. "Medieval Texts and the Two Theories of Oral-Formulaic Composition: A Proposal for a Third Theory." *New Literary History* 16: 31–49.

—. 1993. "Verschriftlichte Mündlichkeit und vermündlichte Schriftlichkeit: Begriffsprüfungen an den Fällen *Heliand* und *Liber Evangeliorum*." In *Schriftlichkeit im frühen Mittelalter*, ed. Ursula Schaefer, ScriptOralia 53, 254–66. Tübingen: Gunter Narr.

Beaman, Karen. 1984. "Coordination and Subordination Revisited: Syntactic Complexity in Spoken and Written Narrative Discourse." In *Coherence in Spoken and Written Discourse*, ed. Deborah Tannen, Advances in Discourse Processes 12, 45–80. Norwood, N.J.: Ablex.

Beck, William. 1986. "Choice and Context: Metrical Doublets for Hera." *American Journal of Philology* 107: 480–88.

Becker, Andrew Sprague. 1992. "Reading Poetry through a Distant Lens: Ecphrasis, Ancient Greek Rhetoricians, and the Pseudo-Hesiodic 'Shield of Herakles.' " *American Journal of Philology* 113: 5–24.

Beekes, Robert S. P. 1972. "On the Structure of the Hexameter: O'Neill Interpreted." *Glotta* 50: 1–10.

Berg, Nils. 1978. "*Parergon metricum*: Der Ursprung des griechischen Hexameters." *Münchener Studien zur Sprachwissenschaft* 37: 11–36.

Beye, Charles Rowan. 1964. Homeric Battle Narrative and Catalogues." *Harvard Studies in Classical Philology* 68: 345–73.

Bolinger, Dwight. 1961. "Syntactic Blends and Other Matters." *Language* 37: 366–81.

Brown, Gillian, and George Yule. 1983. *Discourse Analysis.* Cambridge Textbooks in Linguistics. Cambridge: Cambridge University Press.

Brugmann, K., and A. Thumb. 1913. *Griechische Grammatik.* Munich: Beck.

Bühler, K. 1934. *Sprachtheorie: Die Darstellungsfunktion der Sprache.* Jena: Fischer. 1965. Reprint, Stuttgart: Fischer.

Burkert, Walter. 1987. "The Making of Homer in the Sixth Century B.C.: Rhapsodes versus Stesichoros." In *Papers on the Amasis Painter and His World*, 43–62. Malibu, Calif.: Getty Museum.

Buswell, Guy T. 1935. *How People Look at Pictures: A Study of the Psychology of Perception in Art*, Chicago: University of Chicago Press.

Cable, Thomas. 1974. *The Meter and Melody of Beowulf.* Urbana: University of Illinois Press.

———. 1991. "The Meter and Musical Implications of Old English Poetry." In *The Union of Words and Music in Medieval Poetry*, ed. Rebecca A. Baltzer, Thomas Cable, and James I. Wimsatt, 49–71. Austin: University of Texas Press.

Cairns, Douglas L. 1993. *Aidōs: The Psychology and Ethics of Honour and Shame in Ancient Greek Literature.* Oxford: Clarendon Press.

Cerquiglini, Bernard. 1989. *Éloge de la variante: Histoire critique de la philologie.* Paris: Seuil.

Chadwick, H. M., and N. K. Chadwick. 1932–40. *The Growth of Literature.* Cambridge: Cambridge University Press.

Chafe, Wallace. 1980. "The Deployment of Consciousness in the Production of a Narrative." In *The Pear Stories*, ed. Wallace Chafe, 9–50. Norwood, N.J.: Ablex.

———. 1982. "Integration and Involvement in Speaking, Writing, and Oral Literature." In *Spoken and Written Language: Exploring Orality and Literacy*, ed. Deborah Tannen, 35–53. Norwood, N.J.: Ablex.

———. 1985. "Linguistic Differences Produced by Differences between Speech and Writing." 1985. In *Literacy, Language, and Learning: The Nature and Consequences of Reading and Writing*, ed. David R. Olson, Nancy Torrance, and Angela Hildyard, 105–23. Cambridge: Cambridge University Press.

———. 1987. "Cognitive Constraints on Information Flow." In *Coherence and Grounding in Discourse*, ed. Russel S. Tomlin, Typological Studies in Language 11, 21–51. Amsterdam: Benjamins.

———. 1988. "Linking Intonation Units in Spoken English." In *Clause Combining in*

Grammar and Discourse, ed. John Haiman and Sandra A. Thompson, Typological Studies in Language 18, 1–27. Amsterdam: Benjamins.

—. 1990. "Some Things That Narratives Tell Us about the Mind." In *Narrative Thought and Narrative Language*, ed. Bruce K. Britton and A. D. Pellegrini, 79–98. Hillsdale, N.J.: Lawrence Erlbaum Associates.

—. 1993. "Seneca Speaking Styles and the Location of Authority." In *Responsibility and Evidence in Oral Discourse*, ed. Jane H. Hill and Judith T. Irvine, 72–87. Cambridge: Cambridge University Press.

—. 1994. *Discourse, Consciousness, and Time: The Flow and Displacement of Conscious Experience in Speech and Writing*. Chicago: University of Chicago Press.

—, ed. 1980. *The Pear Stories: Cognitive, Cultural, and Linguistic Aspects of Narrative Production*. Advances in Discourse Processes 3. Norwood, N.J.: Ablex.

Chantraine, Pierre. 1948–53. *Grammaire homérique*. 2 vols. Paris: Klincksieck.

Clanchy, M. T. 1993. *From Memory to Written Record: England 1066–1307*. London: Edward Arnold.

Clark, Matthew. 1994. "Enjambment and Binding in Homeric Hexameter." *Phoenix* 48: 95–114.

Cole, Thomas. 1991. *The Origins of Rhetoric in Ancient Greece*. Baltimore: Johns Hopkins University Press.

Cosset, Evelyne. 1990. "Les formules de Zeus au vocatif dans l'*Iliade*. *L'Antiquité Classique* 69: 5–16.

d'Aquili, Eugene, and Charles D. Laughlin, Jr. 1979. "The Neurobiology of Myth and Ritual." In *The Spectrum of Ritual*, ed. E. d'Aquili, C. D. Laughlin, and J. McManus. New York: Columbia University Press.

Davis, Gerald L. 1985. *I Got the World in Me and I Can Sing It, You Know: A Study of the Performed African-American Sermon*. Philadelphia: University of Pennsylvania Press.

de Jong, Irene J. F. 1987. *Narrators and Focalizers: The Presentation of the Story in the "Iliad."* Amsterdam: Grüner.

Denniston, J. D. 1952. *Greek Prose Style*. Oxford: Oxford University Press.

—. 1954. *The Greek Particles*. Oxford: Oxford University Press.

Derrida, Jacques. 1978. *Writing and Difference*, trans. Alan Bass. Chicago: University of Chicago Press.

Détienne, Marcel. 1967. *Les maîtres de vérité dans la Grèce archaïque*. Paris: Maspéro. 1990. Reprint, Paris: La Découverte.

Devine, A. M., and Laurence D. Stephens. 1993. "Evidence from Experimental Psychology for the Rhythm and Metre of Greek Verse." *Transactions of the American Philological Association* 123: 379–403.

—. 1994. *The Prosody of Greek Speech*. New York: Oxford University Press.

Dik, Helma. 1995. *Word Order in Ancient Greek: A Pragmatic Account of Word Order Variation in Herodotus*. Amsterdam: Gieben.

Dik, Simon C. 1989. *The Theory of Functional Grammar*. Dordrecht: Foris.

Doane, A. N. 1994. "The Ethnography of Scribal Writing and Anglo-Saxon Poetry: Scribe As Performer." *Oral Tradition* 9: 420–39.

Dodds, Eric R. 1951. *The Greeks and the Irrational*. Sather Classical Lectures 25. Berkeley: University of California Press.

Dougherty, Carol. 1991. "Phemius' Last Stand: The Impact of Occasion on Tradition in the *Odyssey*." *Oral Tradition* 6: 93–103.

Dover, Kenneth J. 1968. *Greek Word Order*, 2d ed. Cambridge: Cambridge University Press.

Dry, Helen A. 1983. "The Movement of Narrative Time." *Journal of Literary Semantics* 12: 19–53.

DuBois, John W. 1987. "The Discourse Basis of Ergativity." *Language* 63: 805–55.

Dunkel, George. 1985. "Verse-Internal Sentence Boundary in the *Ṛg-Veda*: A Preliminary Overview." In *Grammatische Kategorien Funktion und Geschichte*, ed. B. Schlerath, 119–33. Wiesbaden: Ludwig Reichert.

Edwards, Mark W. 1966. "Some Aspects of Homeric Craftsmanship." *Transactions of the American Philological Association* 97: 115–79.

——. 1970. "Homeric Speech Introductions." *Harvard Studies in Classical Philology* 74: 1–36.

——. 1987. *Homer: Poet of the "Iliad."* Baltimore: Johns Hopkins University Press.

——. 1991. *The "Iliad": A Commentary.* Vol. 5, Books 17–20. Cambridge: Cambridge University Press.

Eisenhut, Werner. 1974. *Einführung in die antike Rhetorik und ihre Geschichte.* Darmstadt: Wissenschaftliche Buchgesellschaft.

Erbse, Hartmut. 1994. "Milman Parry und Homer." *Hermes* 122: 257–74.

Fenik, Bernard. 1968. *Typical Battle Scenes in the "Iliad": Studies in the Narrative Technique of Homeric Battle Description.* Hermes Einzelschriften 21. Wiesbaden: Franz Steiner.

——. 1986. *Homer and the "Nibelungenlied": Comparative Studies in Epic Style.* Cambridge: Harvard University Press.

Finkelberg, Margalit. 1990. "A Creative Oral Poet and the Muse." *American Journal of Philology* 111: 293–303.

Finnegan, Ruth. 1977. *Oral Poetry: Its Nature, Significance, and Social Context.* Cambridge: Cambridge University Press.

Fish, Stanley E. 1980. *Is There a Text in This Class? The Authority of Interpretive Communities.* Cambridge: Harvard University Press.

Flanagan, Owen. 1992. *Consciousness Reconsidered.* Cambridge: MIT Press.

Fleischman, Suzanne. 1989. "A Linguistic Perspective on the *Laisses Similaires*: Orality and the Pragmatics of Narrative Discourse." *Romance Philology* 43: 70–89.

——. 1990a. *Tense and Narrativity: From Medieval Performance to Modern Fiction.* Austin: University of Texas Press.

——. 1990b. "Philology, Linguistics, and the Discourse of the Medieval Text." *Speculum* 65: 19–37.

Foley, John Miles. 1990. *Traditional Oral Epic: The "Odyssey," "Beowulf," and the Serbo-Croatian Return Song.* Berkeley: University of California Press.

——. 1991. *Immanent Art: From Structure to Meaning in Traditional Oral Epic.* Bloomington: Indiana University Press.

——. 1992. "Word-Power, Performance, and Tradition." *Journal of American Folklore* 105: 275–301.

Ford, Andrew. 1992. *Homer: The Poetry of the Past.* Ithaca: Cornell University Press.

Forster, Leonard. 1989. "Thoughts on the Mnemonic Function of Early Systems of Writing." In *Idee Gestalt Geschichte: Studien zur europäischen Kulturtradition.* Festschrift Klaus von See, ed. G. W. Weber, 59–62. Odense: Odense University Press.

Fowler, Don P. 1991. "Narrate and Describe: The Problem of Ecphrasis." *Journal of Roman Studies* 81: 25–35.

Frame, Douglas. 1988. *The Myth of Return in Early Greek Epic.* New Haven: Yale University Press.

Fränkel, Hermann. 1968. *Wege und Formen frühgriechischen Denkens: Literarische und philosophisch-geschichtliche Studien.* Munich: Beck.

Friedrich, Paul. 1986. *The Language Parallax: Poetic Indeterminacy and Linguistic Relativism.* Chicago: University of Chicago Press.

Frontisi-Ducroux, F. 1986. *La cithare d'Achille: Essai sur la poétique de l' "Iliade."* Rome: Ateneo.

Gaisser, Julia H. 1969. "A Structural Analysis of the Digressions in the *Iliad* and *Odyssey.*" *Harvard Studies in Classical Philology* 73: 1–43.

Gaster, Theodore H. 1954. "Myth and Story." *Numen* 1: 194–212. Reprinted in *Sacred Narrative: Readings in the Theory of Myth,* ed. Alan Dundes, 110–36. Berkeley: University of California Press, 1984.

Geeraerts, Dirk. 1988. "Where Does Prototypicality Come From?" In *Topics in Cognitive Linguistics,* ed. Brygida Rudzka-Ostyn, 207–29. Amsterdam: Benjamins.

Geluykens, Ronald. 1992. *From Discourse Process to Grammatical Construction: On Left-Dislocation in English.* Amsterdam: Benjamins.

——. 1994. *The Pragmatics of Discourse Anaphora in English: Evidence from Conversational Repair.* Berlin: Mouton de Gruyter.

Gentili, Bruno. 1977. "Preistoria e formazione dell'esametro." *Quaderni Urbinati di Cultura Classica* 26: 7–37.

——. 1988. *Poetry and Its Public in Ancient Greek: From Homer to the Fifth Century,* trans. A. Thomas Cole. Baltimore: Johns Hopkins University Press.

Givón, Talmy. 1979. *On Understanding Grammar.* New York: Academic Press.

——. 1984–1991. *Syntax: A Functional-Typological Introduction.* 2 Vols. Amsterdam: Benjamins.

——, ed. 1983. *Topic Continuity in Discourse: A Quantitative Cross-Language Study.* Amsterdam: Benjamins.

Goldman Eisler, Frieda. 1958. "Speech Production and the Predictability of Words in Context." *Quarterly Journal of Educational Psychology* 10: 96–106.

——. 1968. *Psycholinguistics: Experiments in Spontaneous Speech.* New York: Academic Press.

Goody, Jack, and I. Watt. 1968. "The Consequences of Literacy." In *Literacy in Traditional Societies,* ed. Jack Goody, 27–68. Cambridge: Cambridge University Press.

——. 1987. *The Interface between the Written and the Oral.* Cambridge: Cambridge University Press.

Griffin, Jasper. 1980. *Homer on Life and Death.* Oxford: Clarendon Press.

Grimm, Jürgen. 1962. "Die Partikel ἄρα im frühen griechischen Epos." *Glotta* 40: 3–41.

Hainsworth, J. B. 1964. "Structure and Content in Epic Formulae: The Question of the Unique Expression." *Classical Quarterly,* n.s., 14: 155–64.

——. 1976. "Phrase-Clusters in Homer." In *Studies in Greek, Italic, and Indo-European Linguistics,* ed. A. Morpurgo Davies and W. Meid, 83–86. Innsbruck: University of Innsbruck.

——. 1993. *The "Iliad": A Commentary.* Vol. 3, Books 9–12. Cambridge: Cambridge University Press.

Halliday, M. A. K. 1967. "Notes on Transitivity and Theme in English: Part 2." *Journal of Linguistics* 3: 199–244.

Halliday, M. A. K., and Ruqaiya Hassan. 1976. *Cohesion in English.* London: Longman.

Harris, William V. 1989. *Ancient Literacy.* Cambridge: Harvard University Press.

Haslam, M. W. 1976. Review of Gregory Nagy, *Comparative Studies in Greek and Indic Meter. Journal of Hellenic Studies* 96: 202–3.

Havelock, Eric A. 1963. *Preface to Plato.* Cambridge: Belknap Press.

——. 1986. *The Muse Learns to Write: Reflections on Orality and Literacy from Antiquity to the Present.* New Haven: Yale University Press.

Heine, Bernd, Ulrike Claudi, and Friederike Hünnemeyer. 1991. *Grammaticalization.* Chicago: University of Chicago Press.

Herington, John. 1985. *Poetry into Drama: Early Tragedy and the Greek Poetic Tradition.* Sather Classical Lectures 49. Berkeley: University of California Press.

Heubeck, Alfred, Stephanie West, and J. B. Hainsworth. 1988. *A Commentary on Homer's "Odyssey."* Vol. 1, Books 1–8. Oxford: Clarendon Press.

Higbie, Carolyn. 1990. *Measure and Music: Enjambement and Sentence Structure in the "Iliad."* Oxford: Oxford University Press.

Hill, Jane H., and Judith T. Irvine, eds. 1993. *Responsibility and Evidence in Oral Discourse.* Cambridge: Cambridge University Press.

Hock, Hans Henrich. 1986. *Principles of Historical Linguistics.* Berlin: Mouton de Gruyter.

Hoekstra, A. 1965. *Homeric Modifications of Formulaic Prototypes: Studies in the Development of Greek Epic Diction.* Amsterdam: North-Holland.

——. 1981. *Epic Verse before Homer: Three Studies.* Amsterdam: North-Holland.

Holdcroft, David. 1991. *Saussure: Signs, System, and Arbitrariness.* Cambridge: Cambridge University Press.

Hopper, Paul. 1979. "Aspect and Foregrounding in Discourse." In *Discourse and Syntax,* ed. Talmy Givón, Syntax and Semantics 12, 213–41. New York: Academic Press.

Hopper, Paul, and Sandra A. Thompson. 1980. "Transitivity in Grammar and Discourse." *Language* 56: 251–99.

——. 1984. "The Discourse Basis for Lexical Categories in Universal Grammar." *Language* 60: 703–52.

Hopper, Paul, and Elizabeth Traugott. 1993. *Grammaticalization.* Cambridge: Cambridge University Press.

Hymes, Dell. 1981. *"In Vain I Tried to Tell You": Essays in Native American Ethnopoetics.* Philadelphia: University of Pennsylvania Press.

——. 1994. "Ethnopoetics, Oral-Formulaic Theory, and Editing Texts." *Oral Tradition* 9: 330–70.

Immerwahr, Henry R. 1966. *Form and Thought in Herodotus.* Cleveland: Press of Western Reserve University. 1986. Reprint, Atlanta: Scholars Press.

Ingalls, Wayne B. 1972. "Another Dimension of the Homeric Formula." *Phoenix* 24: 1–12.

Jackson, Leonard. 1991. *The Poverty of Structuralism: Literature and Structuralist Theory.* London: Longman.

Jahn, Thomas. 1987. *Zum Wortfeld "Seele-Geist" in der Sprache Homers.* Zetemata 83. Munich: Beck.

Janko, Richard. 1990. "The Iliad and Its Editors: Dictation and Redaction." *Classical Antiquity* 9: 326–34.

——. 1992. *The "Iliad": A Commentary.* Vol. 4, Books 13–16. Cambridge: Cambridge University Press.

Jeffery, L. H. 1961. *The Local Scripts of Archaic Greece.* Oxford: Oxford University Press.

Jensen, Minna S. 1980. *The Homeric Question and the Oral-Formulaic Theory.* Copenhagen: Museum Tusculanum Press.

Kahane, Ahuvia. 1994. *The Interpretation of Order: A Study in the Poetics of Homeric Repetition.* Oxford: Clarendon Press.

——. 1997. "Hexameter Progression and the Homeric Hero's Solitary State." In *Written Voices, Spoken Signs,* ed. Egbert J. Bakker and Ahuvia Kahane. Cambridge: Harvard University Press.

Kannicht, Richard. 1988. *The Ancient Quarrel between Philosophy and Poetry: Aspects of the Greek Conception of Literature.* Christchurch, N.Z.: University of Canterbury.

Kelly, Stephen T. 1974. "Homeric Correption and the Metrical Distinctions between Speeches and Narrative." Diss., Harvard University. 1990. Reprint, New York: Garland.

Kennedy, George. 1963. *The Art of Persuasion in Greece.* Princeton: Princeton University Press.

——, trans. 1991. *Aristotle, "On Rhetoric." A Theory of Civic Discourse.* New York: Oxford University Press.

Kiparsky, Paul. 1976. "Oral Poetry: Some Linguistic and Typological Considerations." In *Oral Literature and the Formula,* ed. Benjamin Stolz and Richard S. Shannon, 73–106. Ann Arbor: Center for the Coördination of Ancient and Modern Studies.

Kirk, G. S. 1962. *The Songs of Homer.* Cambridge: Cambridge University Press.

——. 1966. "Studies in Some Technical Aspects of Homeric Style. Part 2: Verse-Structure and Sentence-Structure in Homer." *Yale Classical Studies* 20: 105–52.

——. 1976. *Homer and the Oral Tradition.* Cambridge: Cambridge University Press.

——. 1985. *The "Iliad": A Commentary.* Vol. 1, Books 1–4. Cambridge: Cambridge University Press.

——. 1990. *The "Iliad": A Commentary.* Vol. 2, Books 5–8. Cambridge: Cambridge University Press.

Klein, Jared S. 1992. "Some Indo-European Systems of Conjunction: *Rigveda,* Old Persian, Homer." *Harvard Studies in Classical Philology* 94: 1–51.

Koch, Peter, and Wulf Oesterreicher. 1985. "Sprache der Nähe—Sprache der Distanz: Mündlichkeit und Schriftlichkeit im Spannungsfeld von Sprachtheorie und Sprachgeschichte." *Romanistisches Jahrbuch* 36: 15–43.

Krieger, Murray. 1992. *Ekphrasis: The Illusion of the Natural Sign.* Baltimore: Johns Hopkins University Press.

Krischer, Tilman. 1971. *Formale Konventionen der homerischen Epik*. Zetemata 56. Munich: Beck.

Kroon, Caroline. 1994. *Discourse Particles in Latin. A Study of "nam," "enim," "autem," "vero," and "at."* Amsterdam: Gieben.

Kühner, R., and B. Gerth. 1898–1904. *Ausführliche Grammatik der griechischen Sprache*. Hannover: Hansche Buchhandlung.

Kuipers, Joel C. 1993. "Obligations to the Word: Ritual Speech, Performance, and Responsibility among the Weyewa." In *Responsibility and Evidence in Oral Discourse*, ed. Jane H. Hill and Judith T. Irvine, 88–104. Cambridge: Cambridge University Press.

Kurylowicz, J. 1970. "The Quantitative Meter of Indo-European." In *Indo-European and Indo-Europeans*, ed. G. Cardona, H. M. Hoenigswald, and A. Senn, 421–30. Philadelphia: University of Pennsylvania Press.

Labov, William. 1972. "The Transformation of Experience into Narrative Syntax." In *Language in the Inner City: Studies in Black English Vernacular*, 354–96. Philadelphia: University of Pennsylvania Press.

Lambrecht, Knud. 1987. "On the Status of SVO Sentences in French Discourse." In *Coherence and Grounding in Discourse*, ed. Russel S. Tomlin, Typological Studies in Language 11, 217–61. Amsterdam: Benjamins.

Lanata, Giuliana. 1963. *Poetica pre-Platonica. Testimonianze e framenti*. Florence: La Nuova Italia.

Lang, Mabel L. 1984. *Herodotean Narrative and Discourse*. Cambridge: Harvard University Press.

——. 1989. "Unreal Conditions in Homeric Narrative." *Greek, Roman, and Byzantine Studies* 30: 5–26.

Latacz, Joachim. 1977. *Kampfparänese, Kampfdarstellung und Kampfwirklichkeit in der "Ilias," bei Kallinos und Tyrtaios*. Zetemata 66. Munich: Beck.

——. 1989. *Homer: Der erste Dichter des Abendlands*. Munich: Artemis Verlag.

——, ed. 1979. *Homer: Tradition und Neuerung*. Wege der Forschung 463. Darmstadt: Wissenschaftliche Buchgesellschaft.

Lattimore, Richmond. 1951. *The "Iliad" of Homer*. Chicago: University of Chicago Press.

Leaf, Walter. 1900–1902. *The "Iliad."* London: Macmillan. 1960. Reprint, Amsterdam: Hakkert.

Leech, Geoffrey N. 1983. *Principles of Pragmatics*. London: Longman.

Lehmann, Christian. 1984. *Der Relativsatz*. Tübingen: Gunter Narr.

Lehmann, Winfred P. 1993. *The Theoretical Bases of Indo-European Linguistics*. London: Routledge.

Levelt, Willem J. M. 1989. *Speaking: From Intention to Articulation*. Cambridge: MIT Press.

Lloyd-Jones, Hugh. 1992. "Becoming Homer." *New York Review of Books* 39, no. 5 (5 March 1992): 52–57.

Lord, Albert B. 1953. "Homer's Originality: Oral Dictated Texts." *Transactions of the American Philological Association* 84: 124–34.

——. 1960. *The Singer of Tales*. Cambridge: Harvard University Press.

——. 1975. "Perspectives on Recent Work on Oral Literature." In *Oral Literature: Seven Essays*, ed. Joseph J. Duggan. New York: Barnes and Noble.

——. 1991. *Epic Singers and Oral Tradition*. Ithaca: Cornell University Press.

Lowenstam, Steven. 1993. *The Scepter and the Spear: Studies on Forms of Repetition in the Homeric Poems*. Lanham, Md.: Rowman and Littlefield.

Lüttel, Verena. 1981. *Κάς und καί: Dialektale und chronologische Probleme in Zusammenhang mit Dissimilation und Apokope*. Göttingen: Vandenhoeck & Ruprecht.

Lynn-George, Michael. 1988. *Epos: Word, Narrative and the "Iliad."* Basingstoke: Macmillan.

Machacek, Gregory. 1994. "The Occasional Contextual Appropriateness of Formulaic Diction in the Homeric Poems." *American Journal of Philology* 115: 321–35.

Maehler, Herwig. 1963. *Die Auffassung des Dichterberufs im frühen Griechentum bis zur Zeit Pindars*. Hypomnemata 5. Göttingen: Vandenhoeck & Ruprecht.

Magoun, Francis P., Jr. 1953. "The Oral-Formulaic Character of Anglo-Saxon Narrative Poetry." *Speculum* 28: 446–67.

Martin, Richard P. 1989. *The Language of Heroes: Speech and Performance in the "Iliad."* Ithaca: Cornell University Press.

Matthews, V. J. 1980. "Metrical Reasons for Apostrophe in Homer." *Liverpool Classical Monthly* 5: 93–99.

Meillet, Antoine. 1937. *Introduction à l'étude comparative des langues indo-européennes*. Paris: Hachette. 1964. Reprint, University of Alabama Press.

Meillet, Antoine, and J. Vendryes. 1968. *Traité de grammaire comparée des langues classiques*. Paris: Librairie ancienne Honoré Champion.

Meister, Karl. 1921. *Die homerische Kunstsprache*. Leipzig: Teubner.

Miller, D. Gary. 1987. "Towards a New Model of Formulaic Composition." In *Comparative Research on Oral Traditions: A Memorial for Milman Parry*, ed. John Miles Foley, 351–93. Columbus, Oh.: Slavica.

Miller, George A. 1956. "The Magic Number Seven, Plus or Minus Two." *Psychological Review* 63: 81–97.

Minchin, Elizabeth. 1992. "Scripts and Themes: Cognitive Research and the Homeric Epic." *Classical Antiquity* 11: 229–41.

——. 1995. "Ring-Patterns and Ring-Composition: Some Observations on the Framing of Stories in Homer." *Helios* 22: 23–35.

Minton, William W. 1965. "The Fallacy of the Structural Formula." *Transactions of the American Philological Association* 96: 241–53.

——. 1975. "The Frequency and Structuring of Traditional Formulas in Hesiod's *Theogony*." *Harvard Studies in Classical Philology* 79: 25–54.

Morris, Ian. 1986. "The Use and Abuse of Homer." *Classical Antiquity* 5: 81–138.

Morrison, James V. 1992. "Alternatives to the Epic Tradition: Homer's Challenges in the *Iliad*." *Transactions of the American Philological Association* 122: 61–71.

——. 1993. *Homeric Misdirection*. Ann Arbor: University of Michigan Press.

Morson, Gary Saul, and Caryl Emerson. 1990. *Mikhail Bakhtin: Creation of a Prosaics*. Stanford: Stanford University Press.

Most, Glenn W. 1990. "Canon Fathers: Literacy, Mortality, Power." *Arion*, 3d ser., 1, no. 1: 35–60.

Mueller, Martin. 1984. *The "Iliad."* London: George Allen and Unwin.

Murray, Penelope. 1981. "Poetic Inspiration in Early Greece." *Journal of Hellenic Studies* 101: 87–100.

Nagler, Michael N. 1974. *Spontaneity and Tradition: A Study in the Oral Art of Homer.* Berkeley: University of California Press.

Nagy, Gregory. 1974. *Comparative Studies in Greek and Indic Meter.* Cambridge: Harvard University Press.

—. 1979. *The Best of the Achaeans: Concepts of the Hero in Archaic Greek Poetry.* Baltimore: Johns Hopkins University Press.

—. 1990a. *Pindar's Homer: The Lyric Possession of an Epic Past.* Baltimore: Johns Hopkins University Press.

—. 1990b. *Greek Mythology and Poetics.* Ithaca: Cornell University Press.

—. 1992a. "Homeric Questions." *Transactions of the American Philological Association* 122: 17–60.

—. 1992b. "Mythological Exemplum in Homer." In *Innovations of Antiquity*, ed. Ralph Hexter and Daniel Selden, 311–31. London: Routledge.

—. 1996. *Poetry as Performance: Homer and Beyond.* Cambridge: Cambridge University Press.

Nesselrath, Heinz-Günther. 1992. *Ungeschehenes Geschehen: "Beinahe-Episoden" im griechischen und römischen Epos.* Stuttgart: Teubner.

Norden, Eduard. 1909. *Die Antike Kunstprosa vom VI. Jahrhundert v. Chr. bis in die Zeit der Renaissance.* Darmstadt: Wissenschaftliche Buchgesellschaft.

Notopoulos, James A. 1949. "Parataxis in Homer: A New Approach to Homeric Literary Criticism." *Transactions of the American Philological Association* 80: 1–23.

O'Brien O'Keeffe, Katherine. 1987. "Orality and the Developing Text of Caedmon's Hymn." *Speculum* 62: 1–20.

Oesterreicher, Wulf. 1993. "*Verschriftung* und *Verschriftlichung* im Kontext medialer und konzeptioneller Schriftlichkeit." In *Schriftlichkeit im frühen Mittelalter*, ed. Ursula Schaefer, ScriptOralia 53, 265–90. Tübingen: Gunter Narr.

—. 1997. "Types of Orality in Text." In *Written Voices, Spoken Signs*, ed. Egbert J. Bakker and Ahuvia Kahane. Cambridge: Harvard University Press.

Olson, David R. 1977. "From Utterance to Text: The Bias of Language in Speech and Writing." *Harvard Educational Review* 47: 257–81.

Olson, David R., Nancy Torrance, and Angela Hildyard, eds. 1985. *Literacy, Language, and Learning: The Nature and Consequences of Reading and Writing.* Cambridge: Cambridge University Press.

O'Neill, Eugene R., Jr. 1942. "The Localization of Metrical Word-Types in the Greek Hexameter: Homer, Hesiod, and the Alexandrians." *Yale Classical Studies* 8: 105–78.

Ong, Walter J. 1982. *Orality and Literacy: The Technologizing of the Word.* London: Methuen.

Onians, R. B. 1951. *The Origins of European Thought.* Cambridge: Cambridge University Press.

O'Nolan, Kevin. 1969. "Homer and Irish Heroic Narrative." *Classical Quarterly* 19: 1–19.

—. 1978. "Doublets in the *Odyssey*." *Classical Quarterly* 28: 23–37.

Panhuis, Dirk. 1984. "Prolepsis as a Discourse Strategy." *Glotta* 62: 26–39.

Parry, Adam. 1966. "Have We Homer's *Iliad*?" *Yale Classical Studies* 20: 175–216.

——. 1972. "Language and Characterization in Homer." *Harvard Studies in Classical Philology* 76: 1–22.

Parry, Anne Amory. 1973. *Blameless Aegisthus.* Leiden: Brill.

Parry, Milman. 1971. *The Making of Homeric Verse: The Collected Writings of Milman Parry,* ed. Adam Parry. Oxford: Oxford University Press.

Peradotto, John. 1990. *Man in the Middle Voice: Name and Narration in the "Odyssey."* Princeton: Princeton University Press.

Perry, Ben Edwin. 1937. "The Early Greek Capacity for Viewing Things Separately." *Transactions of the American Philological Association* 68: 404–27.

Polanyi, Livia. 1982. "Literary Complexity in Everyday Storytelling." In *Spoken and Written Language: Exploring Orality and Literacy,* ed. Deborah Tannen, 155–69. Norwood, N.J.: Ablex.

Porter, H. N. 1951. "The Early Greek Hexameter." *Yale Classical Studies* 12: 3–63.

Pratt, Louise. 1993. *Lying and Poetry from Homer to Pindar: Falsehood and Deception in Archaic Greek Poetics.* Ann Arbor: University of Michigan Press.

Prince, Ellen. 1981. "Toward a Taxonomy of Given-New Information." In *Radical Pragmatics,* ed. Peter Cole. New York: Academic Press.

Pucci, Pietro. 1987. *Odysseus Polutropos: Intertextual Readings in the "Odyssey" and the "Iliad."* Ithaca: Cornell University Press.

Race, William. 1992. "How Greek Poems Begin." *Yale Classical Studies* 29: 13–38.

Redfield, James M. 1994. *Nature and Culture in the "Iliad": The Tragedy of Hector.* 2d ed. Durham, N.C.: Duke University Press.

Ricoeur, Paul. 1981. "What Is a Text? Explanation and Understanding." In *Hermeneutics and the Human Sciences,* trans. John B. Thompson, 145–64. Cambridge: Cambridge University Press.

——. 1991. "Mimesis and Representation." In *A Ricoeur Reader: Reflection and Imagination,* ed. Mario J. Valdez, 137–55. New York: Harvester Wheatsheaf. Reprinted from *Annals of Scholarship: Metastudies of the Humanities and Social Sciences* 2 (1981): 15–32.

Riggsby, Andrew M. 1992. "Homeric Speech Introductions and the Theory of Homeric Composition." *Transactions of the American Philological Association* 122: 99–114.

Risch, Ernst. 1969. "Die verschiedenen Partikeln δέ im Griechischen." In *Studi linguistici in honore di Vittore Pisani.* Brescia: Editrice Paideia.

Rosch, Eleanor. 1973. "Natural Categories." *Cognitive Psychology* 4: 328–50.

——. 1978. "Principles of Categorization." In *Cognition and Categorization,* ed. E. Rosch and B. B. Lloyd, 27–48. Hillsdale, N.J.: Lawrence Erlbaum Associates.

Rosenberg, Bruce A. 1988. *Can These Bones Live? The Art of the American Folk Preacher.* Rev. ed. Urbana: University of Illinois Press.

Rubin, David C. 1988. "Learning Poetic Language." In *The Development of Language and Language Researchers: Essays in Honor of Roger Brown,* ed. Frank S. Kessel, 339–51. Hillsdale, N.J.: Lawrence Erlbaum Associates.

——. 1995. *Memory in Oral Traditions: The Cognitive Psychology of Epic, Ballads, and Counting-out Rhymes.* New York: Oxford University Press.

Ruijgh, C. J. 1967. *Études sur la grammaire et le vocabulaire du grec mycénien.* Amsterdam: Hakkert.

——. 1971. *Autour de τε épique: Études sur la syntaxe grecque.* Amsterdam: Hakkert.

——. 1981. "L'emploi de ἤτοι chez Homère et Hésiode." *Mnemosyne* 34: 272–87.

—. 1990. "La place des enclitiques dans l'ordre des mots chez Homère d'après la loi de Wackernagel." In *Sprachwissenschaft und Philologie: Jacob Wackernagel und die Indogermanistik heute*, ed. Heiner Eichner and Helmut Rix, 213–33. Wiesbaden: Ludwig Reichert.

—. 1995. "D'Homère aux origines proto-mycéniennes de la tradition épique." In *Homeric Questions*, ed. J. P. Crielaard, 1–96. Amsterdam: Gieben.

Russo, Joseph. 1963. "A Closer Look at Homeric Formulas." *Transactions of the American Philological Association* 94: 235–47.

—. 1966. "The Structural Formula in Homeric Verse." *Yale Classical Studies* 20: 219–40.

—. 1994. "Homer's Style: Nonformulaic Features of an Oral Aesthetic." *Oral Tradition* 9: 371–89.

Russo, Joseph, Manuel Fernández-Galiano, and Alfred Heubeck. 1992. *A Commentary on Homer's "Odyssey."* Vol. 3, Books 17–24. Oxford: Clarendon Press.

Russo, Joseph, and Bennett Simon. 1968. "Homeric Psychology and the Oral Epic Tradition." *Journal of the History of Ideas* 29: 483–498. 1978. Reprint, *Essays on the "Iliad": Selected Modern Criticism*, ed. John Wright, 41–57. Bloomington: Indiana University Press.

Sapir, Edward. 1921. *Language: An Introduction to the Study of Speech*. New York: Harcourt, Brace.

Saussure, Ferdinand de. 1972. *Cours de linguistique générale*. Ed. Tullio de Mauro. Paris: Payot.

Schadewaldt, Wolfgang. 1966. *Iliasstudien*. 3d ed. Berlin: Akademie-Verlag.

Schaefer, Ursula. 1988. "The Instance of the Formula: A Poetic Device Revisited." In *Papers on Language and Mediaeval Studies Presented to Alfred Schopf*, ed. Richard Matthews and Joachim Schmole-Rostosky, 39–57. Frankfurt: Peter Lang.

—. 1991. "Hearing from Books: The Rise of Fictionality in Old English Poetry." In *Vox Intexta: Orality and Textuality in the Middle Ages*, ed. A. N. Doane and Carol Braun Pasternack, 117–36. Madison: University of Wisconsin Press.

—. 1992. *Vokalität: Altenglische Dichtung zwischen Mündlichkeit und Schriftlichkeit*. ScriptOralia 39. Tübingen: Gunter Narr.

Schank, R., and R. Abelson. 1977. *Scripts, Plans, Goals, and Understanding: An Inquiry into Human Knowledge Structures*. Hillsdale, N.J.: Lawrence Erlbaum Associates.

Schein, Seth L. 1984. *The Mortal Hero: An Introduction to Homer's "Iliad."* Berkeley: University of California Press.

Schellbach-Kopra, Ingrid. 1991. "Kalevalametrum und Kalevalasprache als Charakteristika des finnischen." In *Metrik und Medienwechsel*, ed. Hildegard L. C. Tristram, ScriptOralia 35, 129–40. Tübingen: Gunter Narr.

Schiffrin, Deborah. 1987. *Discourse Markers*. Cambridge: Cambridge University Press.

Schwyzer, E. 1947. "Zur Apposition." *Abhandlungen der deutschen Akademie der Wissenschaften zu Berlin* (Philosophisch-historische Klasse) 3.

Segal, Charles. 1994. *Singers, Heroes, and Gods in the "Odyssey."* Ithaca: Cornell University Press.

Shive, David M. 1987. *Naming Achilles*. Oxford: Oxford University Press.

Sicking, C. M. J. 1993. *Griechische Verslehre*. Handbuch der Altertumswissenschaft 2.4. Munich: Beck.

Siebenborn, Elmar. 1987. "Herkunft und Entwicklung des Terminus Technicus ΠΕΡΙ-

ΟΔΟΣ: Ein Beitrag zur Frage der Entstehung von Fachterminologien." In *The History of Linguistics in the Classical Period*, ed. Daniel J. Taylor. Amsterdam: Benjamins.

Slings, Simon R. 1992. "Written and Spoken Language: An Exercise in the Pragmatics of the Greek Sentence." *Classical Philology* 87: 95–109.

Smith, Barbara Herrnstein. 1983. "Contingencies of Value." In *Canons*, ed. R. von Hallberg, 5–39. Chicago: University of Chicago Press.

——. 1988. *Contingencies of Value: Alternative Perspectives for Critical Theory.* Cambridge: Harvard University Press.

Smith, John D. 1977. "The Singer or the Song? A Reassessment of Lord's 'Oral Theory.'" *Man*, n.s., 12: 141–53.

Snell, Bruno. 1975. *Die Entdeckung des Geistes: Studien zur Entstehung des europäischen Denkens bei den Griechen.* Göttingen: Vandenhoeck & Ruprecht.

Sobol, Joseph D. 1992. "Innervision and Innertext: Oral and Interpretive Modes of Storytelling Performance." *Oral Tradition* 7: 66–86.

Stock, Brian. 1983. *The Implications of Literacy: Written Language and Models of Interpretation in the Eleventh and Twelfth Century.* Princeton: Princeton University Press.

Stolz, Benjamin A., and Richard S. Shannon, III, eds. 1976. *Oral Literature and the Formula.* Ann Arbor: Center for the Coördination of Ancient and Modern Studies.

Svenbro, Jesper. 1993. *Phrasikleia: An Anthropology of Reading in Ancient Greece.* Ithaca: Cornell University Press.

Tannen, Deborah. 1979. "What's in a Frame? Surface Evidence for Underlying Expectations." In *New Directions in Discourse Processing*, ed. Roy O. Freedle, 137–81. Norwood, N.J.: Ablex.

——. 1985. "Relative Focus on Involvement in Oral and Written Discourse." In *Literacy, Language, and Learning: The Nature and Consequences of Reading and Writing*, ed. David R. Olson, Nancy Torrance, and Angela Hildyard, 124–47. Cambridge: Cambridge University Press.

——. 1989. *Talking Voices: Repetition, Dialogue, and Imagery in Conversational Discourse.* Cambridge: Cambridge University Press.

——, ed. 1982. *Spoken and Written Language: Exploring Orality and Literacy.* Norwood, N.J.: Ablex.

Taplin, Oliver. 1992. *Homeric Soundings: The Shaping of the "Iliad."* Oxford: Clarendon Press.

Tedlock, Dennis. 1972. *Finding the Center: Narrative Poetry of the Zuni Indians.* Lincoln: University of Nebraska Press.

——. 1983. *The Spoken Word and the Work of Interpretation.* Philadelphia: University of Pennsylvania Press.

Thalmann, William G. 1984. *Conventions of Form and Thought in Early Greek Epic Poetry.* Baltimore: Johns Hopkins University Press.

Thomas, Rosalind. 1989. *Oral Tradition and Written Record in Classical Athens.* Cambridge: Cambridge University Press.

——. 1992. *Orality and Literacy in Ancient Greece.* Cambridge: Cambridge University Press.

Thompson, Sandra A. 1987. "'Subordination' and Narrative Event Structure." In *Coherence and Grounding in Discourse*, ed. Russel S. Tomlin, Typological Studies in Language 11, 435–54. Amsterdam: Benjamins.

Thompson, Sandra A., and Anthony Mulac. 1991. "A Quantitative Perspective on the Grammaticization of Epistemic Parentheticals in English." In *Approaches to Grammaticalization*, Vol. 2, ed. Elizabeth Closs Traugott and Bernd Heine, 313–29. Amsterdam: Benjamins.

Thornton, Agathe. 1984. *Homer's "Iliad": Its Composition and the Motif of Supplication.* Hypomnemata 81. Göttingen: Vandenhoeck & Ruprecht.

Thornton, Harry, and Agathe Thornton. 1962. *Time and Style: A Psycholinguistic Essay in Classical Literature.* London: Methuen.

Tichy, Eva. 1981. "Hom. ἀνδροτῆτα und die Vorgeschichte des daktylischen Hexameters." *Glotta* 59: 28–67.

Treitler, Leo. 1974. "Homer and Gregory: The Transmission of Epic Poetry and Plainchant." *Musical Quarterly* 60: 333–71.

Trenkner, Sophie. 1958. *Le style "kai" dans le récit attique oral.* Assen: Van Gorcum.

Tsagarakis, Odysseus. 1982. *Form and Content in Homer.* Hermes Einzelschriften 46. Wiesbaden: Franz Steiner.

Turner, Frederick. 1992. "The Neural Lyre: Poetic Meter, the Brain, and Time." In *Natural Classicism: Essays on Literature and Science.* Charlottesville: University Press of Virginia.

Valdez, Mario J., ed. 1991. *A Ricoeur Reader: Reflection and Imagination.* New York: Harvester Wheatsheaf.

van Groningen, B. A. 1937. "Paratactische compositie in de oudste Grieksche literatuur." *Mededeelingen der Koninklijke Nederlandsche Akademie van Wetenschappen, Afdeeling Letterkunde* 83. Amsterdam: Noordhollandsche Uitgevers-Maatschappij.

—. 1958. *La composition littéraire archaïque grecque: Procédés et réalisations.* Amsterdam: Noordhollandsche Uitgevers-Maatschappij.

van Ophuijsen, Jan M. 1993. "OYN, APA, ΔH, TOINYN: The Linguistic Articulation of Arguments in Plato's *Phaedo.*" In C. M. J. Sicking and J. M. van Ophuijsen, *Two Studies in Attic Particle Usage: Lysias and Plato,* 67–164. Leiden: Brill.

van Otterlo, W. A. A. 1944. *Untersuchungen über Begriff, Anwendung und Entstehung der griechischen Ringkomposition.* Amsterdam: Noordhollandsche Uitgevers-Maatschappij.

van Raalte, Marlein. 1986. *Rhythm and Metre: Towards a Description of Greek Stichic Verse.* Assen: Van Gorcum.

Vernant, Jean-Pierre. 1959. "Aspects mythiques de la mémoire en Grèce." *Journal de psychologie* 56: 1–29. 1965. Reprint, *Mythe et pensée chez les grecs.* Paris: Maspéro.

Visser, Edzard. 1987. *Homerische Versifikationstechnik: Versuch einer Rekonstruktion.* Frankfurt: Peter Lang.

—. 1988. "Formulae or Single Words? Towards a New Theory of Homeric Verse-Making." *Würzburger Jahrbücher für die Altertumswissenschaft,* n.s., 14: 21–37.

Vivante, Paolo. 1982. *The Epithets in Homer: A Study in Poetic Values.* New Haven: Yale University Press.

West, Martin L. 1973. "Greek Poetry 2000–700 B.C." *Classical Quarterly* 23: 179–192.

—. 1982. *Greek Metre.* Oxford: Oxford University Press.

—. 1990. "Archaische Heldendichtung: Singen und Schreiben." In *Der Übergang von der Mündlichkeit zur Literatur bei den Griechen,* ed. Wolfgang Kullmann and Michael Reichl, ScriptOralia 30, 33–50. Tübingen: Gunter Narr.

Whallon, William. 1969. *Formula, Character, and Context*. Washington, D.C.: Center for Hellenic Studies.

Winograd, Terry. 1975. "Frame Representation and the Declarative-Procedural Controversy." In *Representation and Understanding: Studies in Cognitive Science*, ed. Daniel Bobrow and Allan Collins, 185–210. New York: Academic Press.

Witte, Kurt. 1912. "Zur Flexion homerischer Formeln." *Glotta* 3: 110–17.

——. 1913. "Homeros, B) Sprache." Pauly-Wissowa, *Realencyclopädie der classischen Altertumswissenschaft*, 8: 2213–47.

Wyatt, William F., Jr. 1988. "Homeric Language." *Classical World* 82: 27–29.

Yates, Frances A. 1966. *The Art of Memory*. Chicago: University of Chicago Press.

Zanker, G. 1981. "*Enargeia* in the Ancient Criticism of Poetry." *Rheinisches Museum* 124: 297–311.

Zielinski, Taddäus. 1899–1901. "Die Behandlung gleichzeitiger Ereignisse im antiken Epos." *Philologus Suppl.* 8, no. 3: 405–49.

Zumthor, Paul. 1987. *La lettre et la voix: De la "littérature" médiévale*. Paris: Seuil.

——. 1990. *Performance, réception, lecture*. Longueil, Québec: Le Préambule.

Index Locorum

General Index

ABC-scheme, 116–19, 121–22
Activation, 45–46, 58, 91, 93, 103, 105, 108–11, 131. *See also* Consciousness, Reactivation
Active information, 45, 87n. 4, 93–94, 107n. 39, 163
Adding style, 2, 35, 38–39, 41–43, 53, 88, 115, 135, 147, 149
Addition, 85, 88–99, 132, 145, 185, 199–200
Agent, 64–66, 93–96, 101, 103, 105–6, 108, 178, 181
Agreement (syntactic), 96–97, 106–8, 144–45
Allá (particle), 117
Anacoluthon, 102, 104, 107–8
Analogy, 13–15, 194
Anaphoric pronoun, 92, 96, 199–200
And (conjunction), 43, 48–49, 88
Androktasia, 57, 105–8, 115–19
Anti-action, 169–70, 172, 179, 192
Anticipation:
    metrical, 127–28, 138, 147, 152
    syntactic or semantic, 38–39, 54, 61, 73, 85, 88–89, 108, 113, 145, 155
Antimetry, 153–55
Apostrophe, 172–73
Appearance. *See* Epiphany
Apposition, 40–43, 51, 88, 90–91, 96, 103, 135
Appositional relative clause, 91, 108
Ára (particle), 51, 78n. 64, 101, 110n. 43, 178n. 67, 204–5
Archaic style, 40–43, 120
Aristeia, 86n. 1, 177
Aristotle, 36–38, 49, 126–29
Artificial language, 13–16, 139n. 31, 142, 209
Auerbach, E., 55n. 3, 67n. 31
Autár (particle), 96, 100, 109–11, 191nn. 13–14
Author, as maker, 15, 27, 158, 166, 175

Background, 67, 121
Bakhtin, M., 44, 47, 77

Battle narrative, 40, 57–58, 60–61, 68–70, 101–8, 115–18, 177
Beginning, 38, 59–60
Bolinger, D., 157–58
Boundary, 71n. 41, 131–32, 152–53
Boundary marker, 51, 63, 65n. 25
Bucolic diaeresis, 151, 153–54

Caesura, 50, 147–51, 164. *See also* Meter, Hexameter
Canon, 31
Catalogue, catalogic, 55, 56n. 5, 59–60, 68–69, 72, 91, 99, 102, 107, 110, 115–17, 134
Chafe, W., 42, 45–49, 51–52, 77–78, 87, 99, 103, 131, 134
Chant, 133–37
Chantraine, P., 40–41
Chiasmus, 100–103, 119, 122, 139n. 32
Cicero, 37, 139–43
Clanchy, M. T., 25–26
Close up, 57, 69, 88–89, 95–99, 103, 106, 108, 112–13. *See also* Vision and visualization, Perception
Clustering of formulas, 91n. 9, 107n. 40, 193n. 21
Cognition, cognitive, 30, 130–36, 140, 146, 148, 156. *See also* Consciousness
Colon, 140n. 33, 145, 148–50, 164–65, 203
Commemoration, 165–66
Commiseration formula, 173, 192–94
Conception, 8–9, 35–36, 44n. 15. *See also* Oral, Literate conception of language, Speech
Consciousness, 30, 44–50, 52, 54, 56, 58, 63, 69, 75–78, 80, 93, 95, 99, 111, 129–38, 148, 155
Continuation, 62–71, 77, 79–85, 102, 145, 152, 163
Contrast, 83–84, 100–101, 143, 145
Coordination, 70–71, 80. *See also* Parataxis

233

Dé (particle), 51, 62–71, 74–75, 79–85, 88, 92–
93, 96, 100, 102, 104–5, 108–9, 111, 143,
145, 163, 191, 197, 204–5
Dé (particle), 51n. 37, 75–76, 78–79
Denniston, J. D., 112
Deroutinization, 186–87
Description, 55n. 3, 56–58, 64, 67–69, 113, 181
Diachrony, 189
Dialogism, 74–77, 79–81
Diectasis, 209
Digression, 55n. 3, 113n. 50, 114, 118, 121
Dionysius of Halicarnassus, 36
Direct speech. *See* Impersonation
Discourse. *See* Speech
Discourse analysis, 3, 35, 138–39, 207

Economy, of formulaic systems, 10–12, 185,
187, 190, 203
Ecphrasis, 57
Enargeia, 77–79
Enclitics, 51, 101
Enjambement, 36n. 2, 110, 152–55
Epic event, 2, 166–69, 173, 175–81. *See also* Per-
formance
Epic regression, 114–15, 119
Epiphany, epiphanic, 77, 110, 167–83
effected by noun-epithet formula, 162–65,
168–69, 174–80, 189–91
Epithet:
as essential property, 91, 93, 161, 203
as peripheral element, 185, 200–205
Evidence and evidentiality, 55, 75–79, 205
Expansion:
as addition, 55n. 3, 68, 90–91
as aesthetic, 54–55, 90, 189, 202–5
across speech units, 185, 189, 197–99, 203–6
within speech units, 185–86, 189, 200–206
Extension, of formulaic systems, 10–12, 187,
190
Eyewitness, 55, 137

Fate, 165–66, 167n. 24, 169, 179n. 70
Finnegan, R., 18–19, 23
Focus:
of consciousness, 45–49, 50–52, 56, 63–64,
72, 87, 95, 97, 135, 149, 152–53, 202
linguistic concept, 65n. 25
of vision, 56, 67–68, 84–85, 88, 90, 102, 105,
108–10
See also Activation, Consciousness, Intonation
unit
Foley, J. M., 160–61
Folk sermon, 133–36, 146
Ford, A., 77
Foreground, 67, 121
Form (vs. content), 9–11, 42n. 13, 137–38
Formula:
definition of, 11–12, 185
essential idea of, 15, 185, 203–4
as form, 9–10, 15, 137

as idiom, 15–16, 157, 186–87
and oral poetry, 9–16, 24, 39, 156
receptional function of, 24–25
as stylized intonation unit, 53, 92–93, 98,
156–57
Formulaic style, 10–13, 68. *See also* Oral
Framing, frame, 88–89, 95, 100–108, 110, 117–
21, 145, 152, 163, 185, 202
Future (status of epic song), 165–66, 179n. 70,
181

Gár (particle), 51n. 37, 112–15, 117
Goal, 63, 103–4, 108, 113–21. *See also* Anticipa-
tion, Framing, Preview
Gorgias, 142–45
Grammar, 42n. 13, 65, 74, 102, 119, 157–58
as increasing fixity, 190, 193–94, 208
of poetry, 187–206
Grammaticalization, 186n. 3, 208n. 2

Havelock, E., 22
Herodotus, 42n. 13
Hexameter, 49–50, 95, 126, 147–54, 188
Hiatus, 50n. 33, 154
Homeric Question, 189
Hyperbaton, 139nn. 31–32
Hypotaxis, 41, 62, 127–29, 155. *See also* Periodic
and unperiodic style

Idioms, 157–58, 186, 189, 190, 193
Iliad:
plot of, 168, 170–78, 193
poetics of, 181
as secondary action, 166–80
Image, 52, 56–57
Impersonation, 78n. 61, 164, 167–69, 172–73,
191
Inclusion, 71–74
Indo-European syntax, 40–41, 96–97, 99, 106,
135n. 17
Inscription, 28–29
Inspiration, 136–37
Intonation, 47, 49, 51, 135, 142
Intonation unit:
as added name, 65, 92–96, 100, 108–9, 199–
200
as adding unit, 90–98, 106, 112, 135, 152,
163–64
basis for stylization and enhancement, 125,
130, 134–35, 139–45
as clause, 64, 95–98, 101, 104, 106
as *colon,* 140–42, 145, 147–51
defined, 47–48
as formula, 50n. 33, 53, 147, 156–57
as frame, 100–11, 114, 120, 131, 144, 185
as "line," 48, 50, 134, 144, 207
as metrical unit, 129, 147–52, 155, 187, 202–3
as noun-epithet formula, 97, 111, 163, 185,
199
and the "one new idea constraint," 99, 103

MYTH AND POETICS

A series edited by

GREGORY NAGY